4·23·98

NAVIES AND GLOBAL DEFENSE

NAVIES AND GLOBAL DEFENSE

Theories And Strategy

Edited By
Keith Neilson And
Elizabeth Jane Errington

Westport, Connecticut
London

Library of Congress Cataloging-in-Publication Data

Navies and global defense : theories and strategy / edited by Keith
  Neilson and Elizabeth Jane Errington.
      p. cm.
    Includes bibliographical references and index.
    ISBN 0–275–94898–6 (alk. paper)
      1. Sea power—Great Britain.   2. Sea power—United States.
    I. Neilson, Keith.   II. Errington, Elizabeth Jane.
    VA454.N38   1995
    359′.03—dc20   95–2239

British Library Cataloguing in Publication Data is available.

Library of Congress Catalog Card Number: 95–2239
ISBN: 0–275–94898–6

First published in 1995

Praeger Publishers, 88 Post Road West, Westport, CT 06881
An imprint of Greenwood Publishing Group, Inc.

Printed in the United States of America

The paper used in this book complies with the
Permanent Paper Standard issued by the National
Information Standards Organization (Z39.48–1984).

10 9 8 7 6 5 4 3 2 1

This book is dedicated to the memory of Barry Dennis Hunt (1937-1992). A graduate of the Royal Military College (RMC) of Canada and Queen's University, Barry Hunt served his country with distinction as a soldier before returning to RMC to teach in its History Department. A naval historian of note himself, Barry Hunt would have found delight in this volume. He will be missed by all who knew him.

Contents

Acknowledgments

The editors are indebted to the Royal Military College of Canada which hosted the twentieth Military History Symposium, incurred a portion of its expense and provided essential support services and assistance. The symposium and thus this volume would also not have been possible without the financial support of the Social Sciences and Humanities Research Council.

The symposium was truly a collective effort. The day-to-day support and encouragement of colleagues and students within the Department of History were invaluable. We particularly appreciated the help of those cadets who made themselves available throughout the conference and the work of our departmental secretary Mrs. K. Brown and of Mrs. Ellie Hudson. Also thank you to Laura Haycock for her work in keying in and setting up this manuscript. Finally, we wish to express our appreciation for all those who attended the symposium and made it the success that it was.

NAVIES AND GLOBAL DEFENSE

Introduction

Keith Neilson and Elizabeth Jane Errington

"[I]f we lose our sea supremacy we lose our Empire."[1] This remark, penned by the British permanent undersecretary at the Foreign Office in 1907, underlined the significance of sea power for the British of the era. However, this sentiment is capable of generalization, for any attempt to affect events worldwide necessarily has involved the exercise of sea power: there is an inextricable link between naval strength and global power. The intent of this book, which evolved out of a conference held at the Royal Military College of Canada in March 1994, is to explore the nature of this link by considering both the theory and practice of the navies of the two countries--Great Britain and the United States--that have dominated world politics in the last century and a half.

In a broad-ranging paper that set the tone of the conference, Donald Schurman explained why naval history has taken the form that it holds today. Schurman argued that naval history, properly considered, deals with a number of issues--cultural, diplomatic, economic and financial-- that in the British case traditionally were closely linked with the study of the British Empire and the projection of British power overseas. This historical tradition was exemplified by the work of Gerald Graham and Brian Tunstall. Since the early 1950s, however, British naval history-- and naval history generally--has tended to be considered antiquarian and to focus on battle history and narrow nuts-and-bolts issues. How has this come to pass? Schurman explained that it resulted from two facts: the disfavor into which the study of the British Empire fell during the period in which it degenerated into Commonwealth and the undue historical emphasis placed on the role of armies in the long shadow cast by two world wars with Germany. With respect to the latter, the work of Sir

Michael Howard and Paul Kennedy has been particularly pernicious. Howard posited a false dichotomy between the defense of British interests imperially and on the continent, while Kennedy emphasized that changing technology has resulted in the dominant land powers assuming the ascendency over the leading naval power in the twentieth century. Schurman called for a return to the wider view of what constitutes naval history--for its reintegration into the broader stream of historical endeavor--and argued that this would lead to an abandonment of Kennedy's conclusions.

Such an argument would have found favor with Sir Julian Corbett, one of the earliest practitioners of the kind of history that Schurman lauded.[2] As Geoffrey Till pointed out, Corbett was careful to distinguish between what he termed "naval" strategy--the study of sea power alone-- and "maritime" strategy--the study of sea power in connection with military strategy and foreign policy. For Corbett, a maritime strategy meant that the country with control of the sea could utilize it to ensure safe and rapid communications for its commerce and to project its military power ashore. This concept was later developed into what Basil Liddell Hart termed the "British way in warfare."[3]

Till argued that Corbett's ideas explained why Britain was able to obtain and maintain a global empire. Using the Royal Navy (RN) not only as a naval weapon against other fleets but also as a protector of Britain's commerce and a diplomatic bargaining chip and lever, the British were able to ensure their position against all comers. The means of doing so were never constant. At times, Till pointed out, the British lacked the necessary resources to carry on single-handedly; in such circumstances alliances were necessary and naval battles were avoided if the outcome was in doubt or if maritime communications could be maintained without combat. At other times, changing technologies made the maintenance of maritime supremacy difficult. For example, during the First World War, the submarine posed a threat to surface navies and the British position, while after the First World War air power threatened to lessen the value of maritime power generally. However, in both cases, Till concluded, the challenge was met: the first through convoy; the second through naval air power and improved anti-aircraft defenses. The only time that some of Corbett's ideas fell into disfavor with the RN, Till contended, was after the failure of the Dardanelles campaign. This meant that the projection of British power ashore was not contemplated again until the Second World War, and even then there was a reluctance to attempt amphibious operations.

Alfred Thayer Mahan had a rather different concept of the use to which naval power could be put in a global context. Mahan, unlike Corbett, argued that navies needed to engage the enemy in order to assure command of the sea. John Hattendorf explained that Mahan argued in such a fashion not merely out of conviction but also out of a need to create an intellectual framework for the discussion of naval affairs in the United States in the late nineteenth century. In this fashion, Hattendorf explained that Mahan should be considered in the context of his time, as a man with ideas, rather than reduced to a doctrine, a "Mahanian." To further this, Hattendorf pointed out how the religious aspects of Mahan's ideas are generally not considered by those who have reduced this complex man to a strategic formula.

Mahan developed many of his ideas in the periods 1886-89 and 1892-93, while president of the United States Naval War College (itself founded in 1884). This position gave him a public podium from which to advance his ideas during an age when there was much debate about the future of the American navy and its role in possible American expansion beyond the North American continent. Mahan argued that navies were offensive weapons that enabled countries to destroy the commerce of their opponents. The key to doing this effectively was bases and lines of communication. In order to obtain these, navies needed to be decisively strong at the decisive point. This position could normally be obtained only through battle. Hattendorf saw this as an argument, although seemingly historically based on the British experience, speaking directly to the contemporary American concerns about imperial expansion.

The intellectual context of the discussion of navies and their role in global defense having been set, Andrew Lambert took a contentious and aggressive stand with respect to the RN's role in the period from 1856 to 1914. Lambert argued that any suggestion of a decline in British power during this period due to the rise of new land powers and the improvement in land communications due to railways is incorrect. Instead, he declared that the strategic significance of sea power rose. The design of British ships from 1815 to at least 1889 underscored the fact that they were built to undertake offensive operations against fortresses in aid of amphibious operations. This was a result of a British grand strategy intended to deny any opponent the use of the sea by destroying its ports and to force it to defend them in such strength as to tie up large amounts of troops. British naval plans to attack both Kronstadt and Cherbourg, two ports of Britain's most likely opponents, illustrated this approach. Lambert conceded that this British naval grand strategy necessarily took an extended period of hostilities to become decisive. Thus, Britain was unlikely to intervene in any short war, explaining its passive attitude in 1870-71.

No such arguments existed for the United States Navy (USN) in the era from 1889 to 1922. Kenneth Hagan outlined how, after the USN had shown its usefulness in supporting American interests overseas in Samoa against Britain and Germany in 1889, American naval thinking moved away from a strategy based on the ideas of a *guerre de course* and towards a doctrine of fleet engagement. Imperialism and the building of a large battle fleet went forward hand in glove. The Naval Act of 1890 ensured that the USN was sufficiently formidable to back up American diplomatic complaints against Chile in 1892 and, in the following year, to give support to the idea of annexing Hawaii. Further, American imperial interests on either side of the North American continent underscored the need for the development of two--an Atlantic and a Pacific--fleets.

The events of 1898 were the apotheosis of American naval-imperial thinking. The naval battles of Santiago de Cuba and Manila ended Spanish colonial rule in these areas, Hawaii was annexed utilizing the USN and the final settlement of conflicting colonial aspirations at Samoa reflected the burgeoning naval power of the United States. By 1902, Hagan demonstrated, the USN was the world's fourth largest navy, and more than sufficient to ensure that the establishment of Panama was in accordance with American naval and maritime interests. However, the growth of American naval power in the Pacific was not without its drawbacks. The changing constellation of power in that region in the aftermath of the Anglo-Japanese Alliance and the Russo-Japanese War led American leaders to fear that possession of the Philippines might prove to be a strategic liability in the face of rising Japanese naval power. The round-the-world odyssey in 1907 of the so-called "Great White Fleet"--an action initiated by that quintessential naval-imperialist Theodore Roosevelt--was designed to demonstrate American naval power to all real and potential rivals.

The First World War, Hagan argued, was both a challenge and an opportunity to the USN. During the period of American neutrality, the United States found the British blockade odious but was unwilling to push the matter to the brink of war. However, the threat to American ideas about the freedom of the seas allowed the advocates of navalism in 1916 to push through Congress a building program designed to make the USN a "navy second to none." While the USN entered the war in the following year on the side of the RN, the 1916 naval appropriations promised that postwar relations between the two navies would not necessarily be smooth. Indeed, Hagan ended his study by showing that the Washington Naval Conference of 1922--which avoided an Anglo-American naval race through negotiation--achieved what the USN had long desired: parity with the world's preeminent navy, the RN.

David French's examination of the RN's contribution to victory in the First World War made manifest a certain irony in the British use of sea power. Lambert's RN, designed for offensive operations against a continental power, found itself relegated to a more Corbettian role, ensuring that Britain was able to utilize the sea-lanes to move troops, war matériel and foodstuffs in aid of a war of attrition against Germany. This led to several problems. The first was that the RN's building program was aimed at producing vessels designed to fight the enemy at sea, but the war required vessels--particularly destroyers and corvettes--to combat the submarine menace. Second, the requirements of the RN for steel, skilled labor and large-caliber armaments meant that it was competing against other aspects of the British effort for scarce resources. Indeed, in the face of constant losses of merchant ships, by 1917 British authorities were faced with either running short of supplies because of a lack of bottoms or reducing the number of naval ships constructed. The final point was that the RN was incapable of winning the war by itself against a major land power. Had the German Grand Fleet been destroyed at Jutland--the only major engagement between the German navy and the RN during the war--this would have mattered "remarkably little," French noted, to the ultimate outcome of the war, as the German army would have still needed to have been defeated in the field.

However, this did not mean that the RN was not important in the war. Its very existence meant that Germany was denied access to the overseas supplies that fueled the Allied war effort. Allied troops--particularly American troops after 1917--were moved by sea with few restrictions and international trade (which underpinned international finance) was maintained largely unhindered. Only the submarine threatened the RN's rule of the waves. This challenge, French demonstrated conclusively, was met (not by convoy as conventionally maintained) by a more careful usage of the existing merchant fleet. This task was done, first, through import restrictions and, second, through diverting ships into shorter routes, ensuring that they were able to carry more goods in a given period of time.

The period after the First World War meant problems for all navies, since public opinion favored arms limitation, if not complete disarmament. Although the Washington Naval Conference seemingly brought about the former in 1922, Nathan Miller argued that the results of the conference were useful for the USN, since budgetary limitations would have placed restraints on its building programs in any case. During the interwar period, the USN had three problems: maintaining its viability inside treaty limits, coping with new technologies and finding an enemy sufficiently credible to justify naval appropriations. The first problem was met through renovation and modernization, activities that enhanced the strength of the USN but did not violate any treaty restrictions. The second was not resolved, since the highest echelons of the USN favored the battleship and resorted to dubious means--the rigging of fleet exercises, for example--to ensure that the advocates of air power remained only visionaries. The technological inadequacies of the submarine left it a weapon of the future until near the outbreak of the Second World War. The final problem was "solved" through the assumption--inherent in War Plan Orange--that Japan was the likely opponent of the future.

Under Franklin Roosevelt and with the rise of aggressive regimes in Italy, Germany and Japan, the USN received vastly increased funding. While much of it was aimed at alleviating domestic unemployment, the result was that the USN was able to resume its building programs. Further, new ideas, such as amphibious operations, could be explored. Improvements in the submarine meant that it could be integrated into the concept of the "combined fleet," the centerpiece of American naval thinking in the era. By 1941, despite the events of Pearl Harbor, the USN was more than a match for the Imperial Japanese Navy in terms of ships, doctrine and technology.

If the interwar period was kind to the USN, not so to the RN. G.A.H. Gordon believed that the Washington Conference sowed the "seeds of future appeasement," since its two concomitants, the abandonment of the Anglo-Japanese Alliance and the restrictions placed on the RN, meant that the Admiralty could not fulfill its worldwide obligations to the empire. For Gordon, the global nature of British power was at the center of British naval policy. Since Britain had to be able to protect its interests not only in European waters but also in the Mediterranean, the Indian Ocean and the Pacific, naval arms limitation cut across its bows more than it did any other power. Deprived by treaty of the ability to maintain a large fleet and stripped of a reliable ally in the Far East, the Admiralty consistently advocated finding a foreign-policy solution to Britain's security interests. Such a point of view was shared by Neville Chamberlain, who, as early as 1934, called for a return to an Anglo-Japanese arrangement--at whatever cost to good Anglo-American relations. When the Second World War became a global war in 1941, the Admiralty's worst fears were realized, with Britain having to face naval challenges in three different locales. This the Admiralty was manifestly unable to do, and only the acquisition of the USN as an ally ensured navy victory.

After 1945, the USN was the dominant naval power. Despite lacking any credible opponent until the rise of the Soviet Navy, the USN demonstrated that maritime power, in the Corbettian sense, was still essential to the exercise of global power. As Colin Gray argued, the USN underpinned the North Atlantic Treaty Organization (NATO) alliance by ensuring that the sea-lanes to Europe would remain open in all circumstances. In other circumstances, Korea, Vietnam and the Gulf War, it permitted the United States to influence events at the end of very long logistical lines. Finally, the USN provided the means for the United States to exercise its hegemony in the Western hemisphere, as interventions in Latin America demonstrated.

In a concluding paper, Holger Herwig took a dissenting stand. While not denigrating completely the value of sea power, Herwig argued that it was not as ubiquitous in its application as the other contributors suggested. Looking at the German military experience since 1850, Herwig pointed out that sea power had done little either to bring about the rise of Germany or to contribute to its fall. For example, the German wars of unification and the Franco-Prussian War were resolved without any recourse to naval activities. While the efforts of the RN and the USN were important in the First and Second World Wars, without the enormous casualties that Germany had suffered on land, neither of the these conflicts would have ended in a German defeat. In short, then, Herwig suggested that naval power, while enormous, was limited by geography and needed to be considered as only part of a nation's ability to defend its interests globally.

NOTES

1.Nicolson to Hardinge, letter, 19 June 1907, Nicolson Papers, FO 800/337, Public Record Office (Kew).

2.This is not surprising, given that Schurman has written a biography of Corbett: *Julian S. Corbett, 18504-1922: Historian of British Maritime Policy from Drake to Jellicoe* (London: Royal Historical Society, 1981).

3.The phrase has become embedded in writing on British defense policy; see the discussion in David French, *The British Way in Warfare 1688-2000* (London: Unwin Hyman, 1990), xv-xvii.

1

Imperial Naval Defense: Then And Now

Donald M. Schurman

For me, global history means imperial maritime history. The word "naval" implies only a narrow and parochial part of imperial concerns. But in the last forty years, empires have become passé and studies in the British Empire, in particular, have fallen under a broad mantle of opprobrium. In terms of written history, that changeover was marked, almost exactly, by the publication of *Africa and the Victorians* by John Gallagher, Ronald Robinson and Alice Denny.[1] That book raised the question of what drew Britain to the "Cape to Cairo" idea. Robinson and Gallagher's conclusion was that while gold and diamonds at the Cape had attracted *people*, Her Majesty's Government had moved to protect its bases at Alexandria, Aden and Simon's Bay.[2] *Africa and the Victorians* was virtually the last time that the imperial strategic argument flexed its muscles. In the 1970s, the mainstream preoccupations of imperial history became theories about the despoilment of India, investment empire and loutish imperial behavior.

What does all this mean for the topic of "navies and global defense?" It means that for British naval history we are not looking back to global (imperial) defense *merely* across the great divide of the Cold War and empire fragmentation, in political terms, but across a gulf of interpretation. Historians take up that work in fragmented pieces. For naval *history* this has meant that the work that went on from John Colomb[3] to Gerald Graham[4] has been demoted to "naval," by which we usually mean battle lore, logistic development and/or technology; and sea sociology has taken over the *maritime* story, by which we mean sea communications and world social politics. Despite these changes in approach, war itself still means *planning* as well as last minute responses

--such planning was as necessary for imperial defense as it was in a more modern age for the Strategic Defense Initiative. Moreover, *imperial* defense constituted the frame for maritime communications between 1880 and 1945, and this chapter portrays some aspects of this.

Writing about naval history has not always been a rewarding activity, especially in terms of book sales. But I think that our naval handicaps go further. When looking back over nearly a century of warfare, it seems that the purpose and function of participating navies were not always well understood. Moreover, navies fare poorly in the pantheon of memory. Who, for instance, remembers who commanded at the first battle of the Falklands in 1914? Indeed, who was the naval commander at the Falklands in 1982? Even former British prime minister, Margaret Thatcher gives Admiral Sandy Woodward only thirteen golden lines in her 900-page autobiography.[5]

The problem may be seen more clearly if one looks at the antisubmarine campaign in the North Atlantic in the Second World War. The Battle of the Atlantic was at the very heart of a demanding, draining, relentlessly heavy conflict. It also provides much evidence for argument concerning proportion and responsibilities of the Allied participants. I am not playing down the research of British and Canadian scholars, who have done so much to render naval events visible; this has been a great accomplishment. Yet, their work raises all sorts of questions that are not yet put to rest. For example, how really useful were convoys and the convoy method adopted? Where were the Americans? Was Admiral King right or wrong in his approach to the Atlantic war?

Perhaps the Americans did not benefit at the time as much as they might have from the advice of Royal Naval experience. But as Samuel Eliot Morison indicated, Admiral King did not refuse his help with convoys because he thought the method stupid; he did it because he had not the escorts to shepherd the convoys, and because he calculated, in 1942, that in a year the Americans and Canadians could build more ships than the U boats could sink. Certainly, Admiral King did not think merely in terms of casualty lists. Furthermore, he was determined that American troops were not going to drown on their way to Europe. They did not. The U boats were controlled. The invasion of Europe was carried out for the crucial first two weeks without serious interference by U boats, and after that the losses were reduced to what may be called "acceptable." This effort, assisted by the United States Air Force (USAF) and the various Royal air forces, delivered some 2,600,000 Americans, quite apart from British, Poles and Canadians, to the Continent dry-shod and provided them with air cover that was over 90 percent efficient. The campaign itself was a triumph for the Royal Navy and its accumulated experience, to which the Canadian navy and the American navy made significant and essential contributions. (It was the human cost involved to the merchant navies that seems so horrendous, then and now.) But who understands or could name these naval facilitators? Why is it that the world remembers the ground forces that, having landed, took three-quarters of a year to get to the Rhine and that Generals Eisenhower, Bradley, Patton, Montgomery, (Simonds perhaps) are almost household names?

A fellow contributor to David Chandler's volume on the Sandhurst Companies, *Great Battles of the British Army*,[6] wrote that the distinguishing mark of these intelligent generals was that they could win wars without heavy casualties. No doubt they did. All survivors of war must be grateful for this tenderness. But theirs was not the method of the convoy escorts or of the convoys themselves; nor was mere survival the sine qua non of the crews of the various Royal air forces or the U.S. Army Air Force in Europe. Who knows the names of the commanders in Coastal Command, who assisted the convoy war? Naval cause and effect are mostly neglected in policy considerations regarding World War II. The more I think of it, the more I respect judgments at the Canadian government's Directorate of History that have emphasized Canadian protection of convoy, not least by the choice of examining Canadian escort service before the history of Canada in Bomber Command.[7]

For perspective's sake I have referred to the highly emotional evaluations of World War II; but I have used the material to illustrate a point about naval importance that could be made for any period in the twentieth century from the Russo-Japanese War onward. Against this background, this chapter considers the idea of the Royal Navy as a worldwide imperial power between 1880 and 1945. There are two features to this: the deployment and use of the navy as an instrument of state policy and the viewpoint of the various historical interpreters through whose lenses we view that deployment.

Respecting the early naval writers, consider Sir John Colomb, who had, perhaps, the clearest oceanic mind of any of his contemporaries and who remained an imperial communications propagandist all his life. He educated many people and finally received a knighthood as a reward. Howard d'Egville's book, *Imperial Defence and Closer Union*,[8] a biography of this underestimated man, is still worth reading. It highlights the fact that Sir John was a pioneer in grasping the importance of sea communications as the key to imperial sea power and in recognizing that it was constantly interpenetrating with colonial-imperial relations.

Julian Corbett and Herbert Richmond added a particular Cambridge connection to the equation. First of all, Corbett's work represented a sort of harris tweed weave of the imperial and continental themes.[9] Along with Richmond, who was then a battleship commander, Corbett brought into being the publishing venture at the Cambridge University Press known as the Naval and Military Series.[10] It began by publishing the proceedings of a conference just before World War I; it continued publishing after the war. Its two most distinguished works were those by Richmond on the naval war of 1739-48[11] and, after the second war, John Ehrman's outstanding work on King William's War.[12] The Cambridge association was strengthened by the founding of the Vere Harmsworth Chair of Imperial and Naval History, whose occupants included, along with Richmond himself,[13] J. Holland Rose,[14] Eric Walker[15] and E.E. Rich. In a sense I represented the move away from Cambridge when the University Board of Research Studies assented to my foraging for a supervisor in London, where I subsequently worked, in sequence, with Gerald Graham, the Rhodes Professor at King's, and with Brian Tunstall, Reader in International Relations at the London School of Economics.[16] Professors Graham and Tunstall both rigorously maintained the Corbett-Richmond tradition, however, until they retired in the mid-1960s. They kept naval history immured in naval tradition; both of them were also seized with the notion that sea power, though powerful, was still a limited instrument and that it had been perceived as such by practicing politicians from William the Silent to Winston Churchill. This, of course, had been Corbett's and Richmond's view. All of these scholars, with the exception of Alfred Thayer Mahan and possibly John Laughton,[17] refused to be categorized as blue-water historians. (The blue-water label had been used by army propagandists and narrow navalists.)[18]

Graham's contribution to scholarship was to give value to the maritime element in imperial history, and in his Wiles Lectures,[19] he drew attention to the subtlety with which British maritime stage managers of sea power achieved their effects. It was Tunstall's great contribution to take the age of empire, from 1815 to 1915, and draw together the imperial defense aspects. In three masterly articles in *The Cambridge History of the British Empire*,[20] he drew a map of imperial preoccupations that was consistently grounded on parliamentary, and particularly command papers. In consequence, Tunstall provided the reader with a wide viewpoint--foreign policy and naval primacy were not seen to be in conflict.[21] Tunstall searched for unity of structure at home and realized, as Graham had done, that while home policies might not be in conflict with each other, they were, none-the-less, not well coordinated.

Was there a general rejection, in Britain before World War I, of naval primacy in strategic thought? Britain did seem, quite aside from the Japanese alliance, to have become preoccupied with army defenses, and, in 1914, the navy appeared to be fixed in a role that demanded protection for an army in a particular deployment, thus tying its hands somewhat against other functions. However, it is important to remember that in 1911 nobody foresaw Kitchener's armies. The support role the army envisaged did not require over a million men, merely enough for Haldane's small force. Since World War II, Sir Michael Howard, and some of his distinguished graduates from his King's days, writing on the "continental commitment," as it came to be called, seemed to think that Britain had faced an open choice between a predominantly army or navy effort.[22] Certainly, the amount of army power that Britain could muster against powerful coalitions, or even single powers in Europe or America, for that matter, was severely limited. But it can hardly be doubted that the muscle that had given real leverage in various situations in the past was the navy, or the navy and the power of the Bank of England. Put another way, not many can deny that the army was a part of the British arsenal. What is more difficult to see, however, is how this collection of regiments can be considered a primary military force. There has been only one army captain, our "Chief of Men" in England--Cromwell--and nobody wanted another.

After the Boer War, Haldane's Army can not be considered a forerunner to anything except its excellent but limited self. The prewar struggle between the services represented nothing more than the attempt of a scratch team of army supporters to disrupt defense planning by attacking the Navy.[23] They did not really succeed in their attacks then, but their modern interpreters have altered our perceptions of the relative value of the fleet and the army. Paul Kennedy's approach tends to the same effect. This distinguished Yale professor was originally a naval scholar who concentrated on the German marine menace. He made his reputation with articles about the purposes of the German High Seas Fleet[24] at about the same time that Jonathan Steinberg was publishing *Yesterday's Deterrent*.[25] Professor Kennedy subsequently went on to write a tome describing the Anglo-German naval rivalry.[26] Then, using Sir Halford Mackinder as salt for his porridge, he argued in *The Struggle for*

British Naval Mastery that there had been a theory articulated by Mahan and followed by all British navalists that the great powers of the world had had to choose between an army (great-heartland) view of superior world control or a naval (blue-water) pool in which all others who contended for world dominance were condemned to swim--without much hope. Moreover, by seemingly assuming that there was no significant difference between the war aims of Britain and Germany, Kennedy bolstered the work of the army writers. In short, a naval historian seemed to be saying that in the power race, the naval power was doomed.[27] Kennedy contrasted the Mahan scenario with that of Halford Mackinder and awarded the palm for realism to the Englishman. The result was that a navy concerned worldwide with trade and global possessions had somehow been transformed into a consortium at the Admiralty that peered constantly and fearfully at the German naval menace.

This German emphasis is widely, but not universally, held. Certainly, the German fixation of some British policy planners was a factor, but it was not a determining factor in naval policy before, nor even between 1910 and 1914. (A similar difficulty had existed between 1794 and 1815.) Before 1910, the German "card" was cleverly used by politicians, press barons and publicists as excuses for panicking the public to obtain more ships.[28] This move was encouraged by colonial parsimony and the scare tactics of the soldiers. The navy took the ships and let the fixation go, while it really worried more about Russian cruisers hovering around imperial bases abroad.[29] It was no accident, looking back, that the protagonists of the German idea were historians of Germany with the blessed gift of that language. Howard's enduring work was on the Franco-Prussian War,[30] and Kennedy forged his reputation by showing how German ships were not designed for the open sea but were aimed at the Royal Navy in the North Sea.

These studies were considered seminal works at the time. It turned out to be important for strategic development that the events on the western front, not the effects of sea power, were dominant in the public's collective memory thenceforth. The Second World War had done nothing to change the perception that war meant yardage gained, body counts, pillbox captures, and so on--a new view of imperial or global defense.

To go back to the historians. It was assumed that when the Committee of Imperial Defence was set up in 1903, the needed clout was given to defense. The prime minister was a key figure in the planning and a permanent member; outside the secretary, he was the only permanent member. In *Defence by Committee*, Franklin Johnson[31] seems to consider the formation of the committee the entry of the British planning system into paradise. Not so. As John Mackintosh[32] shows, the necessary power to knock Admiralty and army heads together did not materialize after 1903. The Committee for Imperial Defence did not have any affinity for European foreign policy and was shown to be a progressively unfolding empty charade. The cold, hard fact of the situation was that before World War I, the government could not, for political reasons, even apprise its own political members on combined strategy, let alone a group of sailors, soldiers and administrators.

As there is nowadays, there *was* heavy pressure on Victorian imperial naval planners to make the right technological decisions in a fast-moving world. The Royal Navy grappled sensibly with the materiel changes involved in a great naval revolution.[33] The army, for its part, had been dispersed after 1815, hidden away in overseas postings by the great Duke of Wellington, no doubt to keep it from the nervous gaze of the British taxpayer. The army had behaved creditably, but not brilliantly, alongside the French, in the Crimean War, and had also policed and dominated India. In its spare time, at home, it had indulged in fear campaigns designed to shake the British public's confidence in the Royal Navy and peck at its funding. It had not shaken the good sense of such stalwart naval administrators as Sir John Pakenham,[34] Sir Alexander Milne[35] or even Admiral Sir Geoffrey Phipps Hornby,[36] however. The navy had maintained a steady policy of careful preparation and the testing of ship types over thirty years and had eventually handed to an ungrateful Sir John Fisher a legacy of careful planning that neither he nor his biographer was able to recognize. But Fisher *could* see that the finished tool that, in his turn, he did so much to hone, was being challenged by events abroad.[37] So far as Fisher let it appear that foreign European activity was driving naval preparations, he also allowed himself to become its child of fortune. If he merely used the public howl about continental threats as a means to beef up the estimates, he was on a narrow path from which he was lucky to emerge with credit and that, perhaps, he did not always understand.

Into this brew was thrown another army-oriented invasion scare in 1910. But the great national force that had been trained with a vast empire always in focus and whose opponents might be the French or the Russians was being pushed to develop in the face of a third challenge-- Germany. It was *not* that the German menace emerged fully armed on the scene before 1910. Powerful activist Britons, in both politics and the press, *were*, however, attempting to train public opinion in a myopic fear of Germany and away from the empire.[38] At the same time, the colonials and the Britons continued to misunderstand one another, especially over defense spending.

Certainly a lot hinged on viewpoint. When I came to the study of imperial defense some forty years ago, I found these central issues being discussed in three ways. The first was the problem that the British had had in finding a pattern that would be a useful touchstone for appeals to the peripheral empire for defense support. The second had to do with the seriousness with which Dominion and colonial peoples had taken imperial planning. The third was concerned with whether some imperial planning body, a colonial or imperial defense committee, could have been set up that would have commanded the attention of the central government and overridden the departmental rivalries that were endemic in imperial Whitehall.

At the colonial end, there was never any doubt about the direction of such studies. Historians from all over the Commonwealth have written, and are writing, books to show that imperial planning was incompatible with respect to colonial aspirations for independence. All roads, they noted, were expected to lead, eventually, to Marlborough House and to a secretariat for the British Commonwealth of Nations. They did. However, like the thousand-year Reich, the Commonwealth, in the 1950s, seemed to have run its course. There was nowhere else to go, although the change was made to look inevitable.

Such conclusions were partly due to the fact that Whitehall's imperial coordinating machinery had always been weak.[39] Moreover, navies were expensive. Nonetheless, there *had* been lots of goodwill for Britain from its overseas minions, and when, in 1914, for instance, the war had come, the colonies had surprised everyone by their performance on air and land and the extent of their participation; so did our friends in South Africa and the Antipodes.

Yet, even in the 1880s, the imperial need for a proper planning apparatus had lacked colonial credibility and expertise. It is a conundrum that when Sir John Colomb was removed from the list of eligible members of Lord Carnarvon's Royal Commission, he was left off because he had no political clout.[40] The commissioners had wanted colonial information without colonial "voice." Sir John, like Sir Charles Dilke, had written a book to show that imperial defense was an imperial educational problem.[41] This point had been missed by the facilitators in London; it still misses them. Sir John had thought that London kept looking at the empire through the wrong end of the telescope. Although

Disraeli had facilitated the production of a defense plan,[42] Gladstone, typically, tried to ignore it. On Fleet Street the acme of colonial defense had not been the state of the fleet in the Indian Ocean but rather the snapshot of General Charles Gordon catapulted unwisely into a stupid colonial situation. The Gordon affair and the Russian muscle flexing in 1885 nevertheless had dramatically changed the situation. Overseas defense arrived in the budget. By 1887, Lord Salisbury had been able to assert to Lord Randolph Churchill, as he dropped him as chancellor of the exchequer, that everyone now agreed that the defense of our imperial bases was a vital matter.[43] This same Salisbury had made it clear that India, the Cape and Egypt had value as bases from which to project power in the Middle East.[44] Indeed, from Gibraltar to Hong Kong, base defense was respectable by the 1890s. Amid conflicting demands, the importance of Imperial defense had come to lie precisely on how much attention a single powerful figure like Lord Salisbury, the prime minister, and, eventually, his redoubtable colonial secretary, Joseph Chamberlain, could exert upon it. Lord Salisbury understood imperial problems.[45] Yet, the defense of the empire failed to generate high-powered acquiescence from the colonial subjects who were becoming emancipated and wary of the commitment that imperial defense, maritime defense, demanded.

How, in these circumstances, could plans have been activated for imperial defense or any other kind of defense? The planning might be difficult, but the stance was imperial, the training was imperial and the whipped-up fears were continental. How could anyone have contemplated an either/or army or navy scenario in these shifting disparate situations? The Royal Navy nevertheless had a stance and from this stance, it accomplished its purposes in the first war, and met its strains in the second.

It has now become fashionable to talk about the Westerners and Easterners in both these conflicts. The same argument could be used in World War II for the Channel versus Mediterranean arenas of conflict, and endless ink has been spilled over the "right" strategy. But what was it?

It was not nuts-and-bolts approaches. Corbett and S.W. Roskill fought against such history; so did Admiral Morison. The traditional British system enabled the Royal Navy, the Royal Canadian Navy, the Royal Australian Navy, the Royal New Zealand Navy and the U.S. Navy to move troops from Commonwealth and American homelands to British or Mediterranean soil. The cross-Channel invasion was not seriously disturbed by German naval forces. These were enormous feats measured on any military scale in history.

Sanity prevailed. It can be seen that the twentieth-century defense precautions were those that had been advised to Gladstone's Government in 1881 and those adopted by Salisbury's in 1887; and they were the same ones pioneered by those whom the sailors call "Our Fathers." It was an intrinsic part of the safety of the British state that the imperial navy had to be able to defend the home islands and its appendages abroad, in peace or war. It had to project what power it could elsewhere from that basic stance. The concept of the navy held by the Victorians was one of "defend at home and show the flag abroad." There was never a strong offensive strategy based on any idea of a "war to end wars." Even against Napoleon, it had been a policy that did not conceive of British conquest of France.

This presentation has moved back and forth across the interpretations of Britain's oceanic activities and the interpretations given to the historical fact of empire. It has tried to draw a distinction between the recording of naval activity, or navalism, and what Corbett called "maritime strategy"; which, after all, is something more than the mere battle deployment of military hardware. This chapter has not attacked the idea of the fragmentation of empire but rather suggested that to learn about global deployment today one must consider global deployment in the past. It suggests that army primacy and naval primacy were not interchangeable notions. The one was not divided by the other, but rather the two were distinguishable yet subject to the overall oceanic dynamics. In both world wars the maritime strategic capacity to deny resources and movement to the enemy guaranteed the flexible base from which the British, and then the British and the Americans, operated. Under this strategic umbrella, priorities were worked out. In 1914 and again in 1939, Great Britain was at the center of an "imperial maritime fighting force" (as Michael Lewis used to call it), the very fact of which dominated strategic selection and created the strengths and weaknesses the historian records now. Imperialists were not just too old-fashioned to think globally while the empire was supposedly receding; their whole tradition and the tools at hand forced them to do so. Some attention has also been given to the change in thinking that made such imperial historical calculations both unrecognizable and unfashionable. It does not purport to downgrade the soldiers, simply to put their efforts in a proper naval perspective. Navy and empire were not separable concepts in theory or in practice.

Finally, this chapter has not addressed the American naval situation in the period of the Cold War and since. Yet, I have written this chapter with the changing global commitment of the U.S. Navy and its satellites (or colonies) constantly in mind. The same questions of wavering support and fragmented responses still apply. Like the Royal Navy, the U.S. Navy is not a collection of artifacts that can safely be laid up until the next armageddon. In oceanic affairs, armageddon is now, and its naval success depends on the ability to influence maritime planning worldwide. By referring to Admiral King's view of naval precedence, I have tried to show that he was never theater-bound in his general thinking, and so I was implying that a new oceanic empire was even then moving onto the stage. I have always thought that the history of the Royal Navy was a cautionary tale for the successors of John Paul Jones, as well as being absolutely fascinating to contemplate. I thought that in 1952, and I think so still.

NOTES

1. John Gallagher, Ronald Robinson and Alice Denny, *Africa and the Victorians* (London: Macmillan, 1961).

2. *Ibid.*, Conclusion.

3. See Donald M. Schurman, *The Education of a Navy: The Development of British Naval Strategic Thought, 1867-1914* (London: Cassell, 1965), 13-36.

4. Gerald S. Graham was Rhodes Professor of Imperial History at the University of London until the mid-1960s.

5. Margaret Thatcher, *The Downing Street Years* (London: Harper Collins, 1993).

6. David G. Chandler, *Great Battles of the British Army, as Commemorated in the Sandhurst Companies* (London: Arms and Armour Press, 1991), particularly Richard Holmes, "The Battle of Normandy, 1944," 205-225.

7. See W.A.B. Douglas, *The Creation of the National Air Force: The Official History of the R.C.A.F,* Vol.2 (Toronto: University of Toronto Press, 1986).

8. Howard d'Egville, *Imperial Defence and Closer Union* (London: P.S. King and Son, 1913).

9. See Schurman, *The Education of a Navy*, 147-185; idem, *Julian S. Corbett, 1854-1922: Historian of British Maritime Policy from Drake to Jellicoe* (London: Royal Historical Society, 1981), especially, 60-79.

10. Corbett was joint editor, along with H.J. Edwards.

11. Sir Herbert Richmond, *The Navy and the War of 1739-48*, 3 vols. (Cambridge: Cambridge University Press, 1923).

12.John Ehrman, *The Navy in the War of William III, 1689-1697* (Cambridge: Cambridge University Press, 1953).

13.Admiral Sir Herbert Richmond was Vere Harmsworth Professor of Naval and Imperial History in the University of Cambridge, 1934-36.

14.J. Holland Rose was Vere Harmsworth Professor of Naval and Imperial History in the University of Cambridge, 1919-33.

15.Eric Walker was Vere Harmsworth Professor of Naval and Imperial History in the University of Cambridge, 1936-1951.

16.Biographer of Admiral Byng and Lord Chatham, former lecturer at the Royal Naval College, Greenwich, and hon. secretary of the Navy Records Society.

17.Sir John Knox Laughton: prolific naval author, naval "schoolie" and professor of history, King's College, London, and first Honorable Secretary of the Navy Records Society.

18.Ironically, the blue-water view seems to be that adopted by Yale professor Paul Kennedy. Certainly it suited his argument to put all imperial naval advocates into a common mixing bowl. Professor Kennedy wrote about naval mastery and continentalism, not about imperial defense.

19.Gerald S. Graham, *The Politics of Naval Supremacy: Studies in British Maritime Ascendancy* (Cambridge: Cambridge University Press, 1965).

20.W.C.B. Tunstall, "Imperial Defence, 1815-1870," in E.A. Benians, J.R.M. Butler and C.E. Carrington, eds., *The Cambridge History of the British Empire*, vol. 2 (Cambridge: Cambridge University Press, 1940). See also vol. 3, "Imperial Defence, 1870-1897" and "Imperial Defence, 1897-1914" (Cambridge, 1959).

21.The articles did not dwell on colonial nationalist history, a lack that is still being made up in a crowded and ongoing activity.

22.Michael Howard, *The Continental Commitment* (London: Temple Smith, 1972).

23.Press efforts aside, described in Marder's work; also see Schurman, *Julian S. Corbett*, 79-99.

24.Paul M. Kennedy, "Tirpitz, England and the Second Navy Law of 1900: A Strategical Critique," *Militargeschichtliche Mittleilungen*, 1970, vol. 2.

25.Jonathan Steinberg, *Yesterday's Deterrent: Tirpitz and the Birth of the German Battle Fleet* (London: Macmillan, 1965).

26.Paul M. Kennedy, *The Rise of the Anglo-German Naval Antagonism, 1860-1917* (London: Allen and Unwin, 1980).

27.Paul M. Kennedy, *The Rise and Fall of the British Naval Mastery* (London: 1976), Chapter 7.

28.A. J. A. Morris, *The Scaremongers: The Advocacy of War and Rearmament, 1896-1914* (London: Routledge and Kegan Paul, 1984), 364-5. I am far from adopting Morris' general argument, but he clearly highlights the irresponsibility of the debate, and so the book is extremely useful.

29.Keith Neilson, *Strategy and Supply: The Anglo-Russian Alliance, 1914-17* (London: Allen and Unwin, 1980), Chapter 1; also see idem, "Greatly Exaggerated': The Myth of the Decline of Great Britain before 1914," *International History Review*, 13:4 (November, 1991), 697-725.

30.Michael Howard, *The Franco-Prussian War: The German Invasion of France, 1870-1871* (London: Haert Davies, 1961).

31.F. A. Johnson, *Defence by Committee* (Oxford: Oxford University Press, 1960).

32.J. P. Mackintosh, "The Role of the Committee of Imperial Defence Before 1914," *English Historical Review* 77 (1962).

33.For a short, expert description, see Brian Tunstall, *The Realities of Naval History* (London: Allen and Unwin, 1936), 189-198.

34.Sir John Pakenham, who was twice first lord of the Admiralty, in 1858 and 1866, and who commissioned and saw through construction both HMS *Warrior* and HMS *Black Prince*.

35.Admiral Sir Alexander Milne, 1806-86. Twice first sea lord and responsible for the proper husbanding of resources that distinguished the Admiralty in the age of Disraeli.

36.Admiral Sir Geoffrey Phipps Hornby, 1825-1895, who in 1877-78 conducted fleet operations in the Sea of Marmora with circumspection and decision.

37.See Arthur J. Marder, *From the Dreadnought to Scapa Flow: The Royal Navy in the Fisher Era*, 5 vols. (London: Oxford University Press, 1961-70), especially vols. 1 & 2.

38.See Morris, *The Scaremongers*.

39.Sometimes imperial arrangements were patronizing, often inefficient. The problem lay with the use colonials made of constitutional loopholes in order to escape from planning, the most important aspect of large-scale warfare. It is no accident that colonials like to repeat the cant phrase that the British always lose every battle but the last. The numbers of books that bear out these points from Melbourne through Ottawa are impressive monuments to a crumbling worldview.

40.D. M. Schurman, "Imperial Defence, 1868-1887" (Ph.D. diss., Cambridge, 1955).

41.Sir Charles Dilke, *Problems of Greater Britain* (London: Macmillan, 1890).

42.For details of the Carnarvon Commission, which Disraeli set up, see Schurman, "Imperial Defence," and Gerald S. Graham, Empire of the North *Atlantic* (Toronto: University of Toronto Press, 1950).

43.Schurman, "Imperial Defence."

44.See Schurman, "Imperial Defence," 213-241.

45.Robinson and Gallagher, *Africa and the Victorians*, 260-273.

2

Sir Julian Corbett And The British Way In Naval Warfare: Problems Of Effectiveness And Implementation

Geoffrey Till

This chapter seeks to establish whether there was a "British way in naval warfare," using the theories of Sir Julian Corbett as a means of identifying its possible characteristics. It then moves on to the even more difficult area of seeking to reflect on its effectiveness and to establish the main problems of implementation.

SUMMARIZING CORBETT

> "It's a tremendously interesting subject," said Davies, pulling down [in two pieces] a volume of Mahan's *Influence of Sea Power*.
> Dinner flagged [and froze] while he illustrated a point by reference to the much-thumbed pages. He was very keen, and not very articulate. I knew just enough to be an intelligent listener, and though hungry was delighted to hear him talk.
> "I'm not boring you, am I?" he said suddenly.
> "I should think not," I protested. "But you might just have a look at the chops."[1]

The point of this quotation from *The Riddle of the Sands* is to explain that while Alfred Thayer Mahan is all very well in his way, the work of Sir Julian Corbett provides a much more appropriate foundation for this review of the strengths and weaknesses of British sea power over the past several centuries. Corbett came late to maritime affairs and associated with the great men ushering the Royal Navy painfully into the twentieth century. He was very concerned about the poverty of contemporary naval thought and hoped to improve it in his lectures at the Naval War Colleges at Greenwich and Portsmouth. Evidently, he did not enjoy the experience, complaining in one letter, "My strategy lectures are very uphill work. I had no idea when I undertook it how difficult it was to present theory to the unused organs of naval officers."[2]

His teaching was supported by an impressive list of naval histories, including several on the Tudor and post-Tudor Royal Navy, a masterpiece on the Seven Years' War, a hitherto unpublished work on the Russo-Japanese War, *Some Principles of Maritime Strategy in 1911*, and the first three volumes of the Official Naval History of the First World War.

Paradoxically, Corbett did most of his writing in that particularly interesting period just before the First World War, when Britain was, in fact, moving away from the kind of strategy that he advocated. As a lawyer, he had a more judicious sense than Mahan of the limitations of sea power and, quite crucially, of its place in the wider scheme of things. What is special about Corbett is his emphasis on the importance of putting naval operations in that broader context that does so much to explain their form and purpose and that, in his view, was affected so much by their result.

Corbett emphasized that strategy needs to be consciously related to foreign policy, and naval strategy to land strategy:

> Of late years the world has become so deeply impressed with the efficacy of sea power that we are inclined to forget how impotent it is of itself to decide a war against great Continental states, how tedious is the pressure of naval action unless it be nicely coordinated with military and diplomatic pressure.[3]

Naval strategy has to be seen not as a separate entity but simply as part of the art of war. Land power and sea power are *not* in opposition, but their relationship with one another is different for "world wide imperial states, where the sea becomes a direct and vital factor" than it is for those whose geography makes the "German or continental school of strategy" more appropriate. Britain, of course, was preeminently just such a maritime state and had derived enormous benefit from developing a set of principles governing the conduct of war "in which the sea is a substantial factor." But this certainly should not mean that the British should neglect the use of armies.

> Since men live upon the land and not upon the sea, great issues between nations at war have always been decided--except in the rarest cases--either by what your army can do against your enemy's territory and national life or else by the fear of what the fleet makes it possible for your army to do.[4]

Sea powers could not defeat land powers on their own but, in conjunction with allies on land, they could determine the outcomes of wars and the nature of the peace.

Britain, Corbett thought, had developed a style of maritime war that combined naval and military power in a uniquely beneficial way. It had allowed the British to "become a controlling force in the European system"[5] and to maintain and extend their interests by manipulating the balance of power in continental Europe. This they had done by the controlled and careful application of maritime power in peace and in war. Because the secret of British success lay in the combination of land and sea power, Corbett used the word "maritime" when he reviewed the strategy of sea power rather than the much narrower term "naval," which Mahan tended to use. This difference is significant.

Corbett's was a strategic approach that limited liability if things went wrong, for, as Sir Francis Bacon remarked, "this much is certain, that he that commands the sea is at great liberty, and may take as much and as little of the war as he will. Whereas those that be strongest by land are many times nevertheless in great straits."[6]

Power at sea provided opportunities for the British to make limited interventions for limited objectives in unlimited wars. Through this capacity to exert influence on the continent of Europe from outside, the British, unlike many of their more landbound competitors, had been able to develop a uniquely business like approach to the otherwise messy and wasteful processes of war. They generally tried to avoid expensive, large-scale military commitments to the continent of Europe and its ferocious wars. Instead, the British had done their best to limit their involvement to the financial support of continental allies and to the exertion of maritime pressure (through blockade, the threat of amphibious landings, attacks and raids on threatened coastlines, and the seizure of their adversaries' far-flung colonies and bases).

This "British way of warfare," as it was subsequently described, required a strong navy able to seize or maintain command of the sea and to exploit that command in support of strategic objectives ashore. While command of the sea was ideally won or maintained by decisive battle, this was often not easily or quickly achieved against a reluctant enemy; in such cases, a blockade could be imposed either to neutralize or to force the enemy to battle. High levels of such command greatly facilitated the strategic use of the sea but were not always possible and sometimes not a prerequisite.

Those strategic uses were twofold. First, command of the sea implied control of the sea as a medium of communication; the enemy's commercial and military shipping could be attacked, and yours protected. So important was such shipping to a country's war economy and its capacity to move military personnel that the control of sea transportation could play a decisive role in defeat or victory.

Second, the flexibility and mobility conferred by power at sea usually allowed Britain to project significant power ashore. Accordingly, the maritime strategy that Corbett advocated required the kind of army that could work with the navy to conquer overseas territories and outflank land bound adversaries with amphibious operations, "more or less upon the European seaboard designed, not for permanent conquest, but as a method of disturbing our enemy's plans and strengthening the hands of our allies and our own position."[7]

DEFINING CHARACTERISTICS OF THE BRITISH WAY IN NAVAL WARFARE

One of the first things that emerge from a review of Britain's maritime strategy over the past 300 years or so is that it is not, in fact, very easy to generalize about. It was a strategy more stumbled into than consciously developed; indeed, its main theorists appeared only at the very end of the long period during which it seems to have held sway. Britain's use of sea power, in fact, is more a maritime tendency than a maritime strategy.

Certainly, British motivations for a sea-based strategy have been quite diverse. All too often, advocacy of such an approach proceeded from a lively expectation of private gain. Sir Francis Drake set the tone here when he abandoned his battle station astern of the armada, leaving his colleagues in grave danger of running fatally into the back of it, in order to seize the profitable little *Rosario*. Moreover, so far as we know, noone reprimanded him for it. His privatized conduct of warfare (in such striking contrast to the regimentation of the Armada) was, in fact, standard and wholly to be expected. In just the same way, the enthusiasm with which the British declarations of war against the Spanish in 1739 or the Dutch in 1780 were greeted proceeded, in large measure, from expectations of tidy profits from the privateering ventures they legitimatized. There was also something very commercial about the appearance in monthly editions of the *Gentleman's Magazine* of lists of British merchant ships lost and French or Spanish ones taken, complete with details of their cargoes. Indeed, the notion of an effectively self-financing style of war (whether by the interception of plate convoys or rich foreign merchantmen or, indeed, anticipations of prize money among Royal Navy personnel) was a constant, if not altogether constructive, element in the British attitude toward maritime war.

A war like the Seven Years War, which focused on the prospective acquisition of colonies, was much more popular with the trading classes than potentially costly entanglements in Europe. T. Smollet put it like this:

> [M]any friends of their country exclaimed against the projected army of observation in Germany, as the commencement of a ruinous continental war, which it was neither the interest of the nation to undertake, nor in their power to maintain, without starving the operations by sea, and in America, founded on British principles.[8]

The war was therefore largely conducted in America and at sea, because for most Britons, that was what it was essentially about. Such maritime concerns, moreover, were thought to be absolutely central to everything that Britain stood for. Thus, the ringing tones of Robert, Earl Nugent in a debate in the Lords, in September 1745:

> Let us remember that we are superior to other nations, principally by our riches; that those riches are the gifts of commerce, and that commerce can subsist only while we maintain a naval force superior to that of other princes. A naval power, and an extended trade reciprocally produce each other; without trade we shall want sailors for our ships of war, and without ships of war we shall soon discover that the oppressive ambition of our neighbours will not suffer us to trade.
> [If] our trade be lost, who can inform us how long we shall be suffered to enjoy our laws or our liberties, or our religion? Without

trade, what wealth shall we possess? [A]nd without wealth, what alliances can be formed?[9]

Britain's approach to warfare, therefore proceeded as much from its own maritime nature and characteristics as from conscious strategic thought. This is not to say that considerations of national strategy were simply a camouflage for venality--or no more than a retrospective rationalization, for, of course, they were more than that. Very often, Britain's leaders knew exactly what they were about and why. Nonetheless, such motivations should remind us that the way that the British used the sea was as much accidental and as much the product of basic geography as it was the result of a carefully and consciously thought-out grand strategy of the sort that the likes of Corbett would appreciate.

For just such reasons, the form that Britain's maritime strategy took varied greatly, too. Sometimes it comprised attempts on Spanish bullion fleets; sometimes it implied a concentration on the destruction of the enemy's navy and merchant shipping; sometimes it revolved around the seizure of colonies--or possibly raids and limited interventions against the European coastline. The degree of its success altered a good deal from one period to the next. The balance struck between land and sea power varied, too. The British way in warfare was probably at its purest in Corbett's Seven Years' War and at its most decayed during the First World War. Interestingly, though, the defeat of its continental commitment in the summer of 1940 forced Britain back to a maritime war in which "the keys to survival were mobilising the economy, maintaining oceanic supply lines, and helping the USSR to sustain its military effort."[10] Clearly, the British way in warfare was far from being a settled phenomenon.

Nonetheless, despite such variety of form and experience, it is possible to pick out some common defining characteristics:

1. As a rule, the British were very wary about the acceptance of significant military commitments to the continent of Europe. The extent of their commitment was limited by the fact that their aim was merely to act as a balancing power, not as a major protagonist in continental struggles. Wherever possible, the aim was to limit their liability. They were particularly sensitive to the prospect of the Low Countries falling into the hands of an expansionist power. When they had to intervene on the continent of Europe and had the

option, the Low Countries were their usual theater of operations.

2. Land power was provided in the main by their necessary continental allies. The British intervened ashore only when those allies, even when subsidized, were unable to maintain the balance on their own. Even then, the level of intervention was as limited, both in scale and in time, as possible.

3. As a rule, the navy tended to be best favored in defense expenditure priorities, especially in the eighteenth century. Table 2.1, while demonstrating this, also suggests the need for caution. The adversary's relative spending figures and priorities are not included but plainly need to be considered as well; the balance between land and sea power struck by Britain's adversaries was generally far less sympathetic to the needs of their navies. Moreover, high levels of spending on either the army or the navy do not necessarily indicate choice or, indeed, perceived importance; they may be driven by the requirement to repair previous neglect. To put it simply, Britain needed to have stronger naval forces than its adversaries but could make do with significantly smaller land forces. Indeed, the weakness of its army was often seen as a justification for a sea-based strategy, rather than a consequence of it. But sometimes, paradoxically enough, this meant spending more on the army than the navy, as in the nineteenth century.

4. The British preferred their main theaters of operation to be essentially maritime in character. Wars that, so far as they were concerned, meant fighting to the last Prussian or Frenchman but focusing instead on the acquisition of other people's colonies or trade were seen as particularly cost-effective and strategically beneficial.

5. This worked best when there was a synergistic relationship between the navy and the army. In themselves, these two services were seen as complementary; both could serve the interests of the other. The army could be used to protect the Low Countries, preventing their vital ports from falling into the hands of hostile navies--an imperative ranging from Elizabeth's war against Spain in the sixteenth century to the Passchendaele campaign in the twentieth. Indeed, interventions on the mainland were occasionally justified on the grounds that this would protect Britain's position at sea by preventing the emergence of a hostile power or coalition strong enough to generate a dangerous *maritime* threat.[11] Accordingly, as Sir Herbert Richmond remarked, nothing was "more misleading or

objectionable than the attribution of success to (sea power or land power)...separately."[12]

TABLE 2.1
Ratio of Spending on Land and Sea Services in Wartime

	Land	Sea
Nine Years' War	46	54
War of the Spanish Succession	40	60
War of the Quadruple Alliance	35	65
Anglo-Spanish War of 1726-29	40	60
War of Jenkin's Ear/War of Spanish Succession	38	62
Seven Years' War	43	57
American War of Independence	33	67
French Revolutionary War	51	49
Napoleonic War	57	43
Crimean War	58	42
First World War	73	27
Second World War	38	36

Source: David French, *The British Way in Warfare* (London: Unwin Hyman, 1990), 57.

6. Although it had vital roles to play in defending the Hanoverian succession, the home base generally and the colonies, especially India, the army most appropriate to the British way in warfare would seem to be of an expeditionary sort, sensitive to the need for the closest cooperation with the navy. But sometimes this was not the case. In the forty or so years before the First World War, in fact, because the army began to read the international scene differently, it pursued quite contrary aims, and interservice cooperation was poor. In consequence, the famous Committee of Imperial Defence (CID) meeting of 23 August 1911 quite properly concluded that a pure Corbettian strategy was no longer possible.
7. It was no coincidence that throughout this period, Britain avoided

vainglory and total objectives, especially on the continent of Europe. The British were manipulating, not transforming, the European balance of power. To be effective, sea power had to be exercised with restraint, just because, in the words of Eyre Crowe, the senior clerk in the Foreign Office in 1907, "Sea power is more potent...No one now disputes it." However, it was "but natural that the Power of the State supreme at sea should inspire universal jealousy and fear, and be ever exposed to the danger of being overthrown by a general combination of the world."[13] Only by moderate behavior could Britain keep such a possibility in check.

THE EFFECTIVENESS OF THE BRITISH WAY IN NAVAL WARFARE: TOWARD A VERDICT

Now that we have looked at both the theory and the practice of Britain's sea-based strategy from the first Queen Elizabeth to the second, the obvious question is, Did it work? The question can perhaps be split into two parts: did it work as a strategy of war, and did it work in peace as an instrument of diplomacy?

At one level, the answer to the first part of the question seems simple. Britain engaged in twelve major wars between 1688 and 1945, lost one but not too badly, drew three and won eight--with some help from allies. But here the real question is how responsibility for the outcome to these wars should be allocated between British sea power, on one hand, and British and allied land power, on the other--but this would be prohibitively difficult.

Another indicator of the relative success of the British way in maritime warfare would be Britain's transition from being the small, divided collection of rather insignificant and thinly populated islands of the sixteenth century into a global superpower in the nineteenth century. Corbett is quite clear about the reason for this. Command of the sea and the opportunities it provided explained how it was "[t]hat a small country with a weak army should have been able to gather to herself the most desirable regions of the earth, and to gather them at the expense of the greatest military Powers."[14]

It is certainly difficult to believe that Britain's expansion and its sea-based strategy were simply coincidental. At the very least, it seems reasonable to conclude that sea power had a significant role to play in Britain's comparative military success.

The more important question is the extent to which the British way in naval warfare helped Britain secure its political objectives in peace as well as in war. Having digested his Clausewitz, Corbett was well aware of the fact that war was a political act and that the first function of the fleet was "to support or obstruct diplomatic effort."[15]   But, not unnaturally, given his more adversarial age, the focus of most of his writing was on the operational characteristics of sea power. His preoccupation was with war, not peace, although he was always anxious to demonstrate the connections between the objectives of war and its form. It was left, therefore, to analysts of a much later generation to articulate the characteristics of what has since become known as naval diplomacy.[16]

This is not the place for a detailed exposition of their analysis of what naval diplomacy is and how it works. Suffice it to say that their conclusion that the mobility and flexibility of navies make them uniquely useful as instruments of foreign policy would have come as no surprise to the sailors whose activities Corbett studied. Thus, Nelson stated, "I hate your pen-and-ink men; a fleet of British ships of war are the best negotiators in Europe."[17]

It is important to note, however, that there were limits to what sea power could achieve diplomatically, even at the height of Britain's maritime power in the nineteenth century. The point was made, paradoxically enough, by Lord Palmerston, when commenting on the lessons of a Middle East crisis of the time: "Every country that has towns within cannon shot of deep water will remember the operations of the British fleet on the coast of Syria in September, October and November 1840, whenever such a country has a difference with us."[18]

But many countries had towns that were *not* within cannon shot of the coast and/or were relatively impervious to pressure from the sea. British sea power, for example, was not one of Bismarck's chief preoccupations when building Germany. The British were concerned about his victory over Denmark, for example, but could, in fact, do very little to prevent it. In other instances, too, despite its command of the sea, Britain was obliged to stand resentfully on the sidelines watching the unfolding of unwanted events.

This meant that Britain could hope to be no more than a "balancer." It could not hope to transform the European power system. Not infrequently, moreover, the British had to use their successes outside Europe in order to compensate for their relative failures inside it, as, for example, in the 1801 Treaty of Amiens, by which they had to give up their recent overseas conquests. But, as a whole, this approach usually got the British what they really wanted.

PROBLEMS OF IMPLEMENTATION

So how is this level of effectiveness to be explained? The diplomatic and military utility of British sea power and the British way in maritime warfare was partly a function of Britain's difficulty in exerting maritime pressure on its adversaries and partly a function of their intrinsic vulnerability to such pressure. We will consider both issues in turn.

Finding the Necessary Resources

Sea power is sometimes represented as uniquely cost-effective in that its constituents come naturally and easily from the existence of a large and profitable merchant marine, a prosperous empire and the sophisticated financial system that these both encourage. The fact that it requires fewer human resources than large continental armies and greatly reduces the prospect of the homelands being ravaged by foreign invaders reinforces the impression that maritime powers can command at sea and dominate foreign shores with a kind of olympian ease that their less fortunate land-bound competitors might envy. Nor is such an impression wholly without foundation.[19]

Nonetheless, the ease with which the constituents of power and sea can be produced should not be exaggerated. Britain's maritime power in the eighteenth and nineteenth centuries depended on a huge infrastructure. In 1809, the Royal Navy comprised 755 ships, totaling 500,000 tons, but depended on the biggest shipbuilding industry in Europe, by far, and a merchant fleet twice the size of the French, four times the size of the Dutch and ten times the size of the Spanish. The navy's manpower strength peaked at 142,000 in 1810. When, in June 1792, Admiral Russel had brought 64 English ships of the line and 24 fire ships into Torbay, his crews totaled 24,000 men. The effort to support such a vast endeavor can be deduced by the fact that, at that time, the population of Exeter, the county town of Devon was a mere 14,000 souls. It should be remembered that in the eighteenth century, "the Navy was by far the largest and most complex of all government services, and indeed by a large margin, the largest industrial organisation in the western world."[20]

Sea power may be cost-effective, but it does not come cheap.

As we shall see shortly, the exigencies of the maritime situation and the demands of naval operations meant that huge resources were actually needed and consumed. By the end of the nineteenth century, British statesmen were becoming increasingly anxious about their ability to go on paying the necessary price. The problem was exacerbated by the fact that not all British military resources could be devoted to "the sea affair." It was necessary to maintain a significant army, too, for the reasons previously identified. By the end of the nineteenth century, it was getting difficult to do both. As Lord Selborne remarked to the Indian viceroy in 1903, "It is a terrific task to remain the greatest naval power when naval powers are year by year increasing in numbers and in strength and at the same time be a military power strong enough to meet the greatest military power in Asia."[21]

The only solution to the problem was a conscious policy of threat reduction through diplomatic accommodation with at least some of Britain's potentially most dangerous competitors, on one hand and the ardent pursuit of help from "hands across the sea," on the other. The Dominions did their best to help, but it was really the United States that more than filled the gap, especially in the Second World War.

Protection Against Invasion

The Royal Navy's capacity to commit its resources to offensive actions against the enemy was also constrained by the need to keep some forces back against the possibility of the enemy's launching expeditions against British possessions overseas or, still worse, seeking to invade the British Isles themselves. In Erskine Childers' opinion, Germany before the First World War had one great advantage over Britain: "Her hands are free for offence in home waters since she has no distant network of coveted colonies and dependencies on which to dissipate her defensive energies."[22]

The Royal Navy was nearly always totally confident that its power at sea constituted the final guarantee against large-scale invasion of the British Isles. The most serious investigation of the subject in the period before the First World War found in the navy's favor but the nervousness remained. Moreover, for much of the period, there was sufficient doubt about the Hanoverian succession and/or the situation in Ireland to make it dangerous to ignore the prospect of even quite small invasion forces that *might* be able to slip past British blockading squadrons. In 1688, William of Orange had successfully "invaded" with very few men, and in 1745, the Pretender had arrived in Scotland with just six companions. The French expedition to Bantry Bay in 1796 conveyed the same message. The villains of *The Riddle of the Sands* had a similar scheme in mind--a small invasion force landing in the Wash and striking out against Britain's industrial Midlands, spreading terror and confusion as they went.

In the nineteenth century, such prospects, however unlikely in the main, worried the politicians and the people, diverted national defense resources away from the navy to the construction of fortifications along the southern coast and to the formation of national militia forces and necessarily absorbed a proportion of the Navy's own resources. When, in the First World War, an aerial threat was added, this pattern of diversion was even more marked. By the mid-1930s, the aerial threat from continental Europe meant that the leaders of this offshore island were beginning to think that "Britain's new frontier was now the Rhine."[23] Airpower had made Britain more continental. The summer of 1940 took this process even further, and postwar developments, especially the advent of nuclear weapons, completed it.

The Protection of Shipping

Navalists have always tended to emphasize the positive side of sea power, namely, the effect it has on the adversary. They have, by the same token, tended to neglect its negative aspects, the costs rather than the benefits. The benefits are largely about the influence that naval operations have on events ashore, or in the modern terminology, about power "from the sea."[24] But the British have also been hugely concerned with what happens *at* sea and with power *at* sea. The extent to which operations at sea consume the resources of maritime states reduces their relative capacity to prevail over land powers.

British experience showed that the protection of trade was vital for maritime states, was often intensely difficult and consumed resources for defensive purposes that would otherwise have been available for the projection of power ashore. For this reason--and it is a point insufficiently emphasized by Mahan--being maritime, while not a matter of choice, can be a source of fundamental weakness. The prime minister, Ramsay Macdonald, put it like this in 1929:

In our case, our navy is the very life of our nation. We are a small island. For good or for ill, the lines of our Empire have been thrown all over the face of the earth. We have to import our food. A month's blockade, effectively carried out, would starve us all in the event of any conflict. Britain's navy is Britain itself and the sea is our security and our safety.[25]

But a glance at the U-boat campaigns of both world wars, shows how difficult, and profligate in resources the defense of shipping could be. The sheer size of the ocean and the nature of the medium seem to give the offensive, rather than the defensive, the advantage in naval warfare; the attacker usually needs to devote fewer resources to a maritime campaign than does the defender. Resources consumed by the difficult business of protecting shipping could not be applied offensively against the adversary elsewhere, a simple fact that, for example, persuaded Admiral Donitz to continue the U-boat offensive even when he realized he could not win the tonnage war.

The protection of shipping was also inherently different, both in style and in requirement from a campaign to win command of the sea-- and, to a considerable extent, in competition with it. The potential tension between the two was exemplified by British experience in the First World War. The Admiralty is often accused by historians of trying so hard to force battle on the German High Sea Fleet in the North Sea that it foolishly neglected the needs of the defense of shipping. Escorts needed for convoys were tied to the defense of the Grand Fleet, in order to improve British chances against the German battle fleet should it ever have come out after 1916.

However, there is also considerable substance in the Admiralty's claim that the Battle fleet and the command of the sea it generated, provided the conditions in which shipping could best be protected:

To the Grand Fleet has been due the safety of the naval forces employed on patrol and escort, and but for its latent power, the hundreds of small craft protecting trade from submarine attack and actively attacking the submarine would have been swept off the sea by enemy cruisers.[26]

This takes us to the question of command of the sea and decisive battle as elements in the British approach to naval warfare.

The Pursuit of Necessary Battle

The seizure or maintenance of command of the sea has nearly always been the first and primary aim of the Royal Navy, because, as Corbett reminds us, it makes everything else possible. But seizing/maintaining command of the sea in itself takes a good many resources, and Britain has not always had enough. Despite its maritime priorities, Britain has moved through periods of relative weakness, when the naval odds were not particularly favorable for the Royal Navy. The American War of Independence was an example. In 1782, the Royal Navy comprised 94 ships of the line; its adversaries deployed 146, although they were admittedly not concentrated. Britain's inability to maintain an adequate Western Squadron at this time meant that all the naval battles of that conflict were fought in the Western hemisphere, and this played a significant part in Britain's defeat.

In the same way, the naval balance in the decade before the First World War caused concern and necessitated new alliances with Japan, France and Russia and played an important part in the British acceptance of a continental commitment. His apparent inability to deal with the German U-boat threat in 1917 led Admiral Jellicoe to advocate the Passchendaele offensive, which, it was hoped, would drive Germany away from its naval bases in Belgium. The result was a costly, futile waste of scarce resources that exemplified the extent to which a shortage of the naval resources needed for command of the sea sometimes forced Britain to retreat from its preferred maritime posture.

Sometimes technological developments seemed likely to exacerbate the situation. Nonetheless, British experience in the Norway and Crete campaigns demonstrated that the costs of operations within reach of hostile, shore-based aircraft were indeed higher and that the navy needed to provide more and, expensive layers of defense around its offensive forces. While, in the longer run, navies absorbed this new technological challenge, using it, indeed, to add to their own potential, such developments did contribute to the increasing costs of power at sea.

This shortage of resources exacerbated the permanent tension there always is between concentrating the fleet in order to secure command of the sea against hostile battle fleets, on one hand, and dividing the fleet to exploit that command by supporting amphibious operations or protecting shipping, on the other. As we have seen, the requirements of strength *at* sea were often one of the biggest constraints on the British ability to *use* their sea power and to enjoy the strategic benefits it could confer.

There were four possible solutions to this problem, and all were applied at one time or another. The first was to have enough ships to seize command and to exploit it *at the same time*, as in the opium wars, or the Crimean War--but usually the opposition was too strong for this simple solution. Second, perhaps the most elegant of solutions was simply to blockade the enemy coast. The mere presence of the Western Squadron or the Channel Fleet or the Home Fleet as the case might be, should prevent the enemy from going to sea, thereby maintaining command of the sea, protecting commerce and preventing invasions or foreign expeditions against British colonies and bases overseas all in one fell swoop. But over and over again, British experience showed that blockades were rarely a complete answer; some enemy ships, squadrons or commerce raiders always seemed able to escape to the open sea. Blockade made the problem manageable, but it did not solve it.

Third, the British could, in theory, follow the logical sequence of first seizing command and only then exploiting it--but their enemies were rarely that cooperative or the strategic requirements of the war sufficiently leisurely to allow the navy to go through these stately procedures. All too often, as Corbett remarked, the situation on land demanded that shipping and expeditions had to cross a sea that was, at best, only partially commanded.

The final and best solution to this historic dilemma, of course, was to *force* a battle on the enemy's naval forces, destroy them and decide the matter once and for all. The Royal Navy was always attracted by the notion of the decisive battle as the optimum means of winning command of the sea. Their view just before the First World War was usefully summarized for the benefit of the 1902 Colonial Conference:

> The primary object of the British navy is not to defend anything, but to attack the fleets of the enemy, and by defeating them to afford protection to British Dominions, supplies and commerce. This is the ultimate aim....The traditional role of the Royal Navy is not to act on the defensive, but to prepare to attack the force which threatens-- in other words to assume the offensive.[27]

This being the case, it was unwise to engage in any activity whose conduct might undermine the battle fleet's capacity to fight and win the necessary deciding battle(s). The exploitation of command through the conduct of combined operations or the protection of merchant shipping might weaken the seizure/maintenance of command if it required detaching important forces from the battle fleet. In the 1906 *Brassey's Naval Annual*, J. R. Thursfield argued precisely this point when he maintained that one of the Admiralty's guiding principles was, "that the attack and defence of commerce is best effected by concentration of force, and that a dispersion of force for either of these objects is the strategy of the weak and cannot materially influence the ultimate result of the war."[28] Rather than dissipate the main forces of the navy, it might even be best to allow merchant shipping to look after itself until the decisive battle was won.

But Corbett warned that this "old British creed," although generally admirable and effective, could be taken to excess. In some circumstances, it could lead to a distraction from the real aim of the war. He also pointed out that Britain's adversaries, whose naval forces were normally weaker, often sensibly sought to avoid battle with the Royal Navy. The British thus needed to be on their guard against the danger of trying too hard in this direction, lest such purist aspirations undermine their practical capacity to use the sea as fully as they often needed to in the meantime.[29]

In 1918, the Admiralty itself accepted that "the command of the sea...was secured before the actual outbreak of hostilities by the presence in the North Sea in full readiness for action of nearly all the modern ships of the British Fleet."[30] This being the case, Jellicoe, famously the only man who could lose the war in an afternoon, was able at Jutland to conduct himself with becoming caution. Winston Churchill encapsulated the point in a much discussed article in *The London Magazine* in 1916:

> Although the battle squadrons of the Grand Fleet have been denied all opportunity of decisive battle, yet from the beginning they have all enjoyed the fruits of a complete victory. If Germany had never built a Dreadnought, or if all German dreadnoughts had been sunk, the control and authority of the British navy could not have been more effective. . . . There was no need for the British to seek battle at all. . . . A keen desire to engage the enemy impelled, and a cool calculation of ample margins of superiority justified, a movement not necessarily required by any practical need.[31]

Although, in order to avoid the men with blue pencils, Corbett's account of the Battle of Jutland was a subtle matter of nuance, some members of the board who read the draft did not like it, even if they did not quite know why,[32] and had inserted in the final volume a note to the effect that, "Their Lordships find that some of the principles advocated in the book, especially the tendency to minimise the importance of seeking battle and of forcing it to a conclusion, are directly in conflict with their views."[33]

Afterward, this "sea heresy" associated with Churchill, Corbett and Jellicoe was also vigorously attacked by Thursfield and Pollen. An anonymous contributor to the *Naval Review* of 1931 said of Corbett:

> He had a legal training and mind, which was shown in his preference for getting the better of the enemy in some other way than coming to blows...his teaching did not preach that to destroy or to neutralise the enemy's armed force was the primary military aim leading to a military decision. As an example one may look at his "Principles of Maritime Strategy" and see, out of 310 pages, how many are devoted to "Battle." ...Is it too much to say that Lord Fisher's Baltic Scheme, Mr. Churchill's naval Brigade, even the Dardanelles Expedition, were instances of "ill digested Julian Corbett's 'Seven Years War' "?[34]

This comment is interesting for two reasons. First, it nicely illustrates the fact that the vigorous pursuit of command of sea by decisive battle could, indeed, be seen to interfere with the exploitation of command by, say, the conduct of combined operations. Accordingly, Corbett's *maritime* approach to warfare could be undermined by such apparent *naval* necessities.

After the war, the importance of battle continued to be discussed, since it had a bearing on everything else, not least of which was the necessity of ensuring that the Battle fleet was fully prepared for war. The Royal Navy has been criticized by both Arthur Marder and S. W. Roskill for its preoccupation with a major fleet action[35] because it led the British to neglect the requirements of trade protection and amphibious operations.

But there is no doubt that the British were aware of the problem. In 1938, for example, Admiral L. E. Holland (then assistant chief of the naval staff and eventually lost in the battle cruiser *Hood*) certainly believed that this concentration on the fleet action was the right policy to pursue for a war against the Japanese, for they had exactly the same conceptions of war. "It is generally accepted," he said, "that in the case of a war against Japan the same processes which brought about main battle in the past will be again at work and the final round will be fought between the main fleets."[36]

But the Germans might be more of a problem because, for the foreseeable future, they would not have enough naval forces to make a sensible challenge. There was some anxiety that the Royal Navy's preoccupation with the requirements of the decisive action might skew some naval developments, such as aviation. Commenting on what was the most substantial interwar analysis by the British of the role of naval aviation, Admiral Backhouse, then commander in chief of the Home Fleet and later first sea lord, remarked perceptively:

> [t]he memorandum may be said to visualise, almost exclusively, action between two battlefleets both accompanied by carriers. This condition is only applicable at present in a Far Eastern war. It assumes also, that both fleets intend to fight--*so that what might be described as an unorthodox form of battle results.* While it is appreciated fully that these conditions must be given due weight, functions of the Fleet Air Arm in a war much nearer home must be considered also."[37]

This reference to a major fleet action being "an unorthodox form of battle" clearly demonstrates that (in Richmond's unkind phrase) "the fighting blockhead" school of maritime strategy, about which Corbett was so concerned, was far from being the only one helping to determine the British way in naval warfare. In the interwar period, the dangers of concentrating the limited resources available on the battle fleet were realized, but such was the importance of command of the sea that few thought there was really much choice.

PROBLEMS OF EFFECTIVENESS: THE LIMITS OF NAVAL PROJECTION

The effectiveness of the British way in maritime warfare was a function not only of British difficulties in exerting maritime pressure but also of the vulnerability of their adversaries to such pressure.

"Making War As We Must"

When their adversaries' vulnerability to purely maritime pressure was less than decisive, the British had to supplement their maritime pressure with continental land pressure. Not usually having the resources to supply both to the necessary extent, the British had to find continental Europeans ready and able to do their land fighting for them. But in particular states of the European balance of power, this was not always possible, as the campaigns of Marlborough and Wellington both testify. Perhaps the best illustration of this possibility occurred in 1915. In that year, Kitchener ruefully told the Cabinet, "Unfortunately we had to make war as we must and not as we should like to,"[38] and the British began to prepare for continental war on a scale they had never before contemplated. This was the culmination of a process that had, in fact, begun some ten years earlier, when the British began to realize that the rising power of Germany threatened their maritime supremacy.

There was India to worry about as well. The entente with France of the year before had not solved Britain's strategic problem because Germany seemed likely to be too powerful for France to handle on its own.[39] In the following few years, the British commitment to help France increased incrementally and led to the dispatch of the British Expeditionary Force (B.E.F.) in 1914.

The 1915 decision was the product of two things. First and most obviously, it was a recognition of the fact that Britain's chosen allies in the European war, the French and the Russians, needed help badly after their initial reverses in the first year of the war. Second, there was an acceptance of the fact that anything Britain was able to do against Germany from the sea was unlikely to have a significant impact on the dangerous situation both on the western and the eastern fronts. In 1905, the first sea lord had recognized that

> No action by the Navy alone can do France any good. It would amount to little more than the capture of a few colonies from Germany which are of no use to her, and the stoppage of direct overseas trade from her own ports; but as she would probably have direct access to the sea through neutral ports...this would not greatly affect her general trade....The result would depend entirely on the military operations on the French frontier.[40]

In Woodrow Wilson's view neither economic blockade nor traditional types of amphibious operation were likely to be decisive against Germany. Both points merit some examination, because they are both particular examples of general problems that the British had always faced.

Economic Blockade

Wilson clearly had little faith in the prospect of British sea power's being effective through the economic pressure exerted by commercial blockade. This is interesting in that navalists often pinned considerable hopes on this type of action at sea. Mahan, indeed, celebrated "that noiseless pressure upon the vitals of France, that compulsion whose silence when once noted, becomes to the observer the most striking and awful mark of sea power."[41]

This is not the place for a detailed examination of the historical effectiveness of blockade,[42] but in the period before the First World War, the British, on the basis of their own experience of blockades over the previous 300 years or so, did *not* expect it to be decisive on its own, not least because they, like nearly everyone else, anticipated a short war. But in any case, in their previous wars, the British had discovered that the extent to which their adversaries' war economies were, in fact, dependent on either seaborne trade or the resources of their colonies, was frequently exaggerated, not least by those who expected to profit from their attack. There were considerable problems in instituting effective blockades, too. These were partly operational. The sea was a big place, and it was extremely difficult to keep sufficient forces at sea to cover it effectively. The problems were also partly political; a tight economic blockade always risked antagonizing neutral opinion, possibly adding, as in 1812, to the list of adversaries. For this reason, the likes of Eyre Crowe constantly counseled the Admiralty to be moderate in their exercise of maritime power.

So for all these reasons, the British did not go to war in 1914 expecting their sea power to bring about a rapid economic collapse in Germany. Indeed, in many quarters it was widely expected that maritime powers were much more vulnerable to this sort of pressure than were their continental adversaries.

In fact, the war lasted four years, and effects of the blockade, taken with other pressures on the German economy, were greater than the British had anticipated. The Germans certainly *thought* the economic blockade had done them real harm, and, as a result, the British pinned much more faith in it in 1939-40 than they had twenty-five years earlier. This time, the maritime blockade on its own was largely ineffective because of the reach of German land power. Nonetheless, when associated with the effects of strategic bombing, it contributed usefully to the economic destruction of the adversary. Only against maritime Japan could the full potential of the blockade be developed, however.

To summarize, Mahan and other navalists tended to overestimate the relative importance of colonial trade to continental powers, underestimated their autarkic potential and failed to give due weight to the physical difficulties of actually imposing a blockade. In fact, their views may unconsciously have reflected the much greater vulnerability of *maritime* powers to economic blockade. To conclude, although economic blockade did do real harm to the war economies of continental states, it was certainly not to the decisive extent conjured up by Mahan's hyperbole and probably did not justify Corbett's more moderate hopes either.

In some circumstances, however, the imposition of a more or less effective economic blockade was relatively cost-free for the British, being often a by-product of their determination to prevent the concentration of their enemies' naval forces. Especially in the early days, it could also be something of a self-financing strategy and was popular domestically.

Amphibious Operations

After summarizing the strengths of Germany in his 1905 memorandum, the first sea lord went on to propose diversions "on the coast of Germany in France's favour," and over the next few years there were many such schemes against the Low Countries, the Friesian islands, Heligoland and even the Baltic. These varied in nature. All were eventually found insufficient, impractical or both. The nearest approach to a Corbettian strategy was the Dardanelles campaign. This was, arguably, "the one imaginative strategic idea of the war on the Allied side,"[43] but its strategic possibilities were thrown away by the truly appalling way in which the operation was conducted. By the summer of 1915, then, the British preference for projecting their power into Europe from the sea had manifestly failed. Given this, there was no choice but to accept the continental commitment. Critics of the Corbettian approach have used the 1905-1915 period as a striking example of the imperviousness of the continental state to the kind of maritime pressure (either by blockade or by amphibious operations) that maritime Britain could bring to bear.

The Dardanelles campaign illustrates the difficulties quite often encountered by the British in their conduct of the combined operations so central to Corbett's approach; its failure was neither inevitable, nor did it necessarily imply fundamental weakness in his concept of maritime warfare, however. For a combined operation to succeed, there needs to be agreement in advance, at the highest level, about its priority and about its conduct. In 1915, neither was achieved. The campaign was, instead, a scrambling affair that started as a purely naval operation, changed into a limited amphibious operation in support of the navy and ended as full-scale combined operation. If it had been the latter from the start, as Corbett plainly wanted, the story would probably have ended very differently.

But such a thing would have been surprising, given the poor state of joint planning in the prewar period and the inability to agree on an effective command structure for the actual operation. In fact, both the army and the navy were in favor of combined operations, but for neither were they a top priority. The army concentrated on the demands of fighting in France but was interested in minor, largely unopposed operations against the Ottoman Empire, mainly in the western Mediterranean.[44] Army opinion was split over the Dardanelles operation, with many regarding it as an eccentric and probably futile diversion from the real business of defeating the Germans on the western front.

The navy, too, had its reservations. Successive first sea lords were in favor of combined operations, but principally in the north west European theater, where they would help achieve naval objectives. Corbett fair-mindedly pointed out that the appearance of the U-boat, the continuing attack on shipping and the need to support operations in Africa and elsewhere were all putting a strain on the navy's ability to contain the German fleet. Admiral Lord Fisher was willing to dispatch surplus warships to support such secondary operations as the Dardanelles but resigned when the campaign's increasing demands seemed likely to undermine "the plans he was elaborating to secure a perfect control of Home Waters and the Baltic."[45] For just the same reason, Jellicoe protested strongly about losing the Third Battle Squadron to the Mediterranean in the autumn of 1915.

Given these divided counsels, the failure to agree on a combined strategic approach was unsurprising. But in the operational area, cooperation between the forces ashore and afloat was generally much better from the start and steadily improved. By the time of the Suvla operation, things had improved enormously. "[A]s an example of perfect coordination between land and sea...the movement could scarcely be surpassed."[46]

Nor did the Suvla operation seem to support the notion that amphibious operations were *intrinsically* more difficult, say, than their equivalent on the western front. But this had been a reason commonly advanced by the army before the war for avoiding combined operations, especially opposed ones. In the railway age, the adversary could move its defending forces around so fast that early lodgments, even if made, could be brushed off. Even in the eighteenth century, sea-landed forces were often necessarily less mobile and less heavily armed than the forces they had to confront. Technology would surely make this problem worse. Moreover, naval skeptics might have added, the presence of mines and submarines seemed to make the landing operation itself even more hazardous now than they were.

Once again, Corbett's answer was that these problems *had*, in fact, been managed by the end of the Dardanelles campaign. Indeed, the withdrawal of 120,000 troops from under the noses of the Turks was a splendid indication of the level of improvement achieved in all aspects of amphibious warfare.

> In that marvellous evacuation we see the national genius for amphibious warfare raised to its highest manifestation. In hard experience and successive disappointments, the weapon had been brought to a perfect temper, and when the hour of fruition came to show of what great things it was capable, it was used only to effect a retreat.[47]

So, manifestly, combined operations could be made to work, but would they have the desired effect? The failure to agree on a combined approach early enough was at least partly due to skepticism that these difficult and costly operations would have the large-scale strategic consequence that its advocates hoped for. Even in Corbett's favorite example, the Seven Years' War, skeptics argued that amphibious operations in Europe were of dubious utility. British raids on the French coast did not lead to a withdrawal of French troops from Germany. In the end, Frederick the Great had to save himself, aided by the fortuitous death of the Russian empress.[48]

Corbett's conclusions were based on evidence such as the capture of Havana in 1762, Wolfe's Canadian operations in the Seven Years' War, Wellington's Peninsula campaign--surely the quintessential combined operation[49]--and the Crimean War. When amphibious operations were properly conducted, they could, indeed, be the means by which sea powers could really help decide the outcome of wars, because they allowed them to strike at their enemies' weakest points. Nothing in his study of the Dardanelles campaign led Corbett to modify that point. His basic proposition was that "the continental method" of striking decisively "where the enemy's military concentration was highest" made sense only where there was "sufficient preponderance of force to ensure a decision." In his view this was not the situation on the western front, and it was therefore best to "postpone offence in the main theatre and devote our combined energies" to improving the strategic balance by striking elsewhere.[50]

Trying to come to a conclusion over who was right about the Dardanelles, its advocates or its critics, is beyond the scope of this chapter but subsequent events on the western front certainly did not make the apparent alternatives to Corbett's maritime approach seem very attractive to Liddell Hart and most of his contemporaries.

But it was the failure of the campaign that most impressed the Admiralty and that made them shy away from such entanglements in the future. This partly accounts for the neglect of combined operations in the interwar period, although there were other reasons for this, as we have seen. As a result, Corbett's concept of maritime warfare was put into cold storage, and British amphibious operations in the early part of the Second World War were badly handled. But, once again, the necessary lessons were learned, and success followed. Their most important strategic function, however, was to provide the conditions by which Allied armies (predominantly American and Soviet) could actually go on to win the war by "the continental method," once the necessary preponderance of force had been achieved.

However, the apparently heightened utility of amphibious forces in the fifty years since the Second World War, when objectives tended to be local and limited, seems to confirm the continued salience of Corbett's concepts of maritime strategy even today.

NOTES

1. Erskine Childers, *The Riddle of the Sands* (London: Sidgwick & Jackson, 1935), 41.

2.Quoted in Donald M Schurman, *Julian S. Corbett 1854-1922* (London: Royal Historical Society, 1981), 44.

3.J. S. Corbett, *England in the Seven Years' War*, Vol 1 (London: Longmans, Green, 1907), 5.

4.J. S. Corbett, *Some Principles of Maritime Strategy* (Annapolis: Naval Institute Press, 1988), 15-6.

5.J. S. Corbett, *Drake and the Tudor Navy*, vol 1 (London: Longmans, 1917), 6.

6.Cited in Corbett, *Some Principles*, 58.

7.Ibid., 66.

8.T. Smollet, *History of England*, vol 1 (London: 1760), 423.

9.Speech, reported in *Gentleman's Magazine*; September 1745, 465-6.

10.Daniel A. Baugh, "British Strategy during the First World War in the Context of Four Centuries," in Daniel M. Masterton, *Naval History: The Sixth Symposium* (Wilmington, Del: Scholarly Resources, 1987), 100.

11.P. M. Kennedy, *Strategy and Diplomacy 1870-1945* (London: Fontana, 1983), 57.

12.Ibid., 62-3.

13.Cited in N. Tracy, *Attack on Maritime Trade* (London: Macmillan, 1991), 101-2.

14.Corbett, *Some Principles*, 57-8.

15.Corbett, *England in the Seven Years War*, 6.

16.The literature on this subject is vast. Two of the best introductions are James Cable, *Gunboat Diplomacy: Political Applications of Limited Naval Force*, 2d ed. (London: Chatto and Windus, 1981) and Ken Booth, *Law, Force and Diplomacy at Sea* (London: Allen and Unwin, 1985).

17.Cited in A. Mahan, *The Life of Nelson* (London: Sampson, Low, 1899), 463.

18.Cited in A. Lambert, *The Last Sailing Battlefleet* (London: Conway, 1991), 38.

19.Cited in W. H. Parker, *Mackinder: Geography as an Aid to Statecraft* (Oxford: Clarendon Press, 1982), 162.

20.Michael Duffy, "The Establishment of the Western Squadron as the Linchpin of British Naval Strategy," in M. Duffy, ed., *Parameters of British Naval Power 1650-1850* (Exeter: University Press, 1992), 66; N.A.M. Rodger, *The Wooden World: An Anatomy of the Georgian Navy* (London: Collins, 1986), 29.

21.Michael Howard, *The Continental Commitment* (London: Temple Smith, 1972), 17.

22.Childers, *The Riddle of the Sands*, 282.

23.Howard, *The Continental Commitment*, 107-8.

24.This is a reference to the U.S. Navy's strategic formulation of that name, which appeared in September 1993.

25.Ramsay Macdonald, 11 October 1929, quoted in Air 9/108, Public Records Office (PRO).

26.Admiralty Summary: "The British Naval Effort, 4th August 1914 to 11th November 1918," 24 December 1918, Adm 167/57, PRO.

27.Cited by P. M. Kennedy in "The Relevance of the Prewar British and American Maritime Strategies to the First World War and its Aftermath" in J. B. Hattendorf and Robert S. Jordan, eds., *Maritime Strategy and the Balance of Power* (London: Macmillan, 1989), 168.

28.J. R. Thursfield, "The Defence of Trade" in *Brassey's Naval Annual*, 1906, 53-73.

29.Corbett, *Some Principles*, 167.

30."British Naval Effort."

31.Cited in Anthony Pollen, *The Great Gunnery Scandal: The Mystery of Jutland* (London: Collins, 1980), 160.

32.For a useful description of the Jutland controversy, see B. McL Ranft, ed., *The Beatty Papers*, vol. 2 (London: Scholar Press for the Naval Records Society, 1993), 417-28 plus supporting documents.

33.This is the wording of the board's admonition inserted into vol. 3 of J. S. Corbett, *Naval Operations* (London: Longmans Green, 1920).

34.See "Sea Heresies" and "Some Notes on the Early Days of the Royal Naval War College," two anonymous articles in the *Naval Review*, (1931).

35.Geoffrey Till, *Air Power and the Royal Navy*, 1914-1945 (London: Macdonald and Janis, 1979), 169.

36.Ibid.

37.Cited in ibid., 170; emphasis added.

38.French, *The British Way in Warfare*, 170.

39.Howard, *The Continental Commitment*, 43.

40.Cited in ibid.

41.A. T. Mahan, *The Influence of Sea Power on the French Revolution and Empire*, vol. 2 (Boston: Little, Brown, 1892), 184.

42.Tracy, *Attack*, is a useful introduction, but see A. C. Bell, *A History of the Blockade of Germany 1914-18* (London: Historical Section, Committee of Imperial Defence, 1937).

43.Arthur J. Marder, *From the Dardanelles to Oran* (London: Oxford University Press, 1974), 1.

44.This subject is being researched by David Massam at Oxford University, to whom I am indebted for much interesting discussion on this and other points.

45.Corbett, *Naval Operations*, vol. 2, 105-6.

46.Ibid. vol. 3, 93, 241.

47.Ibid.

48.French, *The British Way in Warfare*, 52; M. Howard, *The Causes of Wars* (London: Temple Smith, 1983), 176.

49.Baugh, "British Strategy," 91.
50.Corbett, *Naval Operations*, vol. 2, 41-2.

3

Alfred Thayer Mahan And American Naval Theory

John B. Hattendorf

Theory is not practice; history is not strategy. Yet, there can be important connections between such differing spheres, even though they may be neither sustained nor continuous. Too often, modern writers have jumped to the conclusion that Alfred Thayer Mahan's ideas were identical with the naval strategy of the United States. Mahan was a writer and a historian, and although he was a naval officer, he never held a position in which he had even a remote chance of directing national naval strategy. It is true that Mahan was well known, and he did have influence in some quarters. Nevertheless, the process of directing national power in the United States was so complex, even in his day, that the ideas of a single writer could not possibly outweigh the complex interplay of national and international politics, finance, industrial production, developing technology and bureaucratic decision making that lies behind the exercise of naval power. Just as theory describes a pattern of action, without being the motive force behind it, so Mahan was trying to provide intellectual models that, through historical analogies, gave meaning and understanding to some of the broad events that were occurring around him. In doing this, he made connections with military theory, identifying a few broad principles that were applicable to navies, and developed a few more general ideas about the role of navies.

In a letter to John Knox Laughton in 1896, Mahan wrote, "Our nation [the U.S.] is in Egyptian darkness, from my point of view, as regards its place and mission in the world."[1] Certainly, Mahan wrote to bring a light to this darkness, but this was not his only objective. At the same time, the U.S. Navy did not accept his ideas fully, nor did it implement them fully into any policy or strategy. On the other hand, his books and his ideas were widely read within the navy and created a kind of intellectual currency for discussions about the broad aspects of naval power.

The distinction here is important. Naval strategy is a practical issue and has to do with the broad and comprehensive direction of ships and weapons to achieve specific practical and political ends through forceful control. It is a rare situation in which abstract ideas would, or even could, drive it. We might attribute this either to fundamental differences or, alternatively, only to the common paradox between ideals and actual behavior. But, it is important to understand that theory exists to shed light on our reflections, allowing us to understand the purpose, inner calculus and related elements within a broad theme. Practitioners can use it only as a very vague guide to action, putting the long glass of theory to a blind eye as quickly as current reality presents new factors. In any real-life situation, a competent practitioner must know how to compromise between conflicting optimum solutions and judge when one theoretical consideration outweighs another. This is the judgment of experience, in the light of theoretical understanding.

Historians should never let their appreciation for successful books and good ideas lead them into assuming that abstract ideas drive navies. This is particularly true in trying to understand the U.S. Navy. If there is such a thing as American national character, no one has ever attributed a deep and abiding interest in theory to that character. Americans like to think of themselves as practical people, not abstract thinkers. As a currently serving American admiral exclaimed recently, "Don't give me some abstract explanation; I am a meat and potatoes man."

MAHAN IN CONTEXT

To understand Mahan and what he was saying, one must understand him in just that context. He was providing abstract explanations to an audience that, by and large, was not very interested and fundamentally doubted their value. That situation changed somewhat later, in the Progressive Era in American history, when scholars began to be accepted as experts.[2] This was a result of a tremendous change in American attitudes, but, even today, it is not fully shared in large areas of society.

Certainly, Mahan wrote before that change had made headway, and the navy was no fertile ground for its growth. In 1861, Stephen Luce had complained, "Compared to the Army with their wealth of professional literature, we [in the Navy] may be likened to the nomadic tribes of the East who are content with the vague traditions of the past."[3]

A dozen years later, that situation was slowly beginning to change. By 1873, there were enough officers interested in professional writing to support the establishment of the U.S. Naval Institute. At least some American naval officers were aware of professional thought and events in France and in Britain, reading such periodicals as *Revue Maritime* and *The Journal of the Royal United Services Institution*, as well as their own *Army and Navy Journal*, the Naval Institute's *Proceedings* and the short-lived *United Service*. By 1890, the drive toward professionalization in the armed forces had included a large professional literature. Much of it, however, was scientific, practical and technical. Relatively few were interested in questions of history and policy, although a few wrote in that area. Mahan was not alone.

Mahan's work was a reaction to the overwhelming dominance of technology in the navy. While in command of the USS *Chicago* in 1894, he had complained, "The infinite and infinitely small details of a modern ship consume time while yielding small results."[4] At that moment, he was deep into writing his biography, *Nelson*, and was irritated by shipboard distractions, but his irritation reflected a larger and deeper issue.

In 1884, Admiral Stephen Luce had founded the Naval War College in Newport, Rhode Island, with the express purpose of opposing the overwhelming dominance of technological imperatives in the navy. At a time when many felt that rapidly developing technology had swept away the old wisdom and demanded a completely new basis, Luce and his colleagues looked in another direction:

- to international law and diplomacy as a means to control and to guide warfare,
- to the use of war games as a means of logically controlling, evaluating and directing technological developments and
- to history as a means of revealing important and continuing patterns of thought and guides to behavior.

Each of these areas has its own history of individual development, although Luce linked them together for the navy. Obviously, Mahan is most clearly connected to the third of these categories, but he is also part of the whole school of thought that the Naval War College, as an institution, represented and over which he twice presided in 1886-89 and 1892-93.

The debate continues between those who argue that technology has made the past irrelevant to modern and future military affairs and those who see history as something of continuing value in its midst. Mahan played a role in this debate, in the second of its several phases, while Admiral Luce had been involved at a very early stage and was influential in setting the original agenda for the debate. In this, Mahan made clear his debt to the Naval War College when he wrote in his preface to *The Influence of Sea Power Upon the French Revolution and Empire*:

> [i]n the race for material and mechanical development, sea officers as a class have allowed their attention to be unduly diverted from the systematic study of the Conduct of War, which is their peculiar and main concern. That the author has done so is due, wholly and exclusively to the Naval War College, which was instituted to promote such studies.[5]

Seen in this context, Mahan's work was clearly an attempt to fill a gap in a key area of professional thought, not to provide an overarching explanation of the way in which navies function. Because of this, Mahan's work bypasses the important series of questions that historians wrestle with today, most particularly the question of how the presence of constant technological innovation affects navies.

In laying out the ground on which Mahan was to begin his work, Admiral Luce clearly identified his preference to use history and to relate naval history to military theory. In concluding a lecture during the first session of the Naval War College in 1885, Luce wrote:

> Inspired by the example of the warlike Greeks, and knowing ourselves to be on the road that leads to the establishment of the science of naval warfare under steam, let us confidently look for that master mind who will lay the foundations of that science, and do for it what Jomini did for the military science.[6]

Some twenty years later, Luce recalled this very comment and noted, "He is here; his name is Mahan."[7] Mahan's advent, however, was no bolt from the blue. It was very clearly part of a long-term development in which he had both predecessors and successors.

In attempting to put Mahan's work into perspective, we must look at it through a number of overlapping viewpoints. As already mentioned, we must see him in terms of the growth of professional literature, but more particularly, we must see him:

- as part of the development of the subdiscipline of naval history, linking international politics to naval action
- as part of the development of military and naval theory, with an early application of Jomini's ideas to maritime problems
- as part of the growth of political commentary, using geopolitical ideas and historical examples
- as part of a growing but rudimentary sophistication in general historical studies, at this point somewhat reluctantly accepting the importance of original research
- as a reflection of the social and intellectual values of his times, in terms of understanding the armed forces, international rivalry, economic competition, imperial power and religious belief

When we see Mahan thus, in depth, in breadth and in context, we see him as part of a broad progression. We see others, before him, working in related fields. In this, we can see relationships in the early work being done in the Royal Navy by the two Colomb brothers, John and Philip, and Sir John Knox Laughton. We can see Mahan's debt to Jomini, to his own father's work in that area, to historians in Britain and France. We see Mahan acquire, use, interpret and develop those ideas further. After him, we find another set of writers and thinkers, like Sir Julian Corbett and Sir Herbert Richmond, who reached new conclusions independently and recast and reinterpreted Mahan's ideas in the light of these new insights, new information and more varied experiences. Beyond that, we can find a whole range of writers, historians and commentators who have applied his ideas, sometimes distorting and changing them in the process, creating a "Mahanian doctrine" and attributing to him ideas that are somewhat at variance with what Mahan himself wrote. With that in mind, let us not continue to see Mahan as doctrine, as a lens by which we should interpret naval power, but let us see him as a man with some ideas, in the context of his own time, at a particular stage of development in the progression and refinement of naval thought.

As a keen observer of international events in the late nineteenth century, Mahan saw clear historical parallels with the structure of European international relations between 1660 and 1815. He saw some similarities in terms of imperial responsibility, the competition of empires, naval rivalry, the role of maritime trade and the relationship of naval battles to the general conduct of wars. He seems to have seen his own world as one in a kind of neomercantilist period. This kind of world structure in international relations--a world so very different from what we see about us in the 1990s--provided the striking parallels he wanted to use to excite the minds of his fellow countrymen and his fellow officers. For us today, the seventeenth and the eighteenth centuries are, indeed, "a world we have lost." The historian looking at that period today needs to bridge a large gap with historical imagination and faces an even wider gap in trying to understand the elements in it that attracted a late-nineteenth-century naval officer--and an American, at that.

Mahan was not alone in his interest in the Napoleonic War period. For his generation, it was, after all, the "last great war." In terms of both relative distance in time and popular interest, the Napoleonic Wars had an attraction that could be roughly likened to what the world wars of this century continue to exert on us. As the centenary of the Napoleonic Wars approached, popular interest rose, and much professional writing touched on the same period as well. Army officers consistently turned to Henri Jomini's writings, even as they slowly began to find an interest in works by Carl von Clausewitz.[8] Regardless of quality, there was a host of books and writers on the subject, even in the naval area. Among his exact contemporaries in Britain, John Knox Laughton and Philip Colomb, each independently of Mahan, chose the same period to examine for professional purposes. Given Mahan's own purposes as well as the wide interest in the period, it is not surprising or unusual that he turned to it.

CATEGORIES OF MAHAN'S WRITINGS

Moving beyond the general context, it is worthwhile to see the pattern of Mahan's works. Most of his twenty volumes remain in print today, nearly a century after they were written, yet many commentators have lumped them together as a single *opus*.[9] However, one can distinguish among several different categories of his work, noting, at the same time, various links among them.

Mahan is remembered today largely for his series of books on *The Influence of Sea Power*, yet the common idea of his views on naval strategy come from another series of works. There are five distinct categories:

1. the broad role of sea power in international relations
2. the basic principles of naval operations
3. contemporary events
4. the U. S. role in international affairs
5. personal memoirs and religious beliefs

The last category, touching on personal religious beliefs, has been often ignored as irrelevant to the others.[10] Today, with our recent experience in international relations, one can more readily appreciate the interplay between religious conviction and military force. For Mahan, this connection was certainly present. His view of international relations is clearly consistent with one of his favorite Biblical passages, St. Paul's Epistle to the Romans, 14:4. A ruler, St. Paul wrote, "is the minister of God, a revenger to execute wrath upon him that doeth evil." Not only was the use of military and naval force just and righteous, in his view, but he believed that western international relations were closely tied to a commitment to spread Christian values and to promote Christian evangelism in the areas under Western control and influence. Such fundamental beliefs underlay Mahan's thought on naval affairs and his understanding of history.

Mahan's broadest understanding of history was laid out in his *Sea Power* series, which consisted of four titles: his most famous book, *The Influence of Sea Power upon History*, followed by his study, with a similar title, on *The French Revolution and Empire*. This was followed by *Sea Power in Its Relation to the War of 1812* and his biography, *Nelson*. Today, one often forgets that this biography is part of the same series and that he subtitled it *The Embodiment of the Sea Power of Great Britain*. In his correspondence, he repeatedly declared, as he was writing *Nelson*, "If I succeed in bringing the work up to the mark at which I aim, it will stand as the work of my life--I so intend it."[11] In dealing with Nelson the man, Mahan was "disengaging the figure of the hero from the glory that cloaks it."[12] At the same time, as he was dealing with the external part of Nelson's career, "the same aim is kept in view of showing clearly, not only what he did, but the principles which dominated his military thought, and guided his military actions, throughout his life."[13] Thus, from a literary and conceptual point of view, Mahan was trying to bring together, in his study of a single man, the concepts he had laid out in his earlier volumes through the abstract terms of international relations. "Wars may cease," Mahan wrote, "but the need for heroism shall not depart from the earth, while man remains man and evil needs to be redressed."[14]

In his first *Sea Power* book, Mahan laid out his basic elements of sea power, emphasizing that

> the first and most obvious light in which the sea presents itself from a political and social point of view is that of a great highway; or better, perhaps, of a wide common, over which men may pass in all directions, but on which some well-worn paths show that controlling reasons have led them to choose certain lines of travel rather than others...called trade routes.[15]

Thus, commercial trade was the essence of maritime activity and the fundamental reason for navies. For much of the history Mahan reviewed, he found three key factors supporting commercial trade: (1) production, with the need to exchange goods; (2) shipping, by which the exchange is carried on; and (3) colonies, which enlarge shipping operations and provide additional points of safety for shipping.

For a nation to be successful in such commercial, maritime endeavor, Mahan laid out his six fundamental factors underlying it: geographical position; physical characteristics of its harbors; climate and production, extent of territory and population; character of the people and their aptitude for commercial trade, the character of the government and the national institutions supporting commerce and trade.

Often one finds students stopping at this point, thinking they have grasped Mahan's views, when, in fact, one must move further on, through his other volumes, to see the full range of his ideas. The volumes on the *War of 1812*, in particular, deal with his ideas on the war against trade. "To attack the commerce of the enemy is therefore to cripple him, in the measure of success achieved, in the particular factor which is vital to the maintenance of war," Mahan wrote. "Money, credit, is the life of war; lessen it, and vigour flags; destroy it, and resistance dies."[16]

While fully recognizing its great importance in dealing with a fundamental factor in any war, Mahan found in historical examples some reasons to look beyond commerce destruction as a general aim in naval warfare. He saw that the relative value of commerce warfare varied with the situation. It was a type of warfare to which countries that had no large naval establishment could resort. Even countries with a large naval force could easily engage in this type of warfare, without much preparation. Stressing it did not help the argument he wanted to make, promoting the building of a larger navy in the United States.

Mahan noted that one of the most effective tools a major naval power had was using warships to impose a commercial blockade. A weaker nation's natural response to a commercial blockade was to attack the enemy's trade on the high seas. Thus, Mahan found it difficult to generalize on this subject, since it was largely dependent on the relative position of the nation employing commerce destruction. In order to clarify the issue, Mahan tried to cast it in different terms:

> It is not the taking of individual ships or convoys, be they few or many, that strikes down the money power of a nation; it is the possession of that overbearing power on the sea which drives the enemy's flag from it, or allows it to appear only as a fugitive; and which, by controlling the great common, closes the highways by which commerce moves to and from the enemy's shores.[17]

The importance that Mahan placed on trade led him to take a strong position in the contemporary controversy over the immunity of private property at sea. While some people sought to protect private property from capture or injury during war at sea, Mahan opposed the idea of immunity, arguing that capture of an enemy's commerce "is a means of importance to the ends of war."[18] As he explained in *The War of 1812*, relinquishing the rights of a belligerent to forbid the free use of the sea to an enemy's merchant ships abandons control of the sea in-so-far as it is useful in warfare.[19] Later, he elaborated on this point in another context:

> Which will most promote, and maintain, a steady aversion to war? ...Depend on it, the interest of humanity demands that war is not to be a mere question of champions, land or sea, but that the whole people should be made to feel, individually, that the war will find its way to them, in purse as well as in sorrow.[20]

In the *Sea Power* series, Mahan outlined his broad ideas on the role of sea power in history, but he reserved a detailed study of the basic principles of naval operations for his book *Naval Strategy*. It was a volume of his War College lectures that he had been reluctant to publish, obviously designed for the professional officer and not the general public.[21] While Mahan confessed that he had "never been so sick of anything" he had written,[22] nevertheless, it remains, perhaps, the most important statement of his ideas on naval theory.

AN OUTLINE OF MAHAN'S THEORY

Mahan's was very uncomfortable with his assignment to apply military theory to naval operations. While finding a few principles that he could appropriately link, he stressed the need to look at an ever-widening range of applications in terms of particular cases, rather than a strict recitation of the abstract principles themselves. "Extensive study of cases," he wrote, "gives firmer grasp, deeper understanding, wider views, increased aptitude and quickness to apprehend the critical features."[23]

In general, however, Mahan reiterated the importance of trade to navies, noting that naval strategy has for its end, in peace and in war, the support and increase of a nation's sea power. In contrast to military operations, navies operated on a relatively large geographical scale. This factor dictated the need for concentrating naval force in advance, rather than distributing it widely, using the navy's mobility as a key to maintaining its usefulness in strength. This was a key factor and differentiated navies from armies. While the possession of key strategic positions was an essential point in military theory, Mahan emphasized that, in naval affairs, one could have too many ports, leading one into dispersal of force rather than concentration. Mobility allowed the navy to balance this situation. In the face of opposition, one could not expect to hold the whole field, but it was essential to hold the key points that allow one to control the greater and most important parts of it. Thus, a major factor in naval affairs was the possession of key, advanced positions, ranging from being able to maintain a blockade off an enemy port to holding a distant harbor.

The importance of advance positions lay at the heart of Mahan's theory. "Behind your fleets, thus resting on secure positions and closely knit to the home country by well guarded communications, the operations of commerce, transport, and supply can go on freely. Into such a sea the enemy cannot venture."[24]

Mahan identified two basic factors for consideration in exercising naval strategy: strategic position and strategic lines. When examining strategic position, Mahan saw three principal conditions that determined its value: position, strength and resources.

The first and most important condition for strategic position was its relation to the major trade routes at sea. To be important, it had to lie within the limits of strategic effect. Thus, among the most important positions were the intersections of two or more sea routes, the narrow channels or highways through which trade must necessarily pass in order to gain wide distribution.

The second condition that determined the value of a strategic position was its military strength, both offensive and defensive. In terms of sea-ports, one had to consider both the landward and seaward components of this. In Mahan's view, ports were best defended by land defenses, not naval resources. The navy's true role, he felt, was in the offensive. In this dimension, ports held offensive capability if a large military force of both warships and transports could assemble there, if such force could easily and safely launch itself into open water from that position and if the port could continue to support the force until the end of the campaign.

For Mahan, the final condition for determining the value of a position was the availability of natural and man-made resources. The most important resource was dry docks which, when close to the scene of action, could effect rapid repairs and supply, returning ships to the fleet quickly.

In parallel with strategic position, Mahan emphasized the importance of strategic lines. "The strategic points on a given theatre of war are not to be looked upon merely separately and as disconnected," Mahan wrote. "After determining their individual values by the test of position, military strength, and resources, it will remain to consider their mutual relations of bearing, distance, and the best routes from one to the other."[25]

Taking his cue from Jomini, Mahan noted that one could give a variety of names to these routes, depending on the use one put them to: line of operation, line of retreat, line of communication and so on. The most important at sea, however, were the lines of communication over which the essential supplies passed. Mahan believed that these strategic lines were controlled at sea through the mobility of organized naval force, that is a battle fleet. Thus, the fleet was the heart of an enemy's strength. If an enemy's fleet could be decisively defeated or dislocated, preventing it from controlling commerce at sea, the object of naval strategy was achieved. This, to Mahan, was the determining factor in naval warfare. The decisive defeat of the enemy fleet or rendering it completely inferior resulted in dislocation of the enemy's lines of communication.

In Mahan's mind, the key to success at sea lay in having an

adequate, efficient and numerically superior fleet at sea. Superiority was identical with holding the decisive position at sea, for it prevented an enemy from concentrating a rival force to challenge it. At the same time, naval preponderance at sea meant secure communications. The single most important point in Mahan's view was the need to be superior to the enemy at the decisive point, whatever the relative strength of the two opposing parties as a whole. In cases when superiority was unclear, then one needed to fight a battle. The results of that battle determined which fleet controlled the strategic position and the lines of communication.

When the fleet had won the key to the strategic position, the fleet passed from an offensive role to a defensive one. In joint operations, the navy moved to deal with communications, its natural element, while the army assumed the offensive and continued the campaign ashore.

These were the main points of Mahan's theory, as he worked them out in his study of history. Yet, Mahan was not solely concerned with history. A large proportion of his writing was devoted to it, but, to a degree, he was dissatisfied with historical study. In his 1896 letter to Laughton, Mahan wrote:

> [i]t seems to me we are approaching an age in which events of great political interest will occur--before your and my generation goes under the sod. I feel the impulse more and more strong to turn my attention to the future, from the point of view of Sea Power, and to address the public through magazines.[26]

Later, Mahan collected these articles in books such as *The Problem of Asia, The Interest of America in Sea Power, Present and Future*. In doing this, Mahan used many of the principles he worked out from history. He saw very clearly that, in historical study, a careful observer could trace and formulate the causes of events, showing the various interactions that produced the result. But the situation was different in trying to analyze present situations and even more difficult in trying to predict the future. In his preface to *The Problem of Asia*, Mahan wrote:

> Past history contains indeed lessons which, well digested, are most valuable for future guidance; but when the attempt is made to utilize their teachings, contemporary conditions are found to differ so much from those preceding them that application becomes a matter of no slight difficulty, requiring judgement and conjecture rather than

imparting certainty. Positiveness in such matters, indeed, is the doubtful privilege of the *doctrinaire*, and commonly unfortunate in the result. The instruction derived from the past must be supplemented by a particularized study of the indications of the future.[27]

Within a decade after writing his first *Sea Power* book, Mahan was clearly aware that historical examples and doctrinaire theory could not forecast the future. He continued to believe, however, that one could gain through the study of history. One could, at least, use history to help determine the essential factors and the range of key relationships involved in situations. "Even so much is gain," he concluded.[28]

As Mahan was writing, the historical profession was only just beginning to emphasize the need for constant attention to documents and to detail. The German approach to documentary research had not yet fully taken over, although the first graduate schools in history were already beginning to point toward the future path. In England, Laughton had been a pioneer and among the very first to use the Admiralty archives for research. In this context, it is interesting to see Mahan's reaction to Laughton's suggestion that Mahan might profit from a look at some newly available private papers for his study of Nelson. No, thank you, Mahan replied. "I have practically given up in many cases, accepting ignorance of details as not material to the broad lines I wish to draw."[29]

THE RANGE AND LIMITATIONS OF MAHAN'S THEORIES

The range of Mahan's theory was both broad and limited. He looked at European history over a period of 150 years, focusing on both the British and French navies. But much of what he said was not necessarily applicable to other periods, other countries or other types of naval power. He wrote with an eye toward educating his own countrymen and promoting the development of his own service. Clearly, some of his historical conclusions reflected that bias.

In the terms of his time, much of what Mahan wrote was a revelation. The idea of applying Jominian theory to navies was brilliant, and Mahan did an excellent job of it. It opened up a wide, new range of thought for contemporaries. Like any such intellectual construct, it served its purpose, but it was also limited. Mahan's own hesitancy to stress the abstract principles, preferring instead to study case after case, was indicative of the fundamental problem. The principles were a useful, if limited, guide in the mind of a man who had broad knowledge and could compare and contrast, seeing the variations and vagaries involved. Jomini's principles, however, have always caused difficulty. They left a great opportunity for readers to seize upon such clearly and simply worded statements, forcing them into formulas, as if they were circuit boards rather than abstract impressions. Mahan saw the problem. He dealt with it indirectly and reticently, at first, and explicitly later, but many readers missed that point.

Mahan made some remarkable contributions to historical understanding, but his approach to history was already waning as he wrote. His disregard for documentary and detailed research may seem deplorable today, although he did more of this than many others in his time. Nevertheless, many of his historical explanations no longer stand.[30] His histories are as dated as his contemporary analysis, but his works were important steps in the history of naval theory on its way to modern development. Their role and their limitations represent part of the intellectual heritage of navies.

American naval theory has evolved considerably since the days when Mahan wrote, but its evolution is largely the result of influences from writers in other countries, from academics and civilian analysts working outside the navy, as well as from a much wider and deeper range of historical research and naval experience. Yet, theoretical interests are no more attractive to the U.S. Navy, today, than they were when Mahan wrote. It is rare to find anyone working on them. One can count on the fingers of a single hand the number of Americans who have made any serious contribution to this field. Among those who have been career officers in the U.S. Navy in the eighty years since Mahan's death, only two theoreticians stand out: Rear Admiral Henry E. Eccles (1898-1986), who wrote *Military Concepts and Philosophy*[31] and a series of important conceptual papers on naval logistics, and Rear Admiral J.C. Wylie (1911-93), who wrote *Military Strategy: A General Theory of Power Control.*[32] The last, in particular, had a discernible, conceptual influence on American naval planning in the 1980s.[33]

Although theory is not practice, and history is not strategy, Mahan was the most influential and prolific writer in the United States to show that there can be important connections between such differing spheres. Today, his conceptualizations lie in the far-distant historical background. Since his time, officers of the U.S. Navy have made neither a sustained nor a continuous effort to develop those connections into any new theoretical formulation, and they show no inclination to do so now. Yet, the cultivation of broad connections between theory and practice, history and strategy remain an important part of the work of the Naval War College and of the academic work of the officers who attend its courses. Today, it is not enough to read Mahan's work and cite his principles or, alternatively, to turn to any other abstract formulas. Today, modern naval officers must deal with a broader understanding of history, using it as a guide to critical analysis in thinking about what navies can and cannot do.[34] The modern officer must be his own Mahan.

NOTES

1.National Maritime Museum, Greenwich, MS79/067 (hereafter cited as NMM, MS79/067): Mahan to Laughton, 20 March 1896. This and the following quotations from this manuscript collection are made by permission of the trustees of the National Maritime Museum.

2.Richard Hofstadter, *Anti-Intellectualism in American Life* (New York: Random House, 1964), Chapter 8.

3.Library of Congress, Luce papers: Luce to Commandant of Midshipmen, U.S. Naval Academy, 26 February 1861.

4.NMM, MS79/067: Mahan to Laughton, 31 January 1894.

5.A. T. Mahan, *The Influence of Sea Power upon the French Revolution and Empire* (Boston: Little, Brown, 1892), vol. 1, v-vi.

6.S. B. Luce, "On the Study of Naval Warfare as a Science," U.S. Naval Institute *Proceedings* 12 (1886), 527-46, reprinted in Hayes and John B. Hattendorf, eds., *The Writings of Stephen B. Luce* (Newport, R.I.: Naval War College Press, 1975), Chapter 3.

7.Ibid., 68, fn. 71.

8.Christopher Bassford, *Clausewitz in English* (New York: Oxford University Press, 1994), chapters 1-2.

9.For a list of his works, see John B. Hattendorf and Lynn C. Hattendorf, compilers; *A Bibliography of the Works of Alfred Thayer Mahan* (Newport, R.I.: Naval War College Press, 1986).

10.On this subject, see Leo N. Leslie, Jr., "Christianity and the Evangelist of Sea Power: The Religion of Alfred Thayer Mahan," in John B. Hattendorf, ed., *The Influence of History upon Mahan* (Newport, R.I.: Naval War College Press, 1991), 127-139.

11.NMM, MS79/067: Mahan to Laughton, 31 January 1894; See also Robert Seager II and Doris D. Maguire, eds., *The Letters and Papers of Alfred Thayer Mahan*, Naval Letters Series (Annapolis: Naval Institute Press, 1975), vol. 2, 229, 470, 509.

12.A. T. Mahan, *Nelson: The Embodiment of the Sea Power of Great Britain* (London: Marston Low, 1897), vol. 1, vi.

13.Ibid., vii.

14.Ibid., vol. 2, 397.

15.A. T. Mahan, *The Influence of Sea Power upon History, 1660-1783* (Boston: Little, Brown, 1890), 25-59.

16.A. T. Mahan, *Sea Power in Its Relations to the War of 1812* (Boston: Little Brown, 1905), 284-290.

17.Mahan, *The Influence of Sea Power upon History*, 138.

18.A. T. Mahan, "The Hague Conference: The Question of Immunity for Belligerent Merchant Shipping," *National Review* (June 1907), reprinted in *Some Neglected Aspects of War* (Boston: Little, Brown, 1907), 190-91.

19.Mahan, *Sea Power in Its Relation to the War of 1812*, vol 1, 144-48.

20.A. T. Mahan, "Comments on the Seizure of Private Property at Sea," in Seager and Maguire, *Letters and Papers*, vol. 3, 623-26.

21.A. T. Mahan, *Naval Strategy Compared and Contrasted with the Principles and Practice of Military Operations on Land: Lectures Delivered at the U.S. Naval War College, Newport, R.I., between the Years 1887 and 1911* (Boston: Little, Brown, 1911).

22.Seager and Maguire, *Letters and Papers*, vol. 3, 440: Mahan to T. Roosevelt, 23 December 1911.

23.Mahan, *Naval Strategy*, Chapter 6, reprinted in John B. Hattendorf, ed., *Mahan on Naval Strategy* (Annapolis: Naval Institute Press, 1991), 99.

24.Ibid., 107.

25.Ibid., Chapter 8, 142.

26.NMM, MS79/067: Mahan to Laughton, 20 March 1896. The quote in note 1 directly follows this one.

27.A. T. Mahan, *The Problem of Asia: and Its Effect upon International Policies* (Boston: Little, Brown, 1900), vi - vii.

28.Ibid.

29.NMM, MS79/067: Mahan to Laughton, 21 March 1893.

30.See, in particular, D. M. Schurman, "Mahan Revisited," *Militärhistorisk Tidskrift*, (1982): 29-43, revised and reprinted in John B. Hattendorf and Robert S. Jordan, eds. *Maritime Strategy and the Balance of Power: Britain and America in the Twentieth Century* (London: Macmillan, 1989).

31.Henry E. Eccles, *Military Concepts and Philosophy* (New Brunswick, N.J.: Rutgers University Press, 1965) and *Military Power in A Free Society* (Newport, R.I.: Naval War College Press, 1985). Eccles's extensive collection of papers and correspondence is in the Naval Historical Collection, Naval War College, Newport, Rhode Island. See Evelyn Cherpak, compiler, *Register of the Henry E. Eccles Papers*, 2d ed. (Newport, R.I.: Naval Historical Collection,

1988).

32.J. C. Wylie, *Military Strategy: A General Theory of Power Control* (New Brunswick, N.J.: Rutgers University Press, 1967). Reprinted with an introduction by John B. Hattendorf, a selection of his other key writings and with a postscript by J. C. Wylie in the Classics of Sea Power series (Annapolis: Naval Institute Press, 1989).

33.See "Introduction" to Naval Institute edition of Wylie, *Military Strategy*, xxxiv-xxxv, fn. 25.

34.See George W. Baer, "Conference Summary: Corbett and Richmond ...Mahan and Us," in James Goldrick and John B. Hattendorf, *Mahan Is Not Enough: The Proceedings of a Conference on the Works of Sir Julian Corbett and Admiral Sir Herbert Richmond* (Newport, R.I.: Naval War College Press, 1993), 287 - 294.

4

The Royal Navy, 1856–1914: Deterrence And The Strategy Of World Power

Andrew D. Lambert

This chapter offers an interpretation of the role of the Royal Navy in the grand strategy of the British Empire between 1856 and 1914. The scale of the chapter makes it essential that some definition be imposed on what is being attempted. British strategy is considered in its relation to the other major powers that were believed to have the capacity to threaten the empire: France, the United States, Russia and Germany. These powers possessed, at different times in the period under review, the second or third largest navy in the world and a range of political and economic grievances that made war appear possible. The question at the heart of the chapter is a simple one: how could Britain use the Royal Navy to deter or fight these states?

In contrast to the two concepts that have largely shaped the historiography of this period, the "decline of British power" and the "waning influence of sea power," I argue that a more accurate appreciation of British strategy can be established by reexamining the war fighting and deterrent opportunities provided by naval dominance. These suggest that there was no decline of British power in this period, because the strategic importance of sea power waxed ever stronger. However, the haphazard and belated process of creating a national strategy resulted in a series of errors and interservice rivalries that have obscured the reality of British power. I do not attempt to follow the detail of naval policy, the checkered course of events, design changes or the politics of the service.

Rather than dealing with the concerns of the period, insular security, imperial defense and commerce protection, I concentrate on one issue, the offensive capacity of the Royal Navy. The ability of the Royal Navy to take the initiative against fleets, arsenals and bases gave Britain the power to fight or deter its rivals. The nature of this power can be given some preliminary definition by events in 1856 and 1914.

On 23 April, 1856, St. George's Day, the Royal Navy staged a fleet review at Spithead. The Queen, the two houses of Parliament and a host of interested citizens came to watch the evolutions of 250 vessels, battleships, cruisers, armored batteries, block ships, gunboats, mortar vessels and floating factories. However, the intended audience for this demonstration of British national strategy was not the multitude of taxpayers, but a select group of foreign officers and dignitaries. The following day *The Times* leader declared:

> A new system of naval warfare has been invented....We have now the means of waging a really offensive war, not only against fleets, but harbours, fortresses and rivers--not merely of blockading, but of invading, and carrying the warfare of the sea to the very heart of the land.[1]

The target of this "great armament" was Cronstadt and St. Petersburg. The key to the "new system" lay in the development of a specialist coast assault craft.[2]

In October 1914, British warships played an important role in stopping the advance of the German army along the Belgian Coast. Of the ships used, only three recently purchased Brazilian river monitors had been built for inshore work. These operations led Julian Corbett to consider the role of coast assault craft. The monitor, he observed,

> was a type essential for coastal operations, especially in shallow seas, but in spite of former experience of their utility and the value the Japanese had obtained from such craft, the type was absent from our Navy. The "Blue Water" trend of modern naval opinion inclined to treat all such craft as heretical in that they were unfit to take part in a fleet action, and they had been pilloried with the designation of "Coast Defence Vessels." This unfortunate misnomer had served to throw into oblivion their function of "coast attack," and the type had died like a dog with a bad name. The first breath of war, however, had blown away the misconception.[3]

Corbett was himself guilty of this error; indeed, among the pioneers of modern naval thought active before 1914, only Philip Colomb and Fred Jane had recognized the primacy of offensive coastal operations in nineteenth-century naval warfare. It is hardly surprising that the first major warships ordered by the Admiralty after the outbreak of war were monitors.[4] As Corbett observed, they had a pivotal role in the ambitious strategy developed by the Admiralty in December 1914 "to open the second phase of the war by a rigorous offensive against the enemy's North Sea Ports." Winston Churchill, the first lord, believed that the naval war would end in 1915, when "we shall have smashed up the German Navy in harbour with our monitors, or they will have fought their battle in blue water, or peace will have been signed."[5] Such plans were finally abandoned in favor of the Dardanelles.

Even if the British public had lost sight of the offensive doctrine of the Royal Navy in the intervening years, the "official mind" of the service and, as we shall see, the successors of those foreign observers present on 23 April 1856 proved less forgetful.

THE DECLINE OF BRITISH POWER AND THE WANING INFLUENCE OF SEA POWER

It has become a commonplace that Britain began its "decline" in the second half of the nineteenth century. Evidence has been provided by economic statistics, industrial production and, most temptingly, the gloomy prognoses of British statesmen and service leaders. These show only a relative decline. Proof of weakness is provided by a series of crises from Schleswig-Holstein in 1862 to the creation of the Triple Entente.[6] No attempt is made to square this image with the scale, duration and success of the empire war effort between 1914 and 1918.

Although Britain lost its overall industrial primacy in the second half of the century, overseas investments and the steady growth of economic and industrial strength kept it in the front rank of modern nations. A chain of imperial naval bases, the self-governing Dominions and India, with their reserves of military manpower, gave it a unique global reach and striking power. Britain was the only world power of the age, and if its resources were widely scattered and slow to mobilize, they were also impossible to knock out in a limited war and were securely linked by the sea. The only threat that Britain could not face alone was a war with Europe united under one rule.

After 1815, Britain made a conscious effort to maintain a balance of power in Europe between hostile camps, so that no single nation or even combination of states would risk war with Britain. All feared their neighbors would exploit this situation and, in consequence, were deterred. Only one nation, imperial Germany, believed it had the power to "win" in a time frame that made British sea power seem as irrelevant as its "contemptible little army."

In November 1991, *The International History Review* devoted an issue to the decline of Great Britain. Gordon Martel and Keith Neilson demonstrated that any "decline" did not happen before 1914.[7] However, they left untouched two critical supports of the "decline" argument: the "threat" to India posed by Russia and the "waning influence of sea power."

Although contemporary British soldiers and statesmen were greatly impressed by Russian advances, William Fuller has demonstrated that "no responsible tsarist statesman from the 1860s until the Russian Revolution ever believed it realistically possible for Russia to launch a war of conquest from Central Asia against the British possessions in India."[8] This alarm was manipulated and exploited by the Indian army to increase its role in imperial strategy. While it is necessary to consider the impact of these scares on imperial strategy, there can be no doubt that India was, in fact, a great reservoir of power, not a source of weakness.[9] The Indian slant of imperial strategy after 1857 reflected the success of the military campaign. In practice, the response of Britain to Russian aggression against any vital interest between 1790 and 1885 was to mobilize a fleet for Baltic operations. This global strategic response was uniquely British.[10]

The second point was set out most cogently by Paul Kennedy. He argued that, between 1856 and 1897, "the effectiveness of seapower itself, and the predominance of British naval mastery in particular, was being slowly but surely undermined."[11] Kennedy builds his thesis on the contrast between A. T. Mahan's sea power theories and the "heartland" thesis of Sir Halford Mackinder, propounded in 1904. This ignores the unreal nature of Mackinder's thesis, which was a parody of the more extreme "blue-water" arguments of the day, rather than a profound analysis. Its popularity, then as now, rests more on the Russophobia of the audience than any particular intellectual merit.[12] Mackinder's argument that the railroad would replace the ship as the world's prime mover was, and remains, absurd. Corbett dismissed it as a "breezy generalisation," noting that "the capacity of...inland communications is not unlimited." Significantly, Corbett never assessed the "Heartland," although he held Mackinder in high regard and discussed imperial strategy with him while in Quebec in 1908.[13] The railways of Russia collapsed in 1877 and again in 1904-5.[14]

Gordon Martel has argued that the nineteenth-century British Empire was less powerful than has been supposed, because it was unable to deter Russia, citing the Crimean War and the 1878 crisis as examples.[15] Keith Neilson adopts a similar perspective, quoting Lord Salisbury on the threat to India.[16] At root this is a question of the utility of sea power. While their interpretation may be correct, the evidence provided is far from compelling.

It should be noted that this image of weakness, of sea power reduced to a purely defensive asset by the rise of mass armies and railways, proved congenial to the liberal mind of the late nineteenth century.[17] Perceptions of British strategy in the nineteenth century have long been dominated by the alarmist publications of the two most vocal groups, those seeking higher military spending and radical followers of Cobden and Bright. From such sources it is possible to create the illusion that the Royal Navy was, at one and the same time, criminally weak and so large as to constitute a menace to British taxpayers and international peace. Recognizing the absurdity of both positions, the two groups finally established common ground; the alarmists restricted their claims of inadequacy to the defense of Britain and its oceanic trade, while the radicals relaxed their pressure for reduction. Thus was created the late nineteenth-century liberal illusion that the Royal Navy was the purely defensive force that Arthur Marder termed "the shield of the empire."[18]

It has been customary to refer to the mid-Victorian period as the "Dark Ages" of the Royal Navy and suggest that the fleet was unable to meet its tasks. This reflects alarmist Admiralty memoranda and creative statistics, themselves, at least in part, a response to the attack on the naval role by the army. Between 1865 and 1890 there was no threat to British naval supremacy from any combination of naval rivals.[19] Similarly, it is a commonplace that both the army and the Royal Navy "remained chiefly specialists in colonial warfare" between 1859 and 1897, while "gunboats...formed the bulk of the fleet," reflecting the navy's role as "the policeman of the world's oceans."[20] This argument should not be taken too far. It makes the fundamental mistake of confusing what happened with what was being prepared for. The Royal Navy was never a colonial gunboat force; its policy and strategy reflected the need to maintain battle fleet supremacy in home waters and a working command of the broad oceans.[21]

If the effort required to achieve these ends was small, as it was between 1870 and 1888, that reflected the weakness of potential opponents. That most of its operations were of a colonial nature should not obscure the real thrust of naval policy. To understand the contemporary loss of faith in the Royal Navy that is reflected in the work of Kennedy and others, we need to reconsider the origins of modern British strategic thought and examine the fundamental issues of British strategy, in particular, the offensive contribution of naval power to the national position.

STRATEGY AND TECHNOLOGY

British strategy was profoundly influenced by changes in the balance of power and the rapid development of technology during the nineteenth century. Britain had risen to greatness on its economic strength and the ability to avoid defeat at sea. In 1815, the Royal Navy was, for the first time, as it would remain for most of the century, equal to the rest of the world's navies combined. This was not just a matter of counting ships. Equally important were the expertise and arrogance of British officers and men, the quality of their ships, the scale and distribution of docks and bases and, most fundamentally, economic strength and stable cross-party political support.

As a result, the Royal Navy became more aggressive, basing its tactics and strategy on the destruction of the enemy wherever it might be found. In the absence of policy documentation, the most important indicator of changing strategic concepts is provided by ship design. By 1815, the Royal Navy had shifted the emphasis of new construction from a defensive force of small, slow, heavily armed battleships, a fleet that could not be beaten, to large two- and three-decked ships with superior speed and firepower for pursuit, presuming that the enemy would not willingly risk battle.[22] Steam, in which Britain remained the world leader down to 1914, provided mobility and, later, speed. Iron and steel gave designers greater freedom to fulfill naval requirements. The Royal Navy responded by building ships and fleets that could destroy any seagoing rival, a capability that was critical to a maritime empire.[23] In consequence, as Table 4.1 indicates, British battle fleet sea power, rarely challenged in the nineteenth century, never passed into other hands. When France attempted a quantitative arms race, between 1852 and 1865, Britain responded with a combination of first- and second-class ships, the only occasions when second-class ships were prepared for fleet service between 1815 and 1914. The second-class ships, largely

Table 4.1
Comparison of First-Class Armored Battleships: 1865-1914
(Ships were added to the list when completed. They remain on it while they are considered capable of fleet operations in open waters against the most recent opposition.)

	Britain	France	Russia	Germany	Italy	Japan	USA	Austria	Rest
1865	10	10	2				1		13
1870	26	17	2	3	6				28
1875	27	16	2	8	9				35
1880	20	8	1	8	5				22
1885	24	10	1	8	7				26
1890	20	15	4	6	7				32
1895	28	12	7	4	10				33
1900	28	16	14	6	10	4	6		56
1903*	42	19	13	12	12	6	10		62
1905	49	15	13	16	10	4	12		70
1910	45	18	9	23	11	11	29		101
1914	67	19	7	32	14	13	27	6	134

*Marder, *Anatomy*, from the 1903 Parliamentary Return. The major difference in figures is provided by the inclusion of four large French coast defense ships of the *Terrible* class, which are left off this table in 1900.
It should be noted that British battleships were invariably larger than their competitors, so the tonnage figures would show the Royal Navy to even greater advantage.

conversions of older units, sacrificed range and speed for firepower; they were the direct descendants of the old "Channel Service" battleships.[24] The older "defensive" strategy remained as a "cheap" option in response to a sudden, unsustainable short-term challenge. The threat of Wilhelmine Germany was met without recourse to short-term expedients or second-class battleships.[25] The Royal Navy had to command the sea and therefore emphasized speed and firepower. These were the two elements that found no place in Mahan's vision of battle fleet-based sea power; Mahan favored small, slow battleships.[26]

Mahan's sea power theory did not address British strategy in the round (any more than Clausewitz's work did). It was an American strategy, relying for historical support on selected evidence from aspects of a particular period of British history. Mahan wanted an ocean going battle fleet for hemispheric defense; therefore, his work was dominated by the manner in which sea power was secured. He made little reference to the coastal warfare experience of the nineteenth century. In consequence, the "blue-water" arguments derived from his work policy proved to be almost useless as a British strategy.

In addition to the world's largest battle fleet and major arsenals in home waters, Great Britain maintained a unique chain of bases around the world. These were critical to the global deployment of power, naval or maritime. They were linked by regular steamship services and the expanding net of submarine telegraph lines, areas in which Britain was uniquely powerful. Each base was defended by permanent works and garrisons approximately proportionate to their value as harbors, links in the imperial chain of routes and reserves of coal.

Battle fleet superiority allowed British warships and commerce to use the sea, while those of its enemies could do so only as fugitives. The protection of ocean going merchant shipping was provided by the battle fleet. If Britain lost its working command of the sea, an enemy fleet could stop the movement of merchant shipping altogether, a far more serious issue than the harassing attacks of raiders. The *guerre de course* was always a diversion from the main thrust of war at sea. It could not prove decisive of itself. Even the French *Jeune Ecole* restricted their hopes to causing a panic in British shipping circles and opening the Channel for an invasion.[27]

With rival battle fleets neutralized or destroyed, trade defense could be conducted by cruisers. In the steam age, oceanic cruising required vast amounts of fuel, a nightmare for fleets without an adequate chain of bases. Only Britain had these bases and high grade steam coal. The bases, in turn, provided the logic for some of the less-profitable parts of the empire.[28]

Battle fleet supremacy and overseas bases ensured that no other nation could pose a decisive threat to British commerce. After 1856, the need to convoy merchant shipping declined, in tempo with the abolition of privateering and the decline of hostile cruiser fleets. By 1879, convoy had become wasteful and inconvenient. It was abandoned in favor of patrols because it would be less efficient to convoy. Only a major technological breakthrough and a comprehensive repudiation of *all* accepted laws of war at sea caused convoy to be reintroduced, for merchant shipping, in 1917. Corbett was quite correct on this issue, as it related to surface ships.[29]

The other major change in British strategy in the late nineteenth century, the decision to abandon the close blockade of enemy naval bases, reflected the combination of torpedo boats, mines, long-range artillery, fast battleships and submarines. A close blockade required a superiority in heavy ships that Britain could not afford in the age of the new navalism. The policy was finally accepted in 1904, just as Germany replaced France as the most likely opponent. The German bases were comparatively more difficult to blockade than those of France, but there was the countervailing advantage that they could be masked by a distant blockade that would also interdict German shipping.[30] However, the decision to abandon the close blockade reduced neither the value of destroying an enemy fleet nor the determination of British decision makers to achieve this end.

COASTAL OPERATIONS

The most striking feature of nineteenth-century naval operations is the almost complete absence of fleet-on-fleet encounters. Command of the sea was hardly ever disputed. By contrast almost every war with a significant maritime dimension included operations against forts and naval arsenals. The short range and increased maintenance requirements of steam navies made bases critical to naval operations. Fleets without bases were useless. Even so mundane a task as coaling was impossible without the possession of a secure anchorage, which became ever more difficult to find in the age of the torpedo boat and was more expeditiously conducted in harbor.

Steam and armor forced all navies to reconsider the location and security of their bases, because they were now vulnerable to naval assault. Britain saw the overseas bases of its rivals as an early target for offensive operations. These would reduce the threat to maritime communications and provide a bargaining counter for peace negotiations.[31]

The logic of war at sea after 1805 suggested that the Royal Navy would face its most difficult tasks inshore, or even inside the arsenals of its rivals. In consequence a new strand of naval thought, pioneered during the Napoleonic conflict, employed technology to enhance the capability of warships to act against the shore, both for amphibious power projection and for the direct assault of fortified harbors. The Crimean and American Civil Wars reinforced this trend. Between 1856 and 1890 coastal warfare dominated naval policy. France sustained a "coastal siege train" for offensive operations until 1900, while weaker powers, including Russia, spent their money on monitors for local defense.[32]

To complement battle fleet command, the Royal Navy developed the equipment for offensive operations against fortified bases. The underlying logic was twofold: to preempt a French invasion[33] and to destroy an enemy fleet in harbor. In consequence, the majority of British battleships built between 1870 and 1890 (thirteen out of twenty-two) were low free-board turret ships with very high levels of protection, fully enclosed gun mountings and the heaviest artillery. In the absence of a serious naval challenge, these ships would fight forts; indeed, they were quite unsuited to open ocean combat.

In addition, specialist coast assault battleships were built, with limited range and dubious seaworthiness. These ships, combined with gunboats, were the cutting edge of British strategy. Their function was to destroy fleets sheltering inside their bases, while the Royal Navy's first torpedo boat, HMS *Vesuvius* of 1873, was a "stealth" vessel, designed to penetrate secure anchorages after dark. The liberal conscience revolted at the very idea of "offensive" warships, so these craft were ordered under the "coast defense" label. Unfortunately for their reputations and the reputations of the policymakers of the period, the label has proved more enduring than the ships or the strategy for which they were built. As Theodore Ropp noted, "France, England and the United States originally developed the ram, the unarmoured gunboats, and the coast *defence* battleships primarily for offensive use."[34] The 1889 Naval Defence Act, a victory for "blue-water" concepts, was justified in Parliament by reference to the threat of a growing number of navies with oceanic ambitions, and first class battleships. As a result, the Royal Navy concentrated on oceangoing fighting ships, in place of the turret type. The new *Royal Sovereign* class replaced obsolete broadside ironclads in the front rank. More significant, if less obvious at the time, no more coast assault battleships were built. The fact that the first operations in European waters after the outbreak of war in 1914 were hampered by the lack of such craft made it clear that this had been a mistake. Sea power was still the offensive arm of British strategy. British interest in coastal offensive operations was promoted by the completion of Cherbourg in the mid-1840s and the subsequent invasion scare. By moving naval warfare into the Channel, France created a lever against Britain. As the Duke of Wellington observed, steam facilitated an invasion of Britain, *if* the Royal Navy could no longer be relied on.[35] However, it has been the norm to ignore the clear reservation in Wellington's famous letter and consider the British response as military and defensive in character. This confuses political and service rivalries with national policy and public debate with strategy. Britain could not afford to have its naval and military resources concentrated in home waters by a French army; therefore Cherbourg had to be neutralized. As the Royal Navy had a historical predilection for destroying foreign dockyards or, as Corbett expressed it, attempting "to perfect our command of the sea," offensive operations were the obvious response.[36] Britain responded with a steam harbor at Alderney, the advanced post for blockading squadrons, and the assembly point for coast assault forces built around steam gunboats and steam block ships armed with improved heavy artillery.[37]

Cherbourg and France dominated British strategy in the 1850s. The first lord of the Admiralty refused to divert money to prepare for the war with Russia, which he considered a short-term nuisance, because of the French threat.[38] Eventually, the "Cherbourg strategy" was deployed. In an impressive display of industrial and economic power, the fleet to destroy Cronstadt (or Cherbourg) was built inside a year. At the end of the war the next first lord visited Cherbourg. He was unsettled by the scale of the French base and the work in progress.[39] The preferred countermeasure was a new fleet base at Portland, linked to Alderney by submarine telegraph. This would "draw a chain across the Channel."[40] With a superior fleet based close to Cherbourg, the arsenal could be blockaded and then assaulted.[41]

Cherbourg became a torpedo boat station in the 1880s, but there was "no way to protect the arsenal from bombardment" or from a landing in the rear.[42] This was exactly what Fisher had in mind when he claimed that "the Regular Army should be regarded as a projectile to be fired by the Navy!" He considered Toulon and the Cotentin peninsula as the "vulnerable points for our fleet to act on France" and proposed submarine attacks into the French bases.[43] Cherbourg was the critical target in 1898, and as the defenses were still inadequate, the French moved their Channel fleet to Brest, Cherbourg being too vulnerable for use as a fleet base.[44] Without a fleet at Cherbourg, France could not threaten an invasion of Britain. This simplified British strategy and exposed the fundamental flaw at the heart of French naval policy. France could not match Britain in naval spending, and neither superior education and administration nor temporary and largely illusory technical breakthroughs could offset the superior numbers and commitment of Britain. In 1898, the French were concerned that the vaulting confidence of the British might lead them to provoke a war and "settle" the century-long colonial rivalry.[45] Operations against French bases were still being considered in 1905.[46]

The inevitable question arises: what was the value of such operations against continental powers? As H. Richmond observed, "If the enemy is sufficiently occupied in his home waters he will be unable to detach either forces large enough to be effective, or escort enough to protect them on passage."[47] Further examples of the deterrent impact of the threat of a direct naval assault can be found in 1856, 1861, 1878 and 1885. The strategic logic remained irrefutable. Technological advances after 1914 improved the chances of successful base attacks.

THE GRAND STRATEGY OF THE BRITISH EMPIRE

The origins of the modern misconception of the role of the Royal Navy and the nature of British power in the nineteenth century lie in the curious genesis of British strategic thought.

Britain evolved a grand strategy on an entirely empirical basis. Because this proved to be successful, it was never subjected to the searching analysis accorded to the policies of other, less fortunate, nations. In essence, Britain was a maritime economic power with an auxiliary army. The technological developments of the 1840s allowed the army to argue that the navy could no longer guarantee insular security and that, therefore, the army should be accorded a larger role in strategic decision making.[48] In the absence of an effective spokesman, the naval case, while strong, was rarely heard in Cabinet. Here the constant pressure to respond to new technology at a practical level deprived the service of the leisure to reflect on the strategic implications of the new environment.

When efforts were made to establish a national strategy, the proponents were John Colomb, a retired Royal Marine captain, and John Laughton, a naval instructor specializing in mathematics and astronomy. Their efforts, which culminated in the work of Corbett, were both too little and too late, for, once the defense of Britain had been secured by more forts, the army raised the specter of a Russian invasion of India to keep up its profile. Despite the success of the "blue-water" school in 1889 and 1894, the idea of invasion was still being raised to frighten weak-minded politicians in 1906. It was then dropped in favor of the commitment to send an army to France. Even as Corbett completed his appreciation of national strategy, the army took control. Corbett found the limited horizons of the "over-confident and anti-navy" generals profoundly unsettling.[49]

Although I have argued that there was a major change in one specific aspect of British strategy in the nineteenth century, a change that reflected both new technology and the balance of power, there was no effective discussion of "national" strategy. Naval issues were not debated in the round, largely because there was no need, but also from a marked aversion among the officers of the age to engage in theoretical speculation. Those who did write on professional subjects confined themselves to tactics and the relative merits of new technologies. The basic issues of British strategy had not changed in 200 years, although the capacity to seek and destroy the enemy had increased.

In the 1860s, the problem of trade defense in the age of the steam cruiser was addressed by John Colomb. Donald Schurman has argued that from a specific technical problem, largely coal supply, can be dated the origins of "British" strategy. This is hardly surprising. The Royal Navy had a problem. Colomb persuaded it to address the problem in a methodical manner. The result was the Carnarvon Commission of 1879.[50]

The Royal Navy did not create doctrine in the nineteenth century, in contrast to the French, Russian, American and German navies, because it was neither rebuilding after defeat nor creating a new service. It relied on its corporate memory, its history, for guidance. The transmission of this knowledge was a major part of the intellectual development of career sea officers. From a structural perspective, the position for statesmen was less satisfactory.

The informal transmission of information was placed on a more secure footing in 1893 with the foundation of the Society for Navy Records, which combined the interest naval officers, historians, politicians and journalists had in British naval history. The society provided the intellectual element of the "navalism" of the 1890s. By 1914, it had produced over forty volumes, covering the Armada, the First Dutch War, the Seven Years' War, the War of American Independence, the War of the French Revolution and several dealing with the critical period 1803-5. There were none on the operational aspects of the nineteenth century. It is no coincidence that the founder of the society, Laughton, also opened the debate on a "national" strategy.[51]

Corbett shared Laughton's objective and his method. Both men saw that accurate historical scholarship was the only sound basis for a national strategy. Laughton considered Mahan's seminal book *The Influence of Seapower upon History, 1660-1782* of 1890 "premature," while Corbett viewed it as "unhistorical."[52] Although aware of Mahan's limitations, they acknowledged that his work had succeeded in raising public awareness and supporting the naval case. This proved to be a double-edged benefit, for the "new navalism" of the 1890s was of an extreme "blue-water" variety. Not only was this profoundly antagonistic to the maritime slant of Corbett's and Laughton's work, but it also led the navy into bitter rivalries with the army. In 1911, Corbett published *Some Principles of Maritime Strategy*, the first appreciation of the higher direction of the national war effort that reflected the dominance of the sea in national strategy. Any weakness reflected Corbett's lack of access to the raw material for the nineteenth century. In consequence he, like Mahan, implied that the age of steam, torpedoes and dreadnoughts formed a continuity with the age of wooden sailing ships.

In Corbett, the Royal Navy found a man capable of supplying a combination of historical example and logical extrapolation. This complemented the pragmatic British approach at a time when such methods by themselves were no longer adequate. Schurman has shown that the strategic argument reached the intended audience only through the medium of history years after Corbett's death. Mahan, for all his popularity, was no more successful in the short term. However, the audience that mattered was the one concerned with the higher direction of war, the statesmen, and here at least the message was received, for even Gladstone read Mahan.[53]

BRITISH INTERESTS AND GLOBAL STRATEGY

In the period under review, British reluctance to enter into continental conflicts, notably over Schleswig-Holstein, has been treated as proof of weakness, either physical or moral, when faced by the mass armies and realpolitik of Bismarck's Europe.[54] This oversimplifies the issues involved in the major crises of the era, ignores the manner in which they were settled and confuses the real nature of British power. Britain did not fight Prussia in 1863-64 because it had no desire to engage in war over two duchies that were never part of the kingdom of Denmark, on an issue provoked by the Danes' breach of the 1852 Treaty, not least because the result would have been to enhance the power of Napoleon III.[55] Furthermore, the real issue for Britain was neither Schleswig nor Holstein, but Denmark.

The idea that Britain was too weak to fight Prussia in 1864 is risible. Whatever Bismarck might have said, Great Britain had the power to secure the Danish islands, cripple Prussian trade and open the specter of a two-front war. What could Prussia have done to Britain?

British strategy after 1688 had been built on endurance and economic strength. These were qualities ill suited to the rapid, limited conflicts that characterized European wars in the second half of the nineteenth century and could be deployed only when vital issues were at stake. It is no coincidence that Britain's success in war invariably bore a close relationship to the length of the struggle. Britain could not hope to win a short war against a major rival. This made the decision for war a more momentous issue for British statesmen than for their foreign contemporaries. Their reluctance did not stem from a fear of defeat. It is hard to see how Britain could have been defeated by any practical combination of rivals. Their reluctance came from a recognition of the economic and domestic political costs of war. If Britain was to fight a long war, the government needed to purchase national unity with a reward. The political culture of the age ensured that this would take the form of domestic political, social or economic change. Even limited wars put the existing political balance under severe pressure, as the campaign for "administrative reform" during the Russian War demonstrated.[56] The application of British power was, therefore, heavily conditioned by domestic politics, as Mahan recognized.[57]

Although it was impossible for British power to be decisive in the short term, this was a point of distinction, not weakness, for Britain was the only world power in the nineteenth century. Its weakness, the lack of a continental army, was a short-term problem. However, it placed great pressure on the Royal Navy to strike a major blow at an early stage, cover the mobilization of military power and demonstrate British resolve to enemies and allies alike. Such logic led Sir James Graham to plan his Russian war around two naval assaults, at Reval and Sevastopol.[58] The same issues came into play in 1914.

The elements of British strategy as they applied to a major war with one or more European states in this period can be summarized as follows.

1. Deploy a superior battle fleet in home waters to guarantee insular security and protect commerce against large scale interruption. This was the central position of strength from which all other military operations flowed.

2. Search for allies, especially those with a suitable army and common security interests.

3. Impose an economic and naval blockade.

4. Mobilize the economic and industrial resources of the nation to create a large army and an enlarged navy. This would provide the manpower to deploy a fleet and army for offensive purposes.

5. Capture outlying colonial territories to deprive the enemy of overseas cruiser bases and to secure leverage for the peace settlement. This would have the effect of compressing the naval war, releasing assets for offensive operations.

6. Assault hostile naval bases to destroy both the naval forces and the support facilities that sustained them. This would deprive the enemy of the power to threaten Britain.

7. Wait for exhaustion to set in before negotiating a settlement that maintained and enhanced British security vis-a-vis its enemy and its allies.[59]

In all these areas the Royal Navy was the critical instrument. It provided insular and imperial security, imposed the blockade, protected the maritime communications that sustained and enhanced British war power, maintained contact with allies, crippled hostile naval forces and secured a stable position that no nation, however insular, could tolerate for prolonged periods without suffering internal collapse or becoming prey to avaricious neighbors.

The destruction of European naval arsenals would allow for the most complete exploitation of global reach, amphibious power projection and economic warfare. The Crimean War provided a brief demonstration of this strategy; but it would require a far larger conflict to obtain the real benefits of a maritime strategy based on the qualities of political endurance, economic resource and industrial mobilization. Only Britain of the Crimean War belligerents was growing steadily more powerful as the war ended. Its allies and its enemy had long since passed their peak, for they lacked the industry to build new weapons systems on a strategic scale, and with the wastage of trained manpower, their greatest resource, they became steadily weaker.

STUDIES IN DETERRENCE

Although this chapter has so far largely concentrated on British naval offensive planning against Cherbourg, France was not the only state that was vulnerable to the application of the "Cherbourg strategy." The United States, Russia and Germany all had to face the threat posed by the Royal Navy. United States' strategy between 1815 and 1900 was dominated by concern that the Royal Navy could repeat the War of 1812. To this end successive programs of fortress construction were carried through, one during the Civil War and the last overlapping with the construction of a battle fleet in the 1890s.[60]

Russia was well aware of the threat to its coastal strong points after 1856. Its naval policy concentrated on forts and coast defense until the 1890s, primarily in the Baltic. The threat of war in 1863, 1878 and 1885 reduced the tsar's councils to panic, encouraged major expenditure on coast defense and highlighted the inability of Russia to fight Britain. The crises of 1878 and 1885 were the only occasions between 1856 and 1914 when Britain mobilized fleets against a European power. These were coast assault fleets for Baltic operations. They exercised a major influence on Russian decision making, as the Russian naval exercises between 1879 and 1884 revealed. These examined the problem of keeping a superior fleet away from Cronstadt; every year the "Russian" forces failed, and the exercise ended prematurely.[61]

Only Germany had the ambition and the power to threaten the British Empire. This threat was not laid against colonial territory, nor did it take the form of an oceangoing navy. The threat came from a drive for European hegemony, based on the Triple Alliance and a powerful army. Germany was largely invulnerable to British action in the short term, and its naval assets were located in heavily defended bases originally built to resist French coast assault operations. This made a "limited maritime war" inappropriate, as Corbett recognized in 1912.[62]

Britain's response was colored by the construction of a powerful battle fleet for European service. Admiral Tirpitz's Risk Fleet made it clear that the new navy was to neutralize Britain, allowing German a free hand in Europe. Tirpitz believed there was a "danger period" while the new fleet was being built, a danger given focus by the remarks of the Admiralty civil lord in 1905, when he spoke of the Royal Navy's "getting its blow in first." The result was a "Copenhagen complex" in the German navy, a fear of a preemptive strike against the fleet in harbor.[63]

Louis Napoleon III had adopted a similar logic for his battle fleet between 1852 and 1865. He had learned, to his cost, that Britain would not concede even a strong second place to a powerful continental state with expansive ambitions. Tirpitz, ignorant of modern history, was compelled to repeat the error. Sir Michael Howard has observed, "It was not the German fleet itself that alarmed the British but the intentions that lay behind it."[64]

Britain aligned itself with France and Russia, its imperial rivals, to avert German domination of Europe. It was no coincidence that the pivot of British decision making in 1914 should have been Belgium, as it had been in 1793, 1815 and 1870. Belgium, more than any other European state, demonstrated why Britain had to be concerned with Europe. Britain did not go to war with Germany because of the naval race. Indeed, Britain could not allow Germany to overthrow France, even if it did not have a significant fleet. That was the clear import of the British response to the "war in sight" crisis of 1875. Britain went to war in 1914 to preserve its political and strategic interests.[65]

CONCLUSION

Between 1856 and 1914, the Royal Navy remained unchallenged as a war-fighting force at sea. The legacy of victory, the unequaled size of the fleet and national commitment to maintaining naval mastery ensured that the Royal Navy remained both the foundation and the sword arm of global power. In the absence of a rival battle fleet, new strategic ideas and technological change made it possible for the Royal Navy to destroy the enemy inside fortified harbors. This capacity exercised a considerable deterrent effect on all the major powers of the era; even the Germans developed a "Copenhagen complex."

The British Empire was built on sea power, and while Britain remained preeminent at sea, and the sea remained unfettered as a source of power, then the empire survived. Sea power has never lost its importance in global strategy, but it was subjected to artificial constraints between 1922 and 1936. In this period Britain lost the ability to deter its rivals, and that, in part, explains the loss of its empire. Between 1856 and 1914, the Royal Navy had the offensive power and doctrine to secure the empire by deterrence.

NOTES

1. The *Times*, Leader, 24 April 1856, 2.
2. A. D. Lambert, *The Crimean War: British Grand Strategy against Russia, 1853-1856* (Manchester: Manchester University Press, 1990), 296-347.
3. Julian Corbett, *Naval Operations*, Vol. 1 (London: Longmans, 1930), 96, 219.
4. Ian Buxton, *Big Gun Monitors* (Annapolis: Naval Institute Press, 1978), 11.
5. Corbett, *Naval Operations*, vol 2, 19, 55; Churchill to Fisher, 21 December 1914 in Arthur Marder, ed., *Fear God and Dreadnought: The Correspondence of Admiral of the Fleet Lord Fisher of Kilverstone*, vol 3 (London: Oxford University Press, 1959), 105 (hereafter *FG&DN*); Arthur Marder, *From the Dreadnought to Scapa Flow*, vol 2 (London: Oxford University Press, 1965), 196-98; James Goldrick, *The King's Ships Were at Sea* (Annapolis: Naval Institute Press, 1984).
6. David French, *The British Way in Warfare: 1688-2000* (London: Unwin Hyman, 1990), 155-6.
7. Gordon Martel, "The Meaning of Power: The Decline and Fall of Great Britain," *The International History Review*, 13:4, (November 1991): 662-94; Keith Neilson, "`Greatly Exaggerated': The Myth of the Decline of Great Britain before 1914," ibid., 697-725.
8. William Fuller, *Strategy and Power in Russia: 1600 - 1914* (New York: The Free Press, 1992), 289, reveals Russian weakness and fear when threatened by Britain and makes clear that it would never have fought Britain over Asia while its European frontiers were threatened, as they were for most of the period, by Austria or Germany. French, *The British Way in Warfare*, 144, argues that internal security was the real concern of Indian soldiers and administrators.
9. Ronald Robinson, J. Gallagher and Alice Denny, *Africa and the Victorians* (London: Macmillan, 1961), 10-14.

10.H. Richmond, *Imperial Defence and Capture at Sea in Wartime* (London: Hutchinson, 1932), 21. Although Richmond was unaware of the Baltic dimension of British strategy in the nineteenth century, he saw the Black Sea as the vulnerable point where Britain could defend India from Russia. He considered (p. 120) that local defense would *never* secure the empire.

11.Paul Kennedy, *The Rise and Fall of British Naval Mastery* (London: Scribner, 1976), 178. The pivotal chapter of the book, "Mahan versus Mackinder (1859-97)" is the last in the section "Zenith"; the following chapter, the first in the section "Fall," is "The End of Pax Britannica (1897-1914)."

12.Neville Brown, *Strategic Mobility* (London: Chatto and Windus, 1963), 173; William H. Parker, *Mackinder: Geography as an Aid to Statecraft* (Oxford: Oxford University Press, 1982), 160-63, admits that contemporary concern with Russian expansion provided a basis for the proposal.

13.J. S. Corbett, "The Capture of Private Property at Sea," in A. T. Mahan, ed., *Some Neglected Aspects of War* (London: Simpson, Low and Marston, 1907), 149; Donald Schurman, *Julian S. Corbett, 1854-1922* (London: Royal Historical Society, 1982), 105.

14.J. N. Westwood, *A History of Russian Railways* (London: Osprey, 1968).

15.British sea power brought Russia to the conference table. It destroyed Sevastopol, ruined its southern provinces, dislocated its strategy, destroyed its precarious export-dominated economy and threatened to knock down its capital city. To contrast this unfavorably with the Austrian Ultimatum of December 1855, as has been the norm in modern scholarship concerning the Crimean War, flies in the face of logic and solid evidence. At the time it issued the Ultimatum, Austria was bankrupt and had been forced to demobilise its army. Russia made peace because she could not expect anything but further defeats in 1856. Britain, which was only just getting into its stride as a war-fighting nation, agreed to end the war because France was unwilling and largely unable to continue, and the allies had agreed on the terms that had been accepted. Lambert, *The Crimean War*, 295-326. Fuller, *Strategy and Power* makes clear the pivotal role of sea power technological superiority in the defeat of 1856. He shows how the threat of naval action in the Bosporus in 1878 led the minister of war to counsel the tsar to avoid a rupture with Britain, if possible. He also demonstrates the sense of powerlessness felt by the Ministry of War in the face of a British fleet in the Baltic. Further, he deals with the 1885 crisis in a similar vein. Russia had to back down because it could not risk a war because of European security concerns.

16.Neilson, "Greatly Exaggerated." Salisbury, a lifelong pessimist, possessed a remarkably poor grasp of strategy. See Arthur Marder, *The Anatomy of British Seapower: A History of British Naval Policy in the Pre-Dreadnought Era, 1880-1905* (London: A. A. Knopf, 1940), 77. R. Millman's account, from which Neilson draws his quote, ignores the development of naval threat to

Russia and the Russian climb down at the Congress of Berlin, which was a triumph for Disraeli. Neilson's account of the Penjdeh crisis of 1885 suffers from the same problem, a limited range of evidence. R. Millman, *Britain and the Eastern Question 1875-1878* (Oxford: Clarendon Press, 1979), does not discuss the strategic issues of 1878, completely ignores naval preparations at home for Baltic operations and follows A.J.P. Taylor, *The Struggle for Mastery in Europe 1848-1918* (Oxford: Clarendon Press, 1954), 250. For an alternative approach to 1878 and 1885, see Lambert, *Part of a Long Line of Circumvallation: Great Britain and the Baltic 1809 - 1890* (Lund, forthcoming).

17.Marder, *Anatomy*, 13-16.

18.Ibid., Part 5, 355-416. This image was a congenial one, both at the turn of the century and when Marder wrote.

19.The concept of the "Dark Ages" was set out in O. Parkes, *British Battleships* (London: Arms and Armour Press, 1956), 230-32 and refined by N. A. M. Rodger, "The Dark Ages of the Admiralty," 3 parts, *Mariner's Mirror*, vols. 61-62, 1975-76; J. F. Beeler, "A One Power Standard? Great Britain and the Balance of Naval Power, 1860-1890," *Journal of Strategic Studies* 15:4 (December 1992): 548-96; see Table 4.1.

20.Kennedy, *The Rise and Fall*, 180; French, *The British Way in Warfare*, 137. The original gunboats were built to bombard Cronstadt. They never formed the "bulk" of the fleet by value, manpower or funding.

21.Brian Tunstall, *The Cambridge History of the British Empire* vol. 3 (Cambridge: Cambridge University Press, 1959), 41. Throughout this volume, Tunstall emphasizes the central role of the main fleet. D. C. Gordon, *The Dominion Partnership in Imperial Defence: 1870-1914* (Baltimore: Johns Hopkins University Press, 1965).

22.Andrew D. Lambert, *The Last Sailing Battlefleet: Maintaining Naval Mastery 1815-1850* (London: Conway Maritime Press, 1991); D. J. Lyon, *The Sailing Navy List* (London: 1994).

23.The first foreign ship to exceed the size of the HMS *Warrior*, (1861) was a British built German ironclad (1869, originally ordered by the Turkish navy, and this was the only German ship to do so until 1893. Russia completed one larger ironclad in 1876; a second entered service thirteen years later. France achieved this size in 1876 and again in 1883.

24.A. D. Lambert, *Battleships in Transition: The Creation of the Steam Battlefleet* (London: Conway Maritime Press, 1984); A. D. Lambert, ed., *Steam, Steel & Shellfire: The Steam Warship 1815-1905* (London: Conway Maritime Press, 1992).

25.Minutes of Admiral Richards, First Sea Lord, 31 October 1895, BND, 699: Admiral Kerr to Earl Selborne, 28 April 1902. D. Boyce, ed., *The Crisis of British Power: The Imperial and Naval Papers of the Second Earl of Selborne*, 1895-1902 (London: Historians Press, 1900), 144.

26.R. Seager, *Alfred Thayer Mahan* (Annapolis: Naval Institute Press, 1977), 519-34.

27.Theodore Ropp, *The Creation of a Modern Navy* (Annapolis: Naval Institute Press, 1988), 155-80.

28.Robinson & Gallagher, *Africa and the Victorians*, 462-72.

29.Julian Corbett, *Some Principles of Maritime Strategy* (London: Longmans, Green, 1911), 259-79. In 1914, the cruiser war was "over by Christmas." Marder, *Anatomy*, 99, fn. 34, 104. Mahan's advocacy of convoy in *The Influence of Seapower upon the War of 1812*, vol 2 (London: Longmans, Green, 1905), 20, 130, reflected a war in which the threat came from a myriad of privateers, not the handful of cruisers that were the cause of concern in the late nineteenth century.

30.M. Partridge, "The Royal Navy and the End of the Close Blockade, 1885-1905: A Revolution in Naval Strategy," *Mariner's Mirror*, 75: (1989): 119-32. The sailing navy *never* adopted the close blockade as the *only* system; close and open blockades were used at different times under different circumstances. Corbett's interest in this historical issue, as in many others, reflected the contemporary concerns of the navy.

31.F. T. Jane, *Heresies of Seapower* (London: Longmans, Green, 1906), 125-44.

32.Ropp, *The Creation*, 16; R. Gardiner, ed., *Conway's All the World's Fighting Ships: 1860-1906* (London: Hodden and Stoughton, 1979).

33.Richmond, *Imperial Defence*, 127-33.

34.Ropp, *The Creation*, 17; emphasis added.

35.Michael Partridge, *The Military Planning for the Defence of the United Kingdom 1814-1870* (New York: Greenwod Press, 1989), 90-91.

36.Corbett, *Some Principles of Maritime Strategy*, 68, 343.

37.Lambert, *The Last Sailing Battlefleet*, 11, 106-7; C. I. Hamilton, *Anglo-French Naval Rivalry 1840-1870* (Oxford: Clarendon Press, 1993), 72.

38.Lambert, *The Crimean War*, 36.

39.Sir Charles Wood to Colonel Claremont (Military Attaché in Paris), 17 July 1856. This was a very unusual step. Wood to the queen, 6 August 1856, Add. 49,566 f12-13.

40.Submission by the Surveyor of the navy, Captain Sir Baldwin Walker, 20 May 1858, ADM 1/5968 in *BND*, 657-61. Although Walker's post gave him responsibility for construction programs, he was consulted on strategic questions, where his advice proved superior to that available elsewhere in the Admiralty. Lambert, *The Crimean War*.

41.J. W. King, *The Warships and Navies of Europe in 1880* (London: Oxford University Press, 1982), 49.

42.Ropp, *The Creation*, 11, 136, 169, 213, 260-62.

43.Fisher to Lord Esher, 19 November 1903, *FG&DN*, vol. 1, 291; Fisher to Earl Roseberry, 10 May 1901, 188-191; Fisher to Arnold White, 6 August 1902, 259-62; Fisher to Lord Selborne, 19 July 1902, 253-54.

44.Marder, *Anatomy*, 324-25; Ropp, *The Creation*, 261.

45.Marder, *Anatomy*, 330-31; C. Andrew, *Theophile Delcassé* (London: Macmillan, 1968), 102-3. Delcassé believed France could not defeat Britain, even with Russian aid. The other navies regarded the Royal Navy with a mixture of awe, envy and fear.

46.Marder, *Anatomy*, 550-67, esp. 566.

47.Richmond, *Imperial Defence*, 16. The missing word is "Air," reflecting contemporary concerns. The principle is both timeless and insufficiently understood.

48.Partridge, "The Royal Navy"; Lambert, *The Last Sailing Battlefleet*, 52-55.

49.Schurman, *Corbett*, 159, 173. French, *The British Way*, 159, argues that the poor performance of the British army in the Second Boer War, 1899-1902, "demonstrates that a 'Blue Water' policy could not defend Britain and her Empire." After Fashoda, France would not fight Britain, even with Russian support, while its European interests were dominated by the presence and menace of Germany. Sea-based deterrence remained the cornerstone of British strategy.

50.Donald Schurman, "The Search for Principles and Naval Strategy," in Marc Milner, ed., *Military History and the Military Profession* (Ottawa: Carleton University Press, 1992), 169-80; Bryan Ranft, *Technical Change and British Naval Policy: 1860-1939* (London: Hodden and Stoughten, 1977), Chapter 1.

51.A. Sainsbury, *The Centenary of the Navy Records Society* (London: 1993).

52.G. S. Graham, *The Politics of Naval Supremacy* (Cambridge: Cambridge University Press, 1965), 5.

53.Schurman, "The Search for Principles," 170-81. Azar Gat, *The Development of Military Thought in the Nineteenth Century* (Oxford: Oxford University Press, 1992), 181. Mahan's view of sea power, as developed into the "blue-water" thesis, must be seen as an antidote to the "bricks and mortar" army school, rather than a coherent strategy. This explains the lack of attention to coastal operations after 1890, which the navy *assumed* the army would support. The impact of such slipshod thinking can be seen in the failure to provide either specialist coastal warfare units and the equally inexplicable failure to conduct gunnery training for the provision of indirect fire against shore targets. These two issues go a long way toward explaining the failure at the Dardanelles. These issues were resolved, as the German army discovered on 6 June 1944. F. Dreyer, *The Sea Heritage* (London: Museum Press, 1955), 440.

54.Kennedy, *The Rise and Fall*, 181; French, *The British Way of Warfare*, 131.

55.Lambert, *Part of a Long Line*.

56.Geoffrey Searle, *Entrepreneurial Politics in Mid-Victorian Britain* (Oxford: Oxford University Press, 1993), 89-125. French, *The British Way in Warfare*, stresses the impact of political reform on defense budgets.

57.A. T. Mahan, *The Influence of Seapower upon History 1660-1783* (London: Longmans, Green, 1890), 58-81.

58.Lambert, *The Crimean War*, 83-99.

59.David French, *British Strategy and War Aims 1914-1916* (London: Allen Unwin, 1986), ix, Chapter 2, confirms all these points but point 6, thus revealing the basic "military" assumptions underlying his work. He dismisses the Grand Fleet as a "[f]leet in being" (24), ignores the crucial battle of the Heligoland Bight, operations on the Belgian coast and plans for a more aggressive use of sea power in the North Sea. See Lambert, *The Crimean War*, for the *ad hoc* development of a similar program between 1853 and 1855.

60.E. R. Lewis, *Seacoast Fortifications of the United States* (Washington, D.C.: Smithsonian Institute Press, 1970), 21-87. The security of Canada was based on the deterrent value of the Royal Navy. No other system was either credible or economically viable. R. A. Preston, *In Defence of the Undefended Frontier, Planning for War in North America: 1867-1939* (Montreal: McGill Queen's University Press, 1977), 21, 30, 57, 83, 115-16.

61.Lambert, *Part of a Long Line*.

62.Corbett, *Some Principles*, xlii.

63.J. Steinberg, *Yesterday's Deterrent* (London: Macmillan, 1965) 21; Holger Herwig, *Luxury Fleet: The Imperial German Navy 1888-1918* (London: Allen Unwin, 1980), 37, 59; I. N. Lambi, *The German Navy and Power Politics 1862-1914* (London: Allen and Unwin, 1984), 154n, 176, 209.

64.Michael Howard, "The Edwardian Arms Race," in *The Lessons of History* (Oxford: Clarendon Press, 1991), 96.

65.Zara Steiner, *Britain and the Origins of the First World War* (London: St. Martins Press, 1977), 134.

5

The Apotheosis Of Mahan: American Naval Strategy, 1889–1922

Kenneth J. Hagan

The story is told that upon learning about the new Naval War College in 1884, one admiral exclaimed, "*Teach* the art of war! Well, I'll be damned." A senior captain chided the college's founder, Rear Admiral Stephen B. Luce, "What is that new fangled thing you've got at Newport? You have Cooper's *Naval History* and Parker's *Fleet Tactics*, what more do you want?"[1]

James Fenimore Cooper today is known in the United States for his romantic novels of the frontier, exemplified by the recent movie, *The Last of the Mohicans*. But Cooper's contemporaries, the generation of Americans living immediately after the War of 1812, recognized Cooper as a distinguished naval historian. He was something of a theorist, and in the introduction to the 1839 edition of his *History of the Navy of the United States*, he enunciated "certain great principles that are unchangeable, and which must prevail under all circumstances." He had in mind the great firepower and stupendous endurance of ships of the line, especially when combined in fleets. Regardless of "the introduction of steam into naval warfare," Cooper opined in those early days of the historic revolution in maritime propulsion that, "in the end, it will be found that the force of fleets will be required, in settling the interests of states, as to-day."[2]

Secretary of the Navy James K. Paulding, a friend of Cooper's from the literary circles of New York, ordered a copy of the book placed in the library of every American warship, where naval officers obviously became aware of it. But despite the book's assertion that only fleet operations of major combatants could determine "the interests of states," the U.S. Navy was still relying primarily on frigates and a strategy of *guerre de course* and coastal defense fifty years after its publication.

Stephen B. Luce fully understood that, notwithstanding Cooper, the U.S. Navy had never regularly combined its ships into fighting fleets. In fact, the rampages of the Confederate steamer *Alabama* had served to confirm the wisdom of commerce raiding as the preferred strategy for the post-Civil War generation of American naval officers. In the early 1880s, Luce and his handful of supporters contended that the old way of doing business was no longer appropriate. He and his allies did not want new strategic literature so much as a new navy wide mind-set that accepted *guerre d'escadre* as the correct American doctrine in the dawning age of steam propulsion, large rifled cannon and armor plate.

Luce chaired a naval board that led directly to the general order of 6 October 1884 establishing the Naval War College, and the board's report is replete with references to the importance of fleet operations to the outcome of campaigns and to the value of naval officers' studying "the great naval battles of history...which illustrate...[the] most immutable principles of War."[3] The report persuaded Secretary of the Navy William E. Chandler to establish the war college, but it served an equally important function as the marching orders for Captain Alfred Thayer Mahan, the officer who successfully formulated a curriculum for the study of the history of naval strategy and then distilled his lectures into a book of the highest importance, *The Influence of Sea Power upon History*, 1670-1783.[4] Using Anglo-Dutch and Anglo-French naval warfare in the age of sail as the demonstrable proof, Mahan argued that international greatness rested on mastery of the oceans, and command of the sea depended on victory in engagements between opposing battle fleets.

Professor John Hattendorf has eloquently shown that *The Influence* was more complex than the previous summary suggests, that Mahan went on to write many other books and essays on various aspects of geopolitics, and that after his retirement from active duty in 1896, Mahan was on the sidelines of naval and national affairs most of the time. So it would be incorrect to contend that his book transformed the U.S. Navy. But it would be impossible to deny that the publication of his book and its growing popularity coincided with a fundamental strategic and technological revolution in the navy. Moreover, as the revolution proceeded, Mahan was enshrined as the preeminent American prophet of "sea power." He remains so to this day.

The Influence of Sea Power upon History was the right book at the right time for the U.S. Navy. The year 1889 ushered in a decade of geopolitical realignments destined to transform the United States from a continental power with a modest navy and virtually no overseas territorial possessions into an imperial power with major holdings in the Pacific and undeniable hegemony in the Caribbean and Gulf of Mexico. After testing itself in two decisive actions against the Spanish navy, the new imperial American navy would permanently divest itself of the apparently outmoded strategy of commerce raising and coastal defense in favor of the fashionable Anglo-Mahanian strategy of fleet engagements. The navy's building program, with its emphasis on battleships and cruisers, reflected the new era.

The first hint of the epochal transformation appeared in far-off Samoa, a Pacific archipelago that had long interested American naval officers as a possible location for an overseas coaling station for the "new navy" of steam and steel. Between 1885 and 1889--the years when Mahan was lecturing at the Naval War College and writing his book--the United States and Germany came perilously close to war over possession of Samoa.

The likelihood of armed conflict vanished abruptly on 16 March 1889, when a hurricane "of monumental proportions" struck Samoa.[5] Of all the naval vessels assembled by the United States, Germany and Britain to glower at one another in the Samoan harbor of Apia, only HMS *Calliope* escaped by fighting its way to sea. Three German warships were dashed on the reef or beached. The Americans lost the *Trenton* and *Vandalia*, two relics of the transitional navy of wooden-hulled ships powered primarily by sail and using steam only as an auxiliary. Their consciences stung by the tragedy, the diplomats in June 1889 created a tripartite government for Samoa without infringing on earlier American treaty rights to establish a naval base in Pago Pago.

The Samoan disaster provided grist for the mill of the new Republican secretary of the navy, Benjamin F. Tracy, an ardent imperialist and navalist of the Mahanian stripe. Tracy's annual report for 1889 marks the official beginning of the American battleship navy and the formal adoption of an offensive naval strategy directed principally at major European powers, and to a lesser extent, at Japan. The report featured the American naval loss at Samoa as a vivid illustration of the weakness of the U.S. Navy in the Pacific and as a graphic demonstration of the need for more powerful steam-driven warships.

In the past, the United States had constructed shallow draft gunboats and monitors for coastal defense and seagoing frigates whose purpose was limited to commerce protection, commerce raiding and single-ship

engagements with similarly rigged opponents rated as less than ships of
the line. Henceforth, said the voice of modern American sea power:

> We must have a fleet of battleships that will beat off the enemy's
> fleet on its approach, for it is not to be tolerated that the United
> States...is to submit to an attack on the threshold of its harbours.
> Finally, we must be able to divert an enemy's force from our coast
> by threatening its own.[6]

The United States, said the secretary disingenuously, would always fight
wars "defensive in principle," but hereafter they would be "offensive in
...operations."[7]

Tracy's unprecedented report, Mahan's book and Republican control
of both houses of the Congress led in short order to the Naval Act of 30
June 1890. It provided for three battleships, one protected cruiser, a
torpedo cruiser and one light torpedo boat. At the unprecedented cost of
over $3 million apiece, each battleship displaced more than 10,000 tons,
2,000 more than the *Maine* or *Texas*. These big warriors mounted heavy
main batteries: four 13-inch and eight 8-inch rifled cannon. The large
turrets and low freeboard might remind the unwary citizen of giant
monitors, and to widen their sectional appeal, the ships were named the
Indiana, *Massachusetts* and *Oregon*, a political gambit reminiscent of the
naming of the *ABCs* in 1883.

Any resemblance between the *Indianas* and earlier American
warships was purely deceptive. Their builders exceeded the 5,000-mile
range that astute congressmen had stipulated to pacify the isolationists.
Their armor plate was heavier than that carried by the British *Majestic*
class, rated the world's most powerful battleship at the time. At a
London meeting of the Institute of British Naval Architects in June 1891,
a leading British designer, J. H. Biles, praised them as "distinctly
superior to any European vessels of the same displacement, and...quite
a match for any ships afloat."[8]

Some of those ships were owned by relatively minor powers, which
became threatening simply by possessing one or two major combatants,
and, in 1891, Chile was such a country. Secretary of the Navy Tracy's
annual report for that year coincided with a period of intense anxiety the
nation was facing over its relations with Chile, whose modern warships
outclassed some of the vessels in the U.S. Navy. For almost a year the
Benjamin Harrison administration had been closely monitoring a
revolution in Chile, and Tracy had created a special ad hoc task force,

including the new cruisers *Baltimore* and *San Francisco*, to cruise in Chilean waters. The naval-diplomatic crisis came outside the True Blue Saloon in Valpariso on 16 October 1891, when a riot left two American sailors from the *Baltimore* dead and several badly injured. Talk of war was sweeping the land just as Tracy penned his 1891 report, and shortly thereafter Harrison issued an ultimatum demanding an apology from Chile. On 25 January 1892, he asked Congress to consider a declaration of war. Five days later Chile capitulated.

Chile's compliance with Harrison's demands may be explained, in part, by Secretary Tracy's extraordinary mobilization of the navy in preparation for war. Alfred Thayer Mahan at least thought so. On 28 January 1892, immediately after a meeting with Tracy, Mahan wrote to his most trusted naval colleague, Admiral Luce, that Tracy "feels, and I think justly, that the energy with which he has pushed naval preparation has had much to do with the final pacific outcome."[9]

Mahan, Tracy and the other men who transformed the U.S. Navy in the 1890s commonly blended imperialism with enthusiasm for capital ships, citing the need for coaling stations as their immediate motive. The Samoan crisis of 1889 warned them that the increasing tempo of European imperialism endangered American access to possible coaling sites and markets in the Pacific. Secretary Tracy in 1891 noted, "The rapid extension of commercial relations has doubled the importance of our interests, especially in the Pacific."[10]

Hawaii attracted the new navalists because the islands seemed ideal as a western bastion to guard the approaches of the proposed Central American canal, which the Harrison administration hoped to build through Nicaragua. Tracy was especially keen on rapidly moving warships from one ocean to another. At the moment, the secretary advised the president with palpable cogency:

> [t]he two seaboards are so remote that each requires its separate system of naval defense. Each has its vulnerable points, and each has neighbors that are well prepared for offensive movements ....To protect either seaboard, even when our present authorized fleet is completed, will involve stripping the other at a critical moment.[11]

But if a canal was constructed through Nicaragua, "the strategic situation would be largely modified."[12] Major combatant ships could then be shifted from the Atlantic to the Pacific so rapidly and returned so swiftly that no debilitating naval power vacuum would form in their absence.

This appreciation of the strategic significance of a canal through Central America underlay the administration's unanimous resolve to annex Hawaii.

President Harrison had appointed an annexationist from Maine, John L. Stevens, as minister to the Hawaiian kingdom. In January 1893, Stevens encouraged the islands' wealthy white planters to overthrow the native monarchy and honored their request for naval intervention the moment they seized power in Honolulu.

The flagship of the Pacific squadron, the protected cruiser *Boston*, was docked at Honolulu when the uprising began on 16 January 1893. Captain Gilbert C. Wiltse tersely reported his quick reaction to Secretary Tracy: "At 4:30 PM landed force in accordance with the request of U.S. Minister Plenipotentiary. Tuesday afternoon the Provisional Government was established, the Queen dethroned, without loss of life."[13] Some 164 bluejackets and marines were brandishing Gatling guns and rifles outside the royal palace. The secretary did not question Wiltse's action.

Minister Stevens immediately recognized the new provisional government, declared Hawaii an American protectorate and urged the administration to annex the islands quickly before Great Britain plucked the "Hawaiian pear...now fully ripe" from the American grasp.[14] Harrison hastily negotiated a treaty of annexation and rushed it to the Senate in the last hours of his presidency. His administration expired before the Senate could act, and the new Democratic president, Grover Cleveland, withdrew it for reconsideration. Swallowing of the ripe pear would await the Spanish-American War, and even then, opposition to overseas colonies made the final acquisition take the form of a joint resolution of Congress rather than a treaty requiring two-thirds approval by the Senate.

Initially, the Cleveland administration was unsure of its own attitude toward the navy and particularly toward the Naval War College. The new secretary of the navy, Hilary A. Herbert, soon gave Mahan a chance to move from center stage and hone his growing affection for the British. He ordered him to surrender the presidency of the Naval War College and take command of the cruiser *Chicago*, destined for an Atlantic cruise. This decision, much resisted by Mahan and his coterie of political supporters, would bring the historian/sailor a level of Anglo-American acclaim never matched before or since by a line officer in the U.S. Navy. When he assumed command of the *Chicago* on 1 May 1893, Mahan was unknowingly headed for formal receptions by the highest levels of British society and honorary degrees from Oxford and

Cambridge.

Once the *Chicago* returned to the United States, Mahan retired from the navy to write full-time. He soon finished a biography of Nelson, which brought him added accolades in England, and he spent most of the rest of his life as a popular writer. Only for a few brief weeks in 1897 and during the Spanish-American War did he return to the policy-making circles of the Navy Department, and when he did so, the strategy and course of the war were largely determined by others. But the explosive burst of pro-British sentiment characterized by his experiences and writing after 1892 helped, in some immeasurable way, to bring about the great Anglo-American rapprochement that permitted U.S. emergence as a power of the first rank at the time of the Spanish-American War.

Mahan himself, in any case, was no longer essential to the prosecution of a Mahanian strategy by the U.S. Navy. Former enemies of the Naval War College such as Democratic secretary of the navy Hilary A. Herbert now supported it along with construction of even more battleships. His assistant secretary, William G. McAdoo, son-in-law to the future president Woodrow Wilson, was an ardent navalist who, in a speech at Boston in 1894, said, "An American battleship with a crew of five hundred men might...prevent the destruction of that which a whole army could not save."[15]

The Democrats further demonstrated the bipartisan nature of naval assertiveness during the Sino-Japanese War by ordering the commander of the Asiatic Squadron to "[a]fford every facility for intelligence officers of our fleet to obtain information."[16] Lieutenant William S. Sims, who would shape American naval policy in World War I, was one of the officers who reported on Japan's emerging naval strength and the challenge it posed to American preeminence in the Hawaiian islands.

By 1895, the administration of Grover Cleveland was so cocksure of itself that it meddled in a boundary dispute between British Guiana and Venezuela. Secretary of State Richard Olney strongly protested that British incursions into Venezuela violated the Monroe Doctrine. Proudly christened Olney's "twenty-inch gun" by Cleveland, the secretary's note generated war hysteria among jingoists like Theodore Roosevelt, soon to be assistant secretary of the navy in the William McKinley administration. Congress was shaken enough to authorize three more battleships.

The war clouds were dissipated by arbitration, and never again did the United States and Britain come so close to a military encounter. The amicable settlement of the 1895-1896 Venezuela boundary dispute marks the real beginning of the Anglo-American rapprochement, which is usually dated from Britain's benevolent neutrality during the Spanish-American War.

Historian John L. Offner has labeled the 1898 fight with Spain "an unwanted war," and this is an apt description of the attitude of many Spaniards and Americans, including President William McKinley and secretary of the navy John D. Long.[17] But it certainly does not describe the view of numerous officers within the navy or of the notoriously belligerent assistant secretary, Theodore Roosevelt. From the moment he joined the newly elected McKinley administration in what then was a position directly below cabinet level and one giving him occasional direct access to the president, Roosevelt agitated for a bellicose foreign policy.

In the summer of 1897, when Japan was protesting the still-independent Hawaiian government's prohibition of Japanese immigration to the islands, Roosevelt wrote to Alfred Thayer Mahan: "If I had my way, we would seize those islands tomorrow....[W]e should act before the two new Japanese warships leave England." To facilitate the movement of the major elements of the battle fleet from the Atlantic to the Pacific in future crises with Japan, Roosevelt believed the United States "should build the Nicaragua canal at once, and...build a dozen new battleships, half of them on the Pacific Coast."[18] Japan muted its protests, but Roosevelt pressed the Naval War College to consider what would happen in some future Japanese-American confrontation in which there were simultaneous "complications with another power in the Atlantic."[19]

Because of the revived Cuban insurgency, Spain was the European country that most worried Roosevelt in 1897, as it did Secretary Long, who convened an advisory panel, the Naval War Board, to plan operations in event of a war. Goaded by Roosevelt, the board developed a two-ocean strategy prescribing an attack on the Spanish fleet in the Pacific and destruction of Spain's fleet in the Western hemisphere. Retired captain Alfred T. Mahan was a member of Roosevelt's group, and at one meeting he advocated attacking Manila as a sure way to defeat the mother country, an inspiration he derived from studying British empire building in the seventeenth century. However, he was not alone in this advocacy, and Roosevelt did not consider Mahan to be the key player in the deliberations.[20]

Secretary Long reluctantly approved the plan in October 1897, hoping against hope that war could still be averted. Ultimately, it was not, and in Offner's opinion the war came in April 1898 "because Spain appeared to be unable to end the war and suffering in Cuba."[21]

By the time that the United States declared war against Spain on 26 April 1898, Theodore Roosevelt had resigned as assistant secretary of the navy to become second in command of a volunteer army unit destined to fight in Cuba. But before leaving office, he had ensured that his choice for the Pacific command, Commodore George Dewey, understood that, in event of war, his "duty will be to see that the Spanish squadron does not leave the Asiatic coast and then [take] offensive operations in the Philippines."[22]

The composition of the Asiatic squadron was somewhat anachronistic in a navy that counted ten battleships commissioned or under construction in 1897 and another three authorized after the explosion of the *Maine* in Havana harbor in February 1898. Dewey's flagship was the protected cruiser *Olympia*. It was backed by three other protected cruisers, two gunboats, a Revenue Service cutter and two newly purchased colliers. Dewey had not been assigned a battleship, even though the Navy Department had been anticipating a war in the Pacific for almost a year. The American battle fleet was always concentrated almost entirely in the Atlantic, where it could protect the industrial and demographic heart of the country from European attack.

Dewey was unworried and confident that his ships were newer, faster and heavier than those of the opposing Spanish squadron. In March, he reassured Secretary Long that "with the squadron under my command, the Spanish vessels could be taken and the defenses [of Manila] reduced in one day." In April, he wrote his son, "I think it will be short work for us."[23] Long took him at his word, and two days before McKinley signed the declaration of war, the secretary cabled the commodore: "Proceed at once to the Philippine Islands. Commence operations at once, particularly against the Spanish fleet."[24]

Steaming from Hong Kong, Dewey reached the mouth of Manila Bay about midnight on 30 April. By dawn on 1 May he was ready to open fire on the seven obsolescent Spanish ships anchored below the city. It was, indeed, very short work for George Dewey. The Spanish admiral surrendered just after noon. He had lost his ships and over 400 men; the Americans lost one sailor to heat exhaustion in an engine room. It remained for Dewey and the army to besiege and capture Manila, a chore that dragged on until August. By then the "shattering first of May" had transformed the obscure commodore into a national hero of a scale not known since the Civil War and electrified the nation in its rush to victory and empire.[25]

In preparing for the Spanish-American War, the Navy Department had considered the Pacific theater a sideshow. The main event was to be staged in the Atlantic, where most of the heavy ships were deployed under the overall command of Rear Admiral William T. Sampson.

Confidence ran high in the North Atlantic squadron as war approached. The captain of Sampson's flagship, the armored cruiser *New York*, assured Roosevelt: "This squadron as it stands could wipe up everything Spain has in twenty minutes. Our losses would be nothing. We could no doubt take Havana by assault. But what's the use?"[26] Sampson, an ordnance specialist who had studied Havana as a member of the naval board of inquiry investigating the explosion of the *Maine*, believed he could easily destroy the unfortified guns on the outskirts of the city. "Having silenced the western batteries," he advised Secretary Long, "it would be quite practicable to shell the city, which I would do only after warning given twenty-four hours in advance."[27]

Sampson's plan resonated with the Union navy's experience against Confederate coastal forts and cities in the Civil War, but this was a new age, and the Navy Department would have none of it. After limited consultation with Mahan, who was preparing for a European vacation, Roosevelt and Long rejected the Sampson plan: "The Department does not wish the vessels of your squadron to be exposed to the fire of the batteries at Havana." The "desired object" of naval operations in the Atlantic theater, Long informed Sampson, must be "the destruction of the enemy's vessels, without subjecting unnecessarily our own men-of-war to the fire of the land batteries."[28] Sampson was to find and destroy the enemy fleet at sea, if possible, and if this failed he was to chase it into a port and lock it in with a blockade.

Sampson and his nominally subordinate commander of the "Flying Squadron," Commodore Winfield S. Schley, had a lot of trouble locating the four armored cruisers and two destroyers of Admiral Pascual Cervera y Topete coming from Spain, but by 1 June, they had him penned in at Santiago de Cuba. With a blockading force of ten ships--including the battleships *Iowa*, *Indiana*, *Massachusetts*, *Oregon* and *Texas*--Sampson became Horatio Nelson off Cadiz, waiting for the enemy to sortie. Cervera obliged on 3 July 1898, and he was instantly annihilated. The Spanish lost 160 men killed and 1,800 captured; one American sailor died, and one was wounded. As in the Pacific, land operations were to come, but Spain's hold over Cuba was broken by the naval battle of that July morning. The English historian Stephen Howarth has cogently observed, "Manila Bay and Santiago were two swift, confident American naval victories which between them forever changed the map of the world and America's part in it."[29]

American diplomacy moved almost as rapidly as the U.S. fleet in the summer and fall of 1898. In July, Hawaii was annexed by joint resolution of Congress, partly to thwart any future intervention by Japan on behalf of its overseas population but more directly to secure a naval base for logistical support of the continuing campaign against the Spanish army in the Philippines. In the negotiations with Madrid following the August protocol of peace, the McKinley administration demanded cession of Guam and the Philippines.

Some Americans conceived of the Philippines as a strategic threshold on the "open door" of China market, but John D. Long acquiesced because he could not shut his eyes "to the march of events--a march which seems to be beyond human control."[30] American naval logistics became more important to Long than the historic American tradition of refraining from overseas territorial expansion. By December 1898, he had concluded, "We must establish naval stations at Puerto Rico, Cuba, Guam, and Manila."[31] Unoccupied Wake was also added to the new American empire in the Pacific, forging an unbroken line of communications from San Francisco to Subic Bay and guaranteeing a firmly based naval presence in the western Pacific. Within a year, a final settlement among Great Britain, Germany and the United States would bestow on the United States economic and naval primacy in Samoa.

The new Pacific empire of the United States was not peacefully maintained, even after the defeat of Spain. In early 1899, the Filipino nationalists who had helped Dewey besiege Manila mounted an insurrection against their new masters that resulted in three years of brutal warfare. Later in the year the United States intervened militarily alongside European powers to help defeat the Boxer Rebellion. The pattern was set from the outset: overseas territorial expansion brought with it an imperative to ride roughshod over the aspirations of indigenous peoples. This was an unforeseen reality facing the United States in the new century.

John D. Long was a peaceful man who built a mighty navy. By 1900, the United States stood sixth among the world's naval powers in battleships commissioned or under construction. In the summer of 1901, sixty ships of all classes were under construction, and the $78 million appropriation bill passed that fall was the largest in American peacetime history. When Long retired in April 1902, the navy was rated fourth in the world overall, just behind Britain, France and Russia. Long had made a generous bequest to his former assistant secretary, Theodore Roosevelt, who became president in September 1901.

Theodore Roosevelt was a navalist second to none. As Richard Turk has pointed out, his relationship with Alfred Thayer Mahan cooled during his presidency, but in some ways he was more a forerunner of Mahan than a disciple.[32] In 1882, at the young age of twenty-four, Roosevelt had written a naval history of the War of 1812, and he was lecturing at the Naval War College as a guest while Mahan was still laboring over his magnum opus. As assistant secretary of the navy under McKinley, he had agitated and planned for the war with Spain and the naval victories of 1898. As president, he oversaw a navy that had long since abandoned the *guerre de course* strategy that had prevailed when he had written his naval history, and his two administrations contributed to the continued growth of the U.S. Navy as a battle fleet-based competitor of the British, German and Japanese navies.

In the Roosevelt era, Britain and its navy did not pose an immediate menace to the United States. The Anglo-American rapprochement left the Americans unchallengeable in the Caribbean and granted them the right to build and fortify a transisthmian canal. Roosevelt worked quietly from behind the scenes to detach the state of Panama from Colombia, and when an uprising seemed imminent in November 1903, the Navy Department ordered the gunboat *Nashville* "to prevent [Colombian] Government troops from proceeding to Panama [City]."[33] As had been the case in Hawaii in 1893, the U.S. Navy facilitated a revolution for the purposes of American expansion.

This time the result was a treaty with the new regime giving the United States the sovereign right to build, fortify and maintain a canal across the Isthmus of Panama. The United States was now undisputed master of the Caribbean, and to warn off European naval intervention in the area, especially that of Germany, Roosevelt in 1904 issued his famed "corollary" to the Monroe Doctrine, proclaiming that the United States as a "civilized nation" would serve as the "international police power" of the region.[34]

Once the canal was finished in 1914, the United States could comfortably continue to concentrate the bulk of its battle force in the Atlantic as a shield against European adventurism, which, in the Roosevelt years, meant a German attack on the East Coast cities following acquisition of a naval base of operations in the Caribbean.[35] If Japan became obstreperous, the battleships and heavy cruisers could be moved quickly into the Pacific for temporary basing on the West Coast or perhaps Hawaii, until the show of force cooled off the Japanese. The fear was always that the newly acquired Philippines would prove, in Roosevelt's words, "a heel of Achilles" that could not be defended against a militarily expansionistic Japan.[36] This was the strategic assumption underlying War Plan Orange, which, from at least 1911 until perhaps 1941, provided the scenario for dealing with a Japanese move against Manila and Subic Bay.[37] In a word, the idea was to fall back upon Hawaii, group the battle fleet and move out across the Pacific, searching for a decisive battle fleet engagement as the prelude to bombarding and perhaps invading the home islands.

Japan was especially troublesome to Theodore Roosevelt because of a series of events beyond his control. The negotiation of the Anglo-Japanese Alliance of 1902 deprived the United States of any hope of help from the Royal Navy in a conflict with Japan. The Russo-Japanese War of 1904-1905, especially the Trafalgar-like Battle of Tsushima in May 1905, shook the administration out of any residual admiration for the Japanese and deepened its apprehension for the future security of the Philippine islands. The president arbitrated a settlement to the war at the Portsmouth Naval Base in New Hampshire, but the Japanese were indignant because the final treaty denied them a cash indemnity. By the end of the Russo-Japanese War, the relations of Japan and the United States had begun a slow descent down an inclined plane that ended at Pearl Harbor on 7 December 1941.

Theodore Roosevelt thought in the long term. He wished that the nation "were prepared to look ahead and to build the navy and erect the fortifications [in the Philippines] which in my judgement it should." Even with outrageous anti-Japanese actions occurring in California, Roosevelt believed the Philippines were "all that makes the present situation with Japan dangerous." It was "the possession of the Philippines" that made the United States "vulnerable in Asia for lack of a great fleet."[38]

As a makeshift show of force, Roosevelt in the summer of 1907 ordered the battle fleet on a two-year cruise around the world. The Pacific leg was intended to demonstrate to Japan that he "would rather see this nation fight all her life than to see her give...[the Philippines] up to Japan or any other nation under duress."[39]

The cruise of the "Great White Fleet" was "gunboat diplomacy" with a vengeance. The nineteenth-century version strove to intimidate much weaker powers and peoples who dared to contest American economic penetration of their countries. The instruments of choice had been frigates and sloops. The Roosevelt variation employed battleships and cruisers and was directed at one of the world's leading naval powers. So, too, was the naval construction program that he extracted from Congress. By 1909, the year Roosevelt left office, the U.S. Navy stood second only to the Royal Navy in number of capital ships. In 1908 alone, three predreadnought battleships were commissioned, and by 1911 three dreadnoughts had entered the American service. One of them, the *Nevada*, was at Pearl Harbor and was the only battleship to get under way after the Japanese attack.

Preoccupation with great-power navalism did not mean that the old-style naval intervention was abandoned by Roosevelt or his two immediate successors, William Howard Taft and Woodrow Wilson. All three intervened with the navy and Marine Corps in the island states of the Caribbean, and Wilson embroiled himself in two interventions in Mexico: one with the navy and marines at Veracruz in 1914 and the other with an army commanded by John J. Pershing in the area south of the Mexican-American border in 1916-1917.[40]

The outbreak of World War I in August 1914 did not immediately affect the United States. Unlike the Second World War, when Pearl Harbor and the 1942 German submarine interdiction of Atlantic coastal oil tankers brought the war home in a hurry, the period preceding actual American intervention in April 1917 was characterized by an aloof detachment from the carnage in Europe. The navy did not begin serious contingency planning for a war in the Atlantic until 1915, when the sinking of the *Lusitania* raised the prospect of having to intervene to preserve one of Woodrow Wilson's "Fourteen Points," freedom of the seas. In that year, also, Congress authorized a centralized staff system for the navy, the office of the chief of naval operations.

William S. Benson was selected to be the first chief of naval operations (CNO) over the heads of several gifted senior officers.[41] From the beginning he had to share responsibility for planning with the Naval War College, the Office of Naval Intelligence and the General Board of the Navy, the latter chaired by the aged hero of Manila Bay, four-star admiral George Dewey, until his death in January 1917. When the United States entered the war in April of that year, Benson's authority was further undercut by the confidence that the president and secretary of the navy placed in the American naval representative in London, Rear Admiral William S. Sims.

Regardless of whether they envisioned continued American neutrality, a war against Germany alone or combat against Germany and

Japan, the top naval strategists of the General Board, the Naval War College and the CNO's office concurred that the battleship must remain at the heart of an American navy "equal to the most powerful...by not later than 1925."[42] In terms of hardware, Secretary of the Navy Josephus Daniels and the General Board agreed that the U.S. Navy should have fifty-two battleships and six battle cruisers to face Britain, Germany or Japan or some combination of the three. Daniels requested an authorization for two battleships and two battle cruisers in 1916, the first installment of a five-year building program to cost $100 million annually.

To prod the Congress, President Wilson went to the people in February, calling for "incomparably the most adequate navy in the world."[43] In testimony before the House Naval Affairs Committee, Admiral Benson stated that the U.S. Navy should be prepared "to meet the biggest navy...in the world [the British]" plus "a combination of the two smaller navies [the German and Japanese]."[44] While Britain was fighting for survival, the U.S. Navy was planning for global postwar naval supremacy.

Naval globalism proved a bit much for Congress, and the appropriations measure languished until news of the Battle of Jutland reached Capitol Hill on 3 June 1916. Two big-navy senators, Republican Henry Cabot Lodge and Democrat Claude G. Swanson, quickly revised the administration's naval bill upward. They compressed the General Board's five-year plan into three, to begin in 1916 with four battleships and four battle cruisers--eight capital ships in all. The Senate vote for the largest American naval expansion in history was overwhelming: 71 to 8, with 18 abstentions. But, as the eminent historian William R. Braisted has written, the 1916 act was not a war measure: "It was designed primarily to prepare the nation for a later contest in which the United States might face a coalition attacking in both oceans."[45]

The emergent American challenge to British naval primacy was postponed by the U.S. entry into World War I in April 1917, an event precipitated by one of history's greatest strategic miscalculations, the German resumption of unrestricted submarine warfare. Up to that point, as Richard Compton-Hall has demonstrated, the Americans, like every major maritime nation before the war, had underestimated the potential of the submarine to wage possibly decisive warfare against maritime commerce.[46]

Like the strategists of the Royal Navy, the Americans were anticipating "a new Battle of Trafalgar which would destroy German sea power as decisively as Nelson had destroyed French and Spanish sea power."[47]   This was the legacy of Mahan, the 1890s, the decisive victories of the Spanish-American War and the planning of the Roosevelt era. Coupled with a desire to emerge from World War I as the nation with the largest battle fleet, it remained the guiding principle of the General Board up to 5 April 1917, the day before the American declaration of war.

The CNO, Admiral Benson, continued to agitate for capital ship construction even after U.S. entry into the war. But he was overruled in July 1917, when Secretary Daniels ordered the 1916 building program put on hold in favor of massive construction of destroyers, submarine chasers and transports. The inspiration for the reversal was Rear Admiral William S. Sims, the administration's naval representative in London.

Ten years earlier, Sims had trumpeted the virtues of the all-big-gun battleship, but once Germany unleashed the U-boat in 1917, he recognized that "the convoy system...will be the solution to the submarine question. That is,...it will reduce the losses [of transports] considerably below the rate of the building, and this will mean that the submarine campaign will be defeated."[48]   This was exactly what happened. Historian Paolo E. Coletta notes that because of the successful antisubmarine campaign, the United States in the summer of 1918 was able to send a troop transport or cargo vessel "to France every five hours. To put it another way...the United States was landing seven soldiers and their equipment in Europe every minute of every day and night."[49]

The victory of William S. Sims over Admiral Benson represents a striking bureaucratic achievement in a service as hierarchical as the U.S. Navy. It can also be interpreted as a reflection of Sims's well-known Anglophilia: by canceling its capital ship construction program in 1917, the American navy was postponing its frontal assault on British naval mastery.

The hiatus ended when the Allied Naval Council convened in Paris in late October 1918 to discuss the postwar order. Upon his arrival, Admiral Benson sent Sims back to London so that as CNO he would be the unquestioned head of the American naval delegation. As Benson informed the secretary of the navy, he had set his sights on creating "a homogeneous force far more powerful in offense and defense than anything now contemplated by any naval power."[50]   There ensued between the Anglo-American allies what William R. Braisted has called "the naval battle of Paris."[51] Neither navy was willing to concede primacy to the other, and the two nations quickly resumed the race in naval construction that had been implicit in the suspended 1916 program.

By 1921, two years after the signing of the Versailles treaty, a serious Anglo-American naval race was under way. Economically prostrate, Britain could not afford the competition, and the strongly isolationist United States did not want it. As a result, on 8 July of that year, Secretary of State Charles Evans Hughes proposed "a conference on limitation of armament...to be held in Washington at a mutually convenient time."[52] He invited Britain, Japan, France, Italy, China, Belgium, the Netherlands and Portugal. Hughes approached the Navy Department for a "yard stick" of naval armaments and a standard for reductions.[53] Assistant Secretary of the Navy Theodore Roosevelt, Jr., entrusted Captain William V. Pratt with personally drafting and typing the secret plan Hughes would present at the opening session of the conference in November 1921.

Pratt's sense of kinship with the English was counterbalanced by his distaste for the Japanese. He deplored the Anglo-Japanese alliance and sought a "wise administration of sea power in the hands of an undivided Anglo-Saxon race."[54] A classical Mahanian, Pratt measured naval strength in terms of capital ships, that is, battleships and battle cruisers. Aware that Great Britain was groping to retain parity with the United States, he proposed a tonnage ratio in capital ships to satisfy the Admiralty and give the United States a nearly two-to-one advantage over Japan. The formula for the United States, Britain and Japan became 5:5:3.

The Navy Department's prerequisite for discontinuing construction of capital ships was abrogation of the Anglo-Japanese Alliance. Navy also insisted that the State Department seek a modus vivendi with Japan regarding the Open Door in China and the Pacific Islands mandated to Tokyo at the Paris peace conference. As a League of Nations trustee, Tokyo had acquired three former German archipelagos: the Mariana, Caroline and Marshall Islands. These put it literally athwart the lines of communication running from Hawaii through Wake and Guam to the Philippines. America's strategic Pacific outposts had become surrounded targets, and Admiral Clarence S. Williams, head of the navy's War Plans Division, concluded that implementation of the transpacific campaign contemplated in Plan Orange might already have become "practically impossible" and certainly would be if the Japanese fortified their insular possessions.[55] A preclusive agreement was essential to the defense of the American empire in the Pacific.

On 6 February 1922, after three months of intense negotiations, the diplomats signed the Five-Power Treaty. It established a tonnage ratio in capital ships for the navies of the five greatest powers: the United States, Great Britain, Japan, France and Italy. This was Captain Pratt's formula with two countries added, making the final ratio 5:5:3:1.75:1.75. To win Tokyo's adherence to a less-favorable ratio of capital ships, the United States and Britain agreed not to further fortify their military and naval installations in the western Pacific that lay within striking distance of the Japanese homeland. For the United States, this meant the nonfortification of all possessions west of Hawaii and of the Aleutian chain in Alaska. The Japanese reciprocally bound themselves not to fortify the Bonins, the Ryukyus, Formosa or the Pescadores.

Two other accords negotiated at Washington further diminished Japanese autonomy in East Asia and the western Pacific. Signed by Britain, the United States, Japan and France, the Four-Power Treaty terminated the Anglo-Japanese Alliance, a sine qua non of the American naval staff. In the new nonaggression pact Japan promised to respect American sovereignty over the Philippines and Guam, but no provisions were made for forceful enforcement of this self-denying ordinance. Equally toothless was the Nine-Power Treaty, promising respect for the Open Door in China.

Despite its consultative role in the proceedings, the navy was unhappy. Rear Admiral William L. Rodgers in March 1922 expressed the opinion of the General Board to the secretary of the navy:

> [t]he naval situation of the United States in the Pacific, both as to ships and as to bases, resulting from the Treaty...will be such as greatly to lessen the power of the United States...to defend its interests or...enforce its policies in the Western Pacific, should these be seriously threatened.[56]

A former commander of the Asiatic Fleet, Rodgers distrusted Japan. In a letter to the secretary of the navy he once characterized the Japanese as "the Germans of the East...whose Asiatic version of the Monroe Doctrine is that Japan only is to rule in Eastern Asia."[57]

Rear Admiral Rodgers' internal criticism of the treaties was publicly echoed by Dudley W. Knox, who retired as a captain to become the naval editor of the *Army and Navy Journal*. Knox contended that the tonnage limitation on capital ships and the prohibition against fortifying Guam and the Philippines "virtually doubled Japan's defensive strength and her offensive power in the Orient."[58]   His thin polemic, *The Eclipse of American Naval Power*, became the bible for uniformed critics of naval limitations.

Knox was a key member of the navy's interwar strategy-shaping intelligentsia. In 1936, he published a book-length Mahanian epistle on sea power, *A History of the United States Navy*, for which then vice admiral William L. Rodgers wrote an appreciative introduction.[59] This book was part of a broadly based propaganda campaign undertaken at the time of the international collapse of the Washington agreements to alert the nation to the importance of naval rearmament. It represents the final chapter of the naval dissidents' commentary on the treaties.

More ominously, Knox's *History of the Navy* became the literary bedrock of an orthodox naval historiography intended to embed in the minds of the American people, naval officers, college students and midshipmen a high respect for Mahanian concepts of battle fleet engagements as war-decisive and a corresponding disdain for *guerre de course* as a strategy unworthy of a first-rate naval power. From the mid-1930s until the mid-1950s or later, the Navy Department actively resisted publication of books criticizing the capital-ship dogma symbolized by the name Alfred Thayer Mahan. Cooperative academic departments at leading universities and the Naval Academy did not always resist the temptation to sponsor acceptance of Mahanian orthodoxy by rewarding publication of certain manuscripts, discouraging others and influencing the content of textbooks.[60]

The stakes were high, and the interests reached beyond the scholarly and academic worlds to the naval-industrial complex. The intention was to justify massive appropriations for battleships in the 1930s and for large aircraft carriers in the 1950s. This chilling story lies well beyond the confines of the present chapter, and it must suffice modestly to conclude that the apotheosis of Mahan has been accompanied by a tragic constraint on what should have been a field of unfettered scholarly debate.

NOTES

1. Anonymous officers quoted in Albert Gleaves, *Life and Letters of Rear Admiral Stephen B. Luce, U.S. Navy* (New York: G. P. Putnam's Sons, 1925), 177. The allusion is to James Fenimore Cooper, *The History of the Navy of the United States of America*, 2 vols. (Philadelphia: Lea and Blanchard, 1839), and

Foxhall A. Parker, *Fleet Tactics under Steam* (New York: D. Van Nostrand, 1879). Parker's work concerns mainly maneuvering and need not distract us here.

2.Cooper, *History of the Navy*, xxxv.

3.Luce board report of 13 June 1884, quoted in Gleaves, *Life and Letters*, 175.

4.Alfred Thayer Mahan, *The Influence of Sea Power upon History, 1660-1783* (Boston: Little, Brown, 1890).

5.Paul Kennedy, *Samoan Tangle* (New York: Barnes and Noble, 1974), 86.

6.Walter R. Herrick, Jr., *The American Naval Revolution* (Baton Rouge: Louisiana State University Press, 1966), 55.

7.Benjamin F. Tracy, 1889 report quoted in Herrick, *American Naval Revolution*, 55.

8.Herrick, *American Naval Revolution*, 133.

9.Robert Seager II and Doris D. Maguire, eds., *The Letters and Papers of Alfred Thayer Mahan* (Annapolis: Naval Institute Press, 1975), vol 2, 1890-1901, 64-65.

10.*Annual Report of the Secretary of the Navy* (Washington, D.C.: Government Printing Office, 1891), 30.

11.Ibid.

12.Ibid.

13.Herrick, *American Naval Revolution*, 104.

14.John Stevens quoted in Thomas G. Paterson, J. Garry Clifford and Kenneth J. Hagan, *American Foreign Policy: A History to 1914*, 2d ed. (Lexington, MA: D. C. Heath, 1983), 174.

15.W. G. McAdoo, "The Navy and the Nation," U.S. Naval Institute *Proceedings*, 20 (1894): 421.

16.Hilary Herbert to Carpenter, 24 September 1894, quoted in Jeffery M. Dorwart, *The Office of Naval Intelligence: The Birth of America's First Intelligence Agency 1865-1918* (Annapolis: Naval Institute Press, 1979), 51.

17.John L. Offner, *An Unwanted War* (Chapel Hill: University of North Carolina Press, 1992), 126.

18.Roosevelt, quoted in Herrick, *American Naval Revolution*, 198.

19.Roosevelt, quoted in Ronald H. Spector, *Professors of War: The Naval War College and the Development of the Naval Profession* (Newport, R.I.: Naval War College Press, 1977), 95.

20.Richard Wainwright, the head of the Office of Naval Intelligence, was Roosevelt's main confidant at this time. Roosevelt to Wainwright, 4 November 1915, quoted in Dorwart, *Office of Naval Intelligence*, 55.

21.Offner, *Unwanted War*, 126.

22.Roosevelt to Dewey, *Annual Report, Appendix to the Report of the Chief of the Bureau of Navigation*, vol 2, 1989, 65.

23.Dewey to Long, 31 March 1898, and Dewey to George Goodwin Dewey, 31 March 1898, quoted in Ronald Spector, *Admiral of the New Empire: The Life and Career of George Dewey* (Columbia: University of South Carolina Press, 1988), 49.

24.*Annual Report*, vol 2, 1898, *Appendix*, 67.

25.Phrase is from Stephen Howarth, *To Shining Sea: A History of the United States Navy, 1775-1991* (New York: Random House, 1991), 255.

26.Chadwick to Roosevelt, 24 March 1898, quoted in Doris D. Maguire, ed., *French Ensor Chadwick: Selected Letters and Papers* (Washington, D.C.: University Press of America, 1981), 187-88.

27.Sampson to the Secretary of the Navy, 9 April 1898, *Annual Report*, vol 2, 1898, *Appendix*, 172-73.

28.Long to the Commander in Chief, North Atlantic Station (Confidential), 6 April 1898, *Annual Report*, vol 2, 1898, *Appendix*, 171.

29.Howarth, *To Shining Sea*, 253.

30.Long, quoted in David F. Trask, *The War with Spain in 1898* (New York: Macmillan, 1981), 455.

31.Long, quoted in Paolo E. Coletta, "John Davis Long," in Paolo E. Coletta, ed., *American Secretaries of the Navy, 1775-1913*, vol. 1 (Annapolis: Naval Institute Press, 1980), 449.

32.See Richard W. Turk, *The Ambiguous Relationship: Theodore Roosevelt and Alfred Thayer Mahan* (New York: Greenwood Press, 1987).

33.Paterson, Clifford and Hagan, *American Foreign Policy*, 217.

34.Ibid., 230.

35.For War Plan Black, see David F. Trask, "The American Navy in a World at War, 1914-1919," in Kenneth J. Hagan, ed., *In Peace and War: Interpretations of American Naval History, 1775-1984*, 2d ed. rev. (Westport, Conn.: Greenwood Press, 1984), 206.

36.Roosevelt to William Howard Taft, 21 August 1907, in Elting E. Morison, ed., *The Letters of Theodore Roosevelt*, vol. 5 (Cambridge: Harvard University Press, 1952), 762.

37.For Plan Orange, see Edward S. Miller, *War Plan Orange: The U.S. Strategy to Defeat Japan, 1897-1945* (Annapolis: Naval Institute Press, 1991).

38.Roosevelt to Taft, 21 August 1907, in Morison, *Letters of Roosevelt*, 762.

39.Ibid.

40.For the context of Wilson's interventions in Mexico, see Allan R. Millett and Peter Maslowski, *For the Common Defense: A Military History of the United States of America* (New York: Free Press, 1984), 320.

41.For Benson, see Mary Klachko and David F. Trask, *Admiral William Shepherd Benson, First Chief of Naval Operations* (Annapolis: Naval Institute Press, 1987).

42.Entry of the General Board dated 27 July 1915, quoted in William R. Braisted, *The United States Navy in the Pacific, 1909-1922* (Austin: University of Texas Press, 1971), 188.

43.Wilson quoted in Paolo E. Coletta, "Josephus Daniels," in Paolo E. Coletta, eds., *American Secretaries of the Navy, 1913-1972*, vol. 2, 543.

44.Benson's statement is in U.S. Congress, House of Representatives, Committee on Naval Affairs, *Hearings...on Estimates Submitted by the Secretary of the Navy, 1916*, 3200.

45.Braisted, *United States Navy in the Pacific*, 201.

46.Richard Compton-Hall, *Submarines and the War at Sea, 1914-1918* (London: Macmillan, 1991), 303.

47.Richard Hough, *The Great War at Sea, 1914-1918* (New York: Oxford University Press, 1983), 60.

48.Sims to Captain Dudley W. Knox, 9 July 1917, quoted in David F. Trask, *Captains & Cabinets: Anglo-American Naval Relations, 1917-1918* (Columbia: University of Missouri Press, 1972), 80.

49.Paolo E. Coletta, "Josephus Daniels," in Coletta, *Secretaries*, vol 2, 558.

50.Benson to secretary of the navy, 5 January 1919, quoted in Braisted, *United States Navy in the Pacific*, 421.

51.Braisted, *United States Navy in the Pacific*, 427-440.

52.Hughes telegram of 8 July 1921, quoted in Thomas H. Buckley, *The United States and the Washington Conference* (Knoxville: University of Tennessee Press, 1970), 32.

53.Hughes to secretary of the Navy, 1 September 1921, quoted in Braisted, *United States Navy in the Pacific*, 584.

54.Pratt memorandum of 8 August 1921, quoted in Braisted, *United States Navy in the Pacific*, 582.

55.Williams to the General Board, 19 October 1921, quoted in Braisted, *United States Navy in the Pacific*, 591-92.

56.General Board to secretary of the navy, 29 March 1922, quoted in Gerald E. Wheeler, *Admiral William Veazie Pratt, U.S. Navy* (Washington, D.C.: Government Printing Office, 1974), 196-97.

57.Rodgers to Daniels, 8 July 1919, quoted in Braisted, *United States Navy in the Pacific*, 395.

58.Dudley W. Knox, *The Eclipse of American Sea Power* (New York: American Army and Navy Journal, 1922), 48.

59.Dudley W. Knox, *A History of the United States Navy* (New York: G. P. Putnam's Sons, 1936).

60.For a preliminary study that has elicited concrete examples sustaining these generalizations, see Kenneth J. Hagan and Mark R. Shulman, "Mahan Plus One Hundred: The Current State of American Naval History," in John B. Hattendorf, ed., *Ubi Sumus: The State of Naval and Maritime History* (Newport, R. I.: Naval War College Press, 1994).

6

The Royal Navy And The Defense Of The British Empire, 1914–1918

David French

The existence of the Empire depends on our sea power.[1]

By mid-1918 most British policymakers expected that the war would not end until 1919 or even 1920. Britain's manpower resources were stretched to their limit and the War Cabinet took the momentous decision to allow the British army in France to shrink from its present strength of over fifty divisions to a force of little more than thirty divisions. Britain's partners were most unhappy, and ministers were compelled to justify their decision by reference to Britain's other contributions to the entente alliance's war effort. In August, Lord Milner, one of Lloyd George's closest associates in the War Cabinet, asserted that Britain's maritime effort

> is the foundation of the whole military framework of the [entente] alliance. Without it there would have been no British or American troops in France. Without it Russia could not have received the munitions and supplies which enabled her to stay in the war as long as she did. Without it Italy could never have dreamt of entering the war. Without it there could have been no Allied force at Salonika or, indeed, anywhere outside the continental territories of France and Russia. Without it Germany would have been unblockaded, and free to send her expeditionary forces to threaten the Allied armies in rear, or to capture Allied territories overseas. It is, in fact, the one indispensable factor. The Alliance can survive the loss of even the greatest armies, as the defection of Russia has shown, and gather

fresh strength for a renewed effort. The loss of command of the sea
by the United Kingdom would be the end of the alliance, and mark
the definite victory of Germany.[2]

Sir Maurice Hankey was equally self-congratulatory about the role of the
Royal Navy. "After all," he insisted, "the Navy has entirely secured the
defensive position, so that we have never sustained invasion at any point
of the Empire except the Aden hinterland and East Africa. Moreover it
has enabled us to reap the results of full command of the sea, subject to
some diminution due to the submarine."[3]

But what both writers did not mention was that these achievements
were based upon a strategic paradox. In August 1914, the British
expected that the North Sea would soon witness a battle of annihilation.
The British Grand Fleet would vanquish its opponent in a second
Trafalgar. The British had created a fleet designed to perform that very
mission.   But, much to their disappointment, they actually found
themselves engaged in a protracted war of attrition. The paradox that
underlay Britain's naval strategy during the First World War was that,
although the Royal Navy failed to achieve uncontested command of the
sea, Britain was able to use the oceans for its own strategic purposes and
deny them to their enemies.[4]

The war in the North Sea was a frustrating experience for the Royal
Navy. Despite its numerical superiority, the Grand Fleet failed to secure
the smashing victory it was expected to gain. This disappointed not only
the press and the public but also many sailors.[5] The British had invested
too much money and imperial pride in the navy to be content to see it sit
idly by at the supreme moment of national danger. But, whatever their
hopes, a rapid decision in the war at sea was unlikely. Both belligerents
felt too vulnerable to risk their battle fleets in a major engagement unless
they enjoyed the kind of decisive advantage that eluded them. For a brief
period between November 1914 and February 1915, the numerical gap
between the capital ships of the two fleets narrowed, only for it to shift
decisively in favor of the British.[6] The High Seas Fleet had been created
as an expression of Germany's great power status and as a political lever
to extract political concessions from Britain. The very fact that Britain
entered the war on the side of Germany's enemies in August 1914
represented a decisive defeat for this strategy. The High Seas Fleet had
never been designed to win a war on its own, and, faced by a
numerically superior enemy, the German admirals had no intention of
obliging the Royal Navy by seeking a fleet action, at least not until they

had reduced Admiral Jellicoe's margin of superiority by attrition. Early operations in the North Sea, particularly the British penetration into the Heligoland Bight (28 August 1914) and the battle of the Dogger Bank (24 January 1915), only confirmed the Germans in their belief in the wisdom of this policy.[7]

British capital ship design gave priority to offensive needs over defensive requirements. But as the High Seas Fleet remained in port, the British could not reap the advantages of their higher speeds and bigger guns to bring it to battle. Moreover, the British had gained these advantages only by sacrificing other design features, principally adequate underwater protection, and the Germans tried to exploit this design vulnerability.[8] The fear of underwater attack came to dominate the tactical thinking of the Grand Fleet's commanders.[9] By mid-October 1914, Jellicoe had lost five cruisers to U-boats, including three sunk by a single submarine off the Dutch coast on 22 September, and a light cruiser and the dreadnought *Audacious*, sunk by mines.[10] Determined as they were to bring the High Seas Fleet to battle, Admiral Jellicoe and Beatty were equally determined that they would not risk doing so in waters where they might be ambushed by U-boats and mines. To do otherwise, as Jellicoe explained to Churchill, would be to "jeopardise the future of the country by giving over to the Germans the command of the open seas."[11] Commodore Tyrwhitt's frustration that submarines and mines "completely put the hat on all honest fighting" was understandable.[12] However, as long as the High Seas Fleet remained bottled up in harbor, the British had little to gain and, if they had ill luck, perhaps much to lose by a fleet action.

The German strategy of reducing the Grand Fleet's numerical superiority by underwater attrition failed. The British devoted considerable resources to minesweeping and protecting their fleet bases. When the Grand Fleet put to sea, it did so surrounded by a swarm of destroyers. It adopted fast cruising speeds, and Jellicoe continued to insist that vessels must not be detached from the Grand Fleet lest its fighting strength fall below that of the High Seas Fleet.[13] But these measures were not without their cost. They placed serious constraints on the Grand Fleet's freedom of action. Jellicoe began the war with only 40 destroyers, and the provision of more became a constant source of worry to the fleet's commanders.[14] More significantly, the psychological impact on the fleet's commanders of the underwater threat cannot be exaggerated. As Bryan Ranft has remarked, it "instilled in their planning and conduct of operations a prudent caution which in future was to decrease the likelihood of a decisive fleet action."[15]

The manifold difficulties of securing an overwhelming victory in these circumstances were clearly illustrated at Jutland. On that day, Beatty succeeded in luring the High Seas Fleet under the guns of the Grand Fleet but, in doing so he highlighted the weakness of British gunnery and naval construction. The Grand Fleet's range finders were deficient, its target-plotting machinery was slow and prone to error and the gunnery computers at the battle fleet's disposal were crude and defective.[16] The greater loss of both lives and ships suffered by the British was eloquent testimony to the excellence of German gunnery and the better performance of their shells, armored plate and underwater protection.[17]

Jutland was a major strategic victory for the Royal Navy. Its damaged ships were ready for sea much sooner than those of the High Seas Fleet, and its numerical superiority and the blockade both remained intact. The Royal Navy was also quick to learn the lessons of the engagement.[18] In contrast, although the High Seas Fleet did venture out of harbor on several occasions after June 1916, it never again sought a fleet action with the British, and when it was ordered to make a final attack in October 1918, its crews mutinied. Henceforth, German naval officers looked towards, their U-boats to rupture Britain's commercial lifelines in 1917-18. Jutland also confirmed the naval high command in their belief that they had to do everything they could to preserve the Grand Fleet.[19] In the words of Sir Henry Jackson, the first sea lord, it was "a very defensive strategy, but it is a very safe one."[20]

In 1917, the Admiralty's de facto policy was designed to contain the High Seas Fleet, while it made good the defects in the Grand Fleet's preparations that Jutland had demonstrated. But that did not mean that the Admiralty was intent on shunning battle, only that it wished to fight under the most favorable circumstances it could engineer. At the end of June 1917, for example, Jellicoe urged Beatty to bring the Grand Fleet south to Rosyth in the hope that he could intercept the High Seas Fleet if it was drawn into the North Sea by General Haig's attempt to occupy the Belgium ports.[21] Following the Russian Revolution, this de facto policy became a de jure one. Even before the Bolsheviks signed an armistice with the Central Powers in December 1917, the pressure on the Grand Fleet's resources had been growing. The need to detach destroyers to escort convoys and the work entailed in maintaining minefields in the Heligoland Bight imposed constant strain on its light forces. Following German attacks on Scandinavian convoys, heavy units had to be detached to cover them. In the wake of the Russian armistice it appeared possible that the Russian Baltic fleet might pass into German hands.[22] In time, the threatened shift in the naval balance of power in the North Sea might be partly offset by the arrival of four American oil-burning Dreadnoughts. But it would take some time for them to work up to the same standard of efficiency as the Grand Fleet, and Beatty insisted that for the time being he did not enjoy a sufficient margin of superiority to enable him to continue to try to do everything possible to bring the High Seas Fleet to battle.

At a conference at the Admiralty on 2 January 1918, Beatty argued that his proper role was now to contain the High Seas Fleet in harbor until the overall strategic situation became more favorable. In the meantime he recommended offensive mining operations in the North Sea and air attacks against the enemy's bases on the Flanders coast.[23] The Board of Admiralty endorsed his recommendations but insisted that this was only a temporary change of policy, which would be reassessed when more American destroyers became available. They also ordered the construction of the Northern Barrage, a minefield stretching from the Norwegian coast to the north of Scotland, and the laying of additional minefields in the Heligoland Bight and across the Straits of Dover. This was to be done in the hope that it would hamper the movements of German surface craft and U-boats and release destroyers for convoy escort duties. The War Cabinet approved their recommendations on 18 January, and they became the basis of British naval policy in the North Seas for the remainder of the war.[24]

In the meantime the British could only toy with ways of attacking the German fleet in harbor. Beatty's favorite option was an aerial torpedo attack. In August and September 1917, he had asked the Admiralty to provide him with four aircraft carriers equipped with torpedo bombers capable of attacking the High Seas Fleet.[25] Progress was slow, for Jellicoe was skeptical about the efficacy of aerial torpedo attacks, and the necessary aircraft could not be provided until the second half of 1918.[26] Others proposed more ambitious plans. In July 1917, Churchill had advocated the formation of an "Inshore Aggressive Fleet" of elderly battleships and cruisers. Once the British had occupied one of the Friesian Islands as an advanced base for their flotillas and aircraft, this force would impose a close blockade on the German coast, thus compelling the Germans to recall many of their U-boats to protect their own bases.[27] But the plan's Nelsonic boldness was vitiated by a host of practical difficulties. For one thing, the material requirements for the

"Inshore Aggressive fleet" were massive. The Admiralty war staff estimated that it would require no less than 40 battleships, 43 elderly cruisers and so many light craft that the convoy system would have to be abandoned. Second, such a force could be assembled only by tapping French, Italian and American resources, and they showed little enthusiasm for risking so many vessels in a hazardous operation under British command.[28]

But what positive advantages would have accrued to Britain and its allies if the Royal Navy had sunk the High Seas Fleet at Jutland? Would a major British victory have made that much difference to the course of the war? Such speculative questions can produce only imprecise answers, but on balance it seems probable that the British would have gained remarkably little even if they had inflicted a crushing defeat on the Germans. Such a defeat might have had an adverse impact on German morale. But Professor Marder was right to claim that, as the navy had much less prestige than the army in Germany, it would not have led to an early German surrender. It might have improved the morale of the British army, although that was already high before 1 July 1916, and it is unlikely that any naval victory would have countered the deleterious impact on the British Expeditionary Force's (BEFs) morale of three months of fighting on the Somme. At sea a British victory would have enabled the British to lay mines much closer to the German coast than they were able to do, thus perhaps confining some German U-boats to their bases in 1917-18. But that would have depended on the ability of the British to mass-produce efficient mines. It might have released some of the troops retained in Britain for home defense, but that might have only added to the casualty bill in France. It might have enabled the British to attempt a landing on the German coast, but major obstacles to a successful amphibious operation remained, not least of which were the Germans' powerful coast defenses. If the High Seas Fleet had been sunk in 1916, it is a matter of conjecture whether or not the British might have been able to open a more direct supply route to Russia and whether by doing so they might have prevented its collapse in 1917. However, the British would still have had to find a way of circumventing German mines and submarines at the entrance to the Baltic. The March 1917 revolution did not occur simply because the Russian army was short of supplies. It was the product of a much wider crisis of legitimacy that undermined every aspect of the tsarist government. Finally, even had the British opened a Baltic route to Russia, the amount of supplies they could have sent was limited by other factors, not the least of which were their growing difficulties in financing Russia's overseas purchases.[29]

Perhaps the one major positive advantage that the British might have gained had they annihilated the High Seas Fleet was that by doing so, they would have released themselves from the need to maintain an overwhelmingly powerful battle fleet. That, in turn, might have enabled them to release some of the large number of colliers, oilers and railway trains supporting the Grand Fleet, and they could have been used to meet civilian and Allied demands. An overwhelming victory at Jutland might also have encouraged the Admiralty to reduce its inflated demands for further capital ship construction. It could then have turned over some of the shipyard capacity it controlled to producing the escort craft and merchant ships that Britain and its allies needed so badly in 1917-18. But that would have occurred only if the admirals had been willing to disregard the potential threat posed to Britain's postwar maritime supremacy by the Japanese and United States fleets, and if they had abandoned their obsessive belief that caused them to equate naval power and big-gun battleships.[30]

In September 1918, Beatty's frustration boiled over. "It is terrible to think," he wrote, "that it is possible after all these weary months of waiting, we shall have no opportunity of striking a blow."[31] The Admiralty shared his disappointment. In October, it decided that if it could not annihilate the High Seas Fleet in battle, it would do so at the armistice table.[32] In fact, it had less reason than it believed to be disappointed. The Grand Fleet failed to destroy its German counterpart, but it did succeed in containing it, and that was sufficient for Britain's purpose. That fact had been demonstrated seven months earlier. Britain came closest to losing the war in the spring of 1918, when the Ludendorff offensive came close to splitting the French and British armies in France. But with the exception of a minor sortie by torpedo boats against Dunkirk and La Panne, the German high command made no attempt to coordinate its offensives against the French and British armies in France with naval action in the North Sea, action that might have interrupted Haig's cross-Channel communications.[33] The British were afforded the priceless advantage of being able to reinforce the BEF, and domestic morale was not shaken by the appearance of German soldiers landing on the east coast of England.

Thus, the Royal Navy failed to win the war of annihilation it wished to fight, and in 1917 it came perilously close to losing the war of attrition it was compelled to fight. In 1905 the Royal Commission on the Supply of Food and Raw Materials in Time of War had demonstrated Britain's dangerous dependence on imports for its economic survival.[34] In December 1916, Lloyd George described merchant shipping as "the jugular vein, which, if severed would destroy the life of the nation."[35] Compared with obsessive concern with offensive fleet operations, before 1914, the Admiralty had shown little concern about the possibility that the Germans might mount a *guerre de course* against British merchant shipping. With most of the German fleet based in German ports and with Britain acting as a breakwater against its egress into the Atlantic, the Admiralty was confident of being able to deal with the scattered German squadrons outside the North Sea. Its confidence was justified, for the Royal Navy had little difficulty in disposing of the threat to the entente's merchant marine posed by the German surface fleet outside the North Sea. On 1 November 1914, the German China Squadron did destroy a British squadron at Coronel, off the Chilean coast. But five weeks later, two battle cruisers sent by the Admiralty destroyed the Germans in their turn at the Battle of the Falklands.[36] In the ensuing months the navy was able to deal with the remaining scattered raiders. As a result, German surface raiders accounted for less than half a million tons of entente shipping, less than 8 percent of the tonnage sunk by U-boats.

But that did not mean that the Royal Navy enjoyed unfettered control of the surface of the world's oceans. Mistakes could still happen. In October 1917, for example, the Germans successfully attacked an escorted convoy bound for Norway. Faulty arrangements for transmitting intelligence from the Admiralty to the Grand Fleet meant that Beatty was given insufficient warning to intercept the raiders.[37] Nor did British naval power extend to either the Black Sea or the Baltic. But the failure of the German surface threat in 1914-15 meant that it could do nothing to prevent the transport of Australasian and Indian forces to the Middle East and Europe in 1914-15, nor could they prevent entente forces from occupying most of their African and Asian colonies by the end of 1915.

However, the navy's success in dealing with German surface raiders left it intellectually and materially ill prepared when the Germans began unrestricted U-boat warfare in February 1917. They should not have been, for they already had a taste of what was to come. Between February and August 1915, the Germans mounted the first of their U-boat campaigns against British and Allied merchant shipping. They ended this campaign in August, not because of any countermeasures that the British had taken but because of the vehement protests they received from the U.S. By March 1916, Britain had lost 900,000 tons of merchant shipping because of U-boat attacks, but it had constructed 2 million tons since the start of the war.[38] This apparent success persuaded the Admiralty that it knew how to keep losses within reasonable limits. It was wrong.[39]

The debate on the introduction of convoys has been told before, and it seems pointless to repeat it here. But its prominence in the historiography of the war conceals a significant fact: convoys by themselves played an important, but only a limited, part in enabling the British to survive the period of maximum danger they faced in 1917. The most important reason the Germans failed to achieve their aim of forcing the British to sue for peace by August 1917 was entirely beyond British control.[40] By its own calculations, the German navy simply did not possess sufficient U-boats to do the job. In May 1914, a German naval staff study suggested that it would need 222 submarines to defeat Britain. But in February 1917, the German navy had approximately only 100 operational submarines, and throughout 1917, they never managed to keep more than one-third of them on operational patrols at any one time. The German Admiralty's expectation that its submarines would be able to sink an average of 600,000 tons of shipping per month was therefore, to say the least, optimistic. To compound the error, the German government was also slow to make any concerted attempt to increase the size of this fleet. Not until the second half of 1917 did the government begin its first large-scale U-boat production program.[41]

Given these advantages, the often rather tardy British countermeasures sufficed to contain the danger. Because of Jellicoe's reluctance to adopt the convoy system, it was not until mid-August 1917 that all outward-bound vessels were convoyed. That decision did have a major impact in reducing sinkings. British tonnage lost fell from 358,000 tons in July to 268,813 tons in October and to 173,462 tons in December 1917. The number of attacks made on merchant ships per day also fell by nearly one third between July and December, and that happened despite the fact that in September the Germans had more operational U-boats than ever.[42] The convoy system therefore had a significant, but belated, part in defeating the U-boat offensive.

But, at least in the short term, the introduction of the convoy system was not the only reason the U-boat offensive was overcome. During the critical period between February and August 1917, the crucial problem facing the War Cabinet was to ensure that the population was adequately fed. In December 1916, Britain had stocks of wheat sufficient to last for fourteen weeks. By mid-April 1917 they had fallen to only nine weeks, and there was every likelihood that they would dwindle still further.[43]

Just as the government was slow to introduce convoys, so was it slow to boost shipbuilding and domestic food production. In 1916, new launchings were sufficient to replace only about one-third of the merchant tonnage lost through marine accidents and enemy action.[44] In January 1917, the War Cabinet had agreed to a shipbuilding program based on the assumption that the war "will last through the year 1918." But in the first half of 1917 Britain launched only 495,000 tons of merchant shipping. There was some acceleration in output in the second half of the year, following the War Cabinet's acceptance of the Geddes programme to produce 3,100,000 tons of merchant shipping per annum by the end of 1918. But the total of 1,163,000 tons launched in 1917 was well below the 3,729,785 tons struck off the British register in 1917 due to enemy action.[45] Nor did Britain survive because the government was able to increase domestic food production by compelling farmers to switch from pastoral to arable farming. The Corn Production Act did not reach the statute book until August 1917, too late to have any impact on the food situation until 1918.[46]

In the period of maximum danger, between February and August 1917, when the Germans hoped that Britain would surrender rather than face famine, two quite different policies defeated the U-boat offensive: the government's attempts systematically to reduce unnecessary imports and its efforts to maximize the carrying capacity of the merchant fleet by concentrating it on the shorter North Atlantic routes rather than employing it on longer voyages to Australasia and India. In February 1917, the War Cabinet reconvened a committee under Lord Curzon to prepare an import restriction program.[47] The programme was promptly put into operation. The main loser was the Ministry of Munitions, whose import programme was sharply reduced in favor of greater food imports.[48] But by 1917, such a sacrifice could be made without any appreciable impact on munitions supplies. The ministry now had a stockpile of 15 million heavy shells, shell production reached its wartime peak in 1917 and the number of artillery pieces produced by the ministry in 1917 was nearly 75 percent more than had been produced in 1916.[49] This policy, in turn, enabled the Ministry of Shipping to divert half a million tons of shipping to bring wheat from North America.[50] The War Cabinet's decision was timely. By early May 1917, stocks of wheat had fallen to less than seven weeks' supply, close to the danger point that the Royal Commission on Wheat Supply had identified in February. However, in June the corner was turned. By 1 July wheat stocks were at their normal level, and by 1 August there was a stockpile equivalent to thirteen weeks' supply in Britain.[51]

In the medium term, the U-boat offensive helped, rather than hindered, the British war effort. After the collapse of the Russian army in the spring and summer of 1917, the French mutinies following the disastrous Nivelle offensive and the near collapse of the Italian army at Caporetto, the one major factor that gave the British grounds for believing that the entente would eventually win the war was the promise of large-scale American military assistance in 1918 and 1919. It was the ultimate irony of the U-boat offensive that it both conjured up that hope by causing the U.S. to enter the war and failed to prevent it from materializing.

In most other respects Milner and Hankey were right to highlight the fact that British naval strategy was a litany of success. Thanks to the continued existence of the Grand Fleet, the Germans were never able to invade Britain.[52] However, the possibility that they might be able to mount a major raid remained a constant worry for British strategists. In November 1914 Jellicoe was concerned that because he had withdrawn cruiser patrols from the central North Sea owing to the U-boat threat, the Admiralty would receive little prior warning of an invasion attempt.[53] By January 1916, a joint Admiralty-War Office committee had concluded that Germany had sufficient shipping to transport 135,000 men across the North Sea in a single day and that they might enjoy a two-day respite before the Royal Navy arrived to interrupt their landing. Consequently, despite the fact that the British were now committed to large-scale participation in the continental land war, a significant number of troops were retained in Britain to combat just such a raid. In January 1917, the Admiralty and the General Staff informed the War Cabinet that, as a German invasion was not out of the question, a force of 500,000 men was required to garrison the defended ports, provide for the air defense of Britain and repel an invading force.[54] There were occasions when such fears placed serious limitations on the government's freedom of action. In the spring of 1915, for example, at a moment when there were few trained and fully equipped troops left in Britain after the dispatch of the BEF to France, it made Lord Kitchener reluctant to dispatch his last remaining regular division, the Twenty-Ninth, to the eastern Mediterranean.[55] The result was that in March, the navy was left to try, and fail, to force the Dardanelles alone.

Behind the shield formed by the Grand Fleet, the British were able to project their growing military power overseas. The Germans did not attempt to interfere with the transport of the original BEF from Britain to France. The British merchant marine became the packhorse of the entente alliance. In January 1917, the British Empire possessed approximately 16 million tons of oceangoing vessels. Half of that tonnage was available to carry the imports required by Britain's civilian population and industries or was engaged abroad in local trades. The rest was employed supporting the army and navy, the Allies and Dominions.[56] By 1918, the British merchant marine had transported nearly 23 million personnel, over 2 million animals and 52 million tons of military stores.[57]

But there were limitations on the Royal Navy's ability to enable the British to project their power across the oceans. In 1914-15 Churchill and Admiral Fisher toyed with the idea of either mounting amphibious operations in the Baltic or seizing an island base off the German coast as an advanced base from which they could use torpedo boats to attack the High Seas Fleet in harbor. Neither plan came to anything. Most naval officers were adamant that such operations would fail in the face of the Germans' defenses. They deplored the diversion of ships from the Grand Fleet, and they knew that since 1905 the War Office had refused to make troops available for an operation they regarded as highly dangerous and likely to fail.[58] The outcome of the Dardanelles operation seemed to justify their caution. When an Anglo-French fleet attempted to force the Dardanelles in March 1915, it was forced to turn back when it lost six capital ships sunk or damaged after they had blundered into a minefield. The failure of the subsequent amphibious landings also underlined the fact that the British lacked a combined services doctrine for amphibious operations. A superior navy alone would not enable the British to project their military power across the oceans against a defended coast unless the two services found some way of working in close cooperation.[59]

The conduct of the Dardanelles campaign also raised another question about the utility of British naval power. Even if the operation had succeeded, there was no guarantee that the strategic benefits that the British hoped to achieve--the relief of Russia, a Turkish surrender and a Balkan alliance--would have fallen into their laps. In late 1915 and early 1916, the Ministry of Munitions was struggling to find supplies for the British army. It had precious little to spare for Russia and supplies ordered in the U.S. on Russia's behalf were slow in arriving because of production difficulties.[60] Even if the Allies had occupied their capital, the Turks might have been capable of continuing the war for a time in Anatolia. The Balkan neutrals, with no naval tradition of their own, were unlikely to be impressed by British promises of ships and a handful of soldiers when they saw the German army overrunning Russian Poland in the summer of 1915. In addition, the movement of troops by sea was sometimes too slow to forestall the Germans if they had command of the central European railway system. When the Admiralty was called upon to transport troops to Salonika in the autumn of 1915 to save the Serbian army and prevent the Germans from opening railway communications to Constantinople, it correctly calculated that British and French troops would arrive at least a month too late.[61]

Britain fought the First World War as a member of an alliance, and throughout the war Britain's allies took for granted the Royal Navy's ability to keep open the entente's maritime communications. But as the war progressed, they became less willing to play the role assigned to them by British strategists, that of Britain's continental cat's-paws. They demanded direct British military assistance. The Royal Navy was rarely able to provide it. In May 1916, when the War Committee considered how it might help Russia if the Germans attacked, the Admiralty rejected a landing on the north German coast because of the strength of the enemy's coast artillery, minefields and the proximity of the High Seas Fleet.[62] Similarly, in October 1917, with the Germans on the point of capturing Reval and perhaps Petrograd, the Russian premier, Aleksander Kerensky, asked the Royal Navy to force its way into the Baltic to save the seat of his government.[63] Again the Naval Staff rejected the operation as impractical, unless the High Seas Fleet had first been destroyed. The most the Grand Fleet could do was to send a weak force into the Kattegat at the end of October in the vain hope of luring the High Seas Fleet into the North Sea.[64]

By 1915-16 it was becoming increasingly apparent that British ships and money would not be enough to hold the entente together. With varying degrees of reluctance, in 1916-18, the British committed a continental-scale army to fight in France and Flanders. But that did not mean that the prestige of the Royal Navy was without diplomatic utility within the entente alliance. On 1 October 1918, the War Cabinet agreed to send two Dreadnoughts to the Aegean. They wanted to be certain that, in the event of a Turkish armistice, Britain would be the preponderant naval power in the region, that a British, and not a French, admiral would control the armistice negotiations and that a British, and not a French, admiral would lead the Allied fleet through the Dardanelles to Constantinople and into the Black Sea.[65] As the British army was primarily responsible for defeating Turkey, the War Cabinet was determined that the Royal Navy would be first on the scene to exploit the victory.

The Grand Fleet was also the basis of the entente's economic blockade of the Central Powers, for had it ceased to exist, the High Seas Fleet would have had little difficulty in brushing aside the cruisers that enforced the blockade. Mines and torpedoes, whether launched by torpedo boats or submarines, ruled out a repetition of the kind of close blockade that the British had mounted against France a hundred years earlier. In its place the Royal Navy mounted a distant blockade. The Straits of Dover were blocked by mines and light craft, supported by the Channel fleet of predreadnought battleships, and the Shetland-Norway gap was blocked by the 10 Cruiser Squadron, supported by the Grand Fleet at Scapa Flow.[66] But the blockade did not operate with the rapidity with which the British hoped that it would. In 1915, Fisher bemoaned the fact that although, "[t]he pressure of sea power to-day is probably not less but greater and more rapid in action than in the past; but it is still a slow process and requires great patience."[67] By 1917, patience was wearing thin, and there was some debate even in the Admiralty about its efficacy. Beatty remained convinced that the blockade could still win the war for the entente, whereas Jellicoe believed that although it would cause the Germans a good deal of suffering, the Germans would surrender only after their army had been defeated in France and their navy in the North Sea.[68]

Nor was the blockade a painless weapon for the British themselves. Between 1914 and 1916 the Asquith government and many businessmen were ambivalent about stopping all trade with Germany. Despite the Orders-in-Council of March 1915, some Anglo-German trade continued. Britain was a merchant state, dependent on exports to pay for its imports. As the blockade was gradually tightened in 1916 it contributed to Britain's own already worsening balance of payments problem and made more difficult the problem of financing the external purchases that Britain needed to sustain its war effort.[69] However, these inconveniences were nothing compared with the impact of the blockade on Germany. In May 1916, food riots led the imperial government to establish its own War Food Office to nationalize the food supply system, and by the end of the year all major foodstuffs were rationed. Even so, in the winter of 1916-17 turnips became part of the staple diet of most Germans who were too poor to buy on the black market. Morale was sapped by the need to queue for rations, food was short and there was a marked rise in mortality.[70] The navy does not deserve all of the credit for this, for as the war proceeded, its work was supplemented, and in 1917 superseded, by the use of diplomatic and financial pressure applied to neutrals to ensure that Germany was denied sustenance from or through contiguous neutrals. But without the Royal Navy there could have been no effective blockade.

Before the war the Admiralty believed that Britain's status as a great power rested on its imperial, financial and economic strength and that all three were underpinned by the Royal Navy.[71] On the outbreak of war British strategic policy rested on four pillars. The Royal Navy was sufficiently powerful to keep open the entente's maritime communications; Britain was sufficiently rich to act as paymaster to the entente; the French and the Russian armies could contain the armies of the Central Powers on the continent of Europe with only minimal direct British assistance until, Kitchener predicted, in early 1917, when the armies of all of the belligerents were exhausted. Britain's New Armies could then intervene decisively in the land war, inflict a final defeat on the Central Powers and enable the British government to dictate the peace settlement. When he came to power, Lloyd George did not intend fundamentally to depart from Kitchener's strategy. But between December 1916 and May 1917 three of these pillars began to crumble. The collapse of the exchange rate in New York called into question Britain's continued ability to act as paymaster to the Entente. The Russian Revolution, coupled with the failure of the Nivelle offensive and the subsequent mutinies in the French army, called into question whether Britain's major continental allies would for much longer be able to contain the armies of the Central Powers. But thanks to the Royal Navy, the Germans were never able to stop the movement of Allied shipping across the world's oceans. The Royal Navy did not win the war for the entente. But had it not contained the High Seas Fleet in harbor, had it not helped to defeat the U-boat offensive, had it not contributed to the weakening of the Central Powers' resistance through the blockade and had it not enabled the entente powers to project their military power across the seas, Britain and its allies would not have won the war.

The war therefore gave further grist to the mill of those who insisted that the navy was the foundation of British security. It was hardly surprising, therefore, that when he examined Woodrow Wilson's proposals concerning the "freedom of the seas," the first sea lord Admiral Wemyss, was aghast. "[I]t was clear," he wrote, "that the step was directed absolutely against the British Navy. If it were adopted we should lose enormously in prestige, and enormously in power."[72] Britain could not surrender on this point and remain a great imperial power for, "[o]n this basis the British Empire has been founded, and on no other can it be upheld."[73]

NOTES

1. Beatty to Hankey, 23 October 1918 and enclosure, Churchill College, Cambridge (henceforth CCC) Hankey mss HNKY 4/10. I am grateful to the following for permission to quote from material to which they own the copyright: the Masters and Fellows of Churchill College, Cambridge, in the University of Cambridge; Lord Robertson; the clerk of the Records of the House of Lords Record Office; the controller of HM Stationary Office.

2. Public Record Office (henceforth PRO) CAB 24/62/GT5532, Milner, British manpower, 28 August 1918.

3. Hankey to Esher, 18 September 1918, CCC Hankey mss HNKY 4/10.

4. This is a fact remarked upon by several recent writers. See, for example, P. M. Kennedy, "The Relevance of the pre-war British and American Maritime Strategies to the First World War and Its Aftermath, 1898-1920," in J. B. Hattendorf and R. S. Jordan, eds., *Maritime Strategy and the Balance of Power: Britain and America in the Twentieth Century* (London: Macmillan/St. Anthony's College, 1989), 166-170; J. A. English, "The Trafalgar syndrome: Jutland and the Indecisiveness of Modern Naval Warfare," *Naval War College Review*, 32 (1979): 61.

5. B. Ranft, "The Royal Navy and the War at Sea," in J. Turner, ed., *Britain and the First World War* (London: Unwin Hyman, 1988), 53, 56-57; A. J. Marder, *From the Dreadnought to Scapa Flow. The Royal Navy in the Fisher Era, 1904-1919*, vol 2 (Oxford: Oxford University Press, 1965), 49-50.

6. See PRO CAB 42/2/24. Churchill appendix to memorandum by the first sea lord on the position of the British fleet and its policy of steady pressure, 27 January 1915; PRO CAB 37/128/29, Churchill, the naval situation at home, 30 May 1915; Marder, *From the Dreadnought to Scapa Flow*, 43.

7. English, "The Trafalgar Syndrome," 63-65; H. Herwig, *"Luxury Fleet": The Imperial German Navy 1888-1918* (London: Allen & Unwin, 1980), 149.

8. As Charles Fairbanks, Jr., has noted, British dreadnoughts were built for speed and generally carried bigger guns than their German counterparts. German dreadnoughts were designed according to a philosophy that insisted that "[t]he supreme quality of a ship is that she should remain afloat." See C. H. Fairbanks, Jr., "Choosing among Technologies in the Anglo-German Naval Arms Competition, 1898-1915," in W. B. Cogar and P. Sine, eds., *Naval History. The Seventh Annual Symposium of the U.S. Naval Academy* (Wilmington, Del.: Scholarly Resources, 1988), 128-30, 139-40.

9. As early as 18 August 1914, Jellicoe was expressing fears that the Germans would soon lay mines in the North Sea. See Jellicoe to Battenberg, 18 August 1914 in A. Temple Patterson, ed., *The Jellicoe Papers. Volume I, 1893-1916* (London: Naval Record Society, 1966), 50. See also, for example, Beatty to Keyes, 18 September 1914; Keyes to wife, 10 October 1914, in P. G. Halpern, ed., *The Keyes Papers. Selections from the Private and Official*

Correspondence of Admiral of the Fleet Baron Keyes of Zeebrugge (London: Naval Records Society, 1972), 28-29, 39.

10. A. Temple Patterson, *Jellicoe* (London: Macmillan, 1969), 63.

11. Jellicoe to Churchill, 30 September 1914, in Patterson, *The Jellicoe Papers*, 71.

12. Tyrwhitt to Keyes, 14 April 1916 in Halpern, *The Keyes Papers*, 350; Marder, *From the Dreadnought to Scapa Flow*, 64-77.

13. On the last point see, for example, Jellicoe to the Admiralty, 12 November 1914, in Patterson, *The Jellicoe Papers*, 83-86. In February 1915-16, capital ships underwent a refit about every ten months. See PRO CAB 42/8/3, H. B. Jackson, summary of the Naval situation, 8 February 1916.

14. See, for example, PRO ADM 137/995. Jellicoe to Secretary of the Admiralty, 4 December 1914; Patterson, *Jellicoe*, 94-95; PRO CAB 42/8/3. H. B. Jackson, summary of the naval situation, 8 February 1916.

15. Ranft, "The Royal Navy and the War at Sea," 58.

16. J. T. Sumida, "The Best-Laid Plans: The Development of British Battle-Fleet Tactics, 1919-1942," *International History Review* 14 (1992): 683-84.

17. Herwig, *Luxury Fleet*, 145-46.

18. Patterson, *Jellicoe*, 132, 137-40; Marder, *From the Dreadnought to Scapa Flow*, vol. 3, 213-32.

19. Patterson, *Jellicoe*, 139; Marder, *From the Dreadnought to Scapa Flow*, vol. 3, 227-30, 250-54.

20. Patterson, *Jellicoe*, 148.

21. Jellicoe to Beatty, 30 June, 4 July 1917, in Patterson, ed., *The Jellicoe Papers*, vol. 2, 173, 179.

22. PRO ADM 116/1805, Paget to FO, 8 November 1917; PRO CAB 24/33/GT2715, Admiralty, naval situation in the Baltic, 22 November 1917; PRO CAB 23/16/WC281A; War Cabinet, 23 November 1917; Hankey diary, 23 November 1917, CCC Hankey mss HNKY 1/3.

23. PRO ADM 116/1806, Memorandum: Discussions at Admiralty on occasion of visit of Commander in Chief, Grand Fleet, on 2 and 3 January 1918; Marder, *From the Dreadnought to Scapa Flow*, vol. 5, 132-35.

24. PRO CAB 23/5/WC325, War Cabinet, 18 January 1918; Hankey diary, 18 January 1918, CCC Hankey mss HNKY 1/3.

25. PRO ADM 116/1804. Beatty, Notes--operations and mining policy, 23 August 1917; Beatty to Admiralty, 11 September 1917, in S. W. Roskill, ed., *Documents Relating to the Naval Air Service. Volume 1. 1908-1918* (London: Naval Records Society, 1969), 541-43.

26. Admiralty to Beatty, 25 September 1917, in Roskill, *Documents Relating to the Naval Air Service*, 549-54.

27. PRO CAB 24/19/GT1397, Churchill, naval war policy, 7 July 1917.

28.PRO CAB 24/28/GT2211. Report of a naval conference of powers united against Germany, 4-5 September 1917; notes of a conference held on board HMS *Queen Elizabeth*, 24 August 1917, in Patterson, *The Jellicoe Papers*, vol. 2, 197-202.

29.For Russia's demands for money and Britain's inability to raise it, see PRO CAB 42/25/8, Hanbury Williams to War Committee, 18 November 1916; PRO CAB 37/162/9, Dessino to War Cabinet, 22 December 1916; PRO FO 371/3075/860, Balfour to Buchanan, 29 December 1916; K. Neilson, *Strategy and Supply. The Anglo-Russian Alliance 1914-1917* (London: Allen and Unwin, 1984), 237-8.

30.J. T. Sumida, "British Naval Operational Logistics, 1914-1918," *Journal of Military History* 57 (1993): 459-60, 466-78; J. T. Sumida, "Forging the Trident: British Naval Industrial Logistics, 1914-1918," in J. A. Lynn, ed., *Feeding Mars. Logistics in Western Warfare from the Middle Ages to the Present* (Boulder, Colo.: Westview Press, 1993), 228-29.

31.Beatty to his wife, 22 September 1918, in Bryan McL. Ranft, ed., *The Beatty Papers. Selections from the Private and Official Correspondence of Admiral of the Fleet Earl Beatty*, vol. 1 (London: Scholar Press and Naval Records Society, 1989), 554.

32.Beatty to Wemyss, 2 October 1918, CCC Wemyss mss WMYSS 11; PRO CAB 24/67/GT6042. Wemyss, naval conditions of armistice, 19 October 1918; Wemyss, memoirs, CCC Wemyss MSS WMYSS 11; PRO CAB 23/14/WC489A, War Cabinet, 21 October 1918.

33.Ranft, *The Beatty Papers*, vol. 1, 506-7; Wemyss to Beatty, 7 February 1918, CCC Wemyss mss WMYS 11.

34.D. French, *British Economic and Strategic Planning, 1905-1915* (London: Allen and Unwin, 1982), 51-54.

35.*Hansard* 88 HC Deb 5s, col. 1348, 19 December 1916.

36.G. Bennett, *Coronel and the Falklands* (London: Pan Books, 1967); English, "The Trafalgar syndrome," 65.

37.Notes on visit of director of Intelligence Division to Beatty, 19 December 1917, in Ranft, *The Beatty Papers*, vol. 1, 454; see also Wemyss, memoirs, [n.d] CCC Wemyss mss, WMYS 11.

38.PRO CAB 42/12/7. War Committee, British merchant vessels lost by hostile action from August 1914 to March 1916.

39.Kennedy, "The Relevance of the Pre-War British and American Maritime Strategies," 175-76.

40.British intelligence discovered the German plan and the timescale of their operations within a few days of the start of the campaign. See PRO FO 371/2939/30373, Howard to FO, 6 February 1917; PRO FO 371/3078/32997, Rumbold to FO, 10 February 1917.

41. P. K. Lundberg, "The German Naval Critique of the U-Boat Campaign: 1915-1918," *Military Affairs*, 27 (1963): 105-18; H. H. Herwig, "The Dynamics of Necessity: German Military Policy During the First World War," in A. R. Millett and W. Murray, eds., *Military Effectiveness. Volume 1. The First World War* (Boston: Allen and Unwin, 1988), 99.

42. PRO CAB 24/20/GT1495, Admiralty, the submarine situation, 24 July 1917; PRO CAB 23/4/WC235. War Cabinet, 18 September 1917; PRO CAB 24/23/GT1744. Naval Staff, naval weekly appreciation, number 12, 15 August 1917; PRO CAB 24/32/GT2645, Naval Staff, naval weekly appreciation, no. 25, 15 November 1917; PRO CAB 24/42/GT3641, Naval Staff, naval weekly appreciation, 14 February 1918; Marder, *From the Dreadnought to Scapa Flow*, vol. 4, 258-88.

43. PRO CAB 23/40/IWC-10, Imperial War Cabinet 13 April 1917; PRO CAB 23/2/WC118, War Cabinet, 13 April 1917; PRO CAB 24/10/GT403, Maclay, loss of British and Allied tonnage during the first nine days of April 1917, 9 April 1917.

44. PRO CAB 24/6/GT6. A. E. A. Grant, merchant shipping, 10 February 1917.

45. Marder, *From the Dreadnought to Scapa Flow*, vol. 4, 64-5; PRO CAB 24/38/GT3289. E. Geddes, Merchant shipbuilding, 8 January 1918; Sir A. Fitzroy, *Memoirs* (London: Hutchinson, nd), vol. 2, 666; Lord Riddell, *Lord Riddell's War Diary* (London: Ivor Nicolson & Watson, 1933), 300; PRO CAB 24/35/GT2908. Naval Staff, Admiralty weekly appreciation, 6 December 1917; PRO CAB 24/39/GT3217. Naval weekly appreciation, 10 January 1918 PRO CAB 24/43/GT3765; Liverpool steamship-owners Association, The submarine menace, 25 February 1918; PRO CAB 24/19/GT1312. Geddes, Report on shipping situation, 5 July 1917; K. Grieves, *Sir Eric Geddes. Business and Government in War and Peace* (Manchester: Manchester University Press, 1989), 42-3.

46. L. M. Barnett, *British Food Policy during the First World War* (London: Allen and Unwin, 1985), 196-97; J. Turner, *British Politics and the Great War. Coalition and Conflict 1915-1918* (London: Yale University Press, 1992), 173-76, 214.

47. PRO CAB 1/24/3. Watson and Elderton, position of shipping during 1917, 19 February 1917; PRO CAB 24/6/GT40, Stanley, petrol consumption, 2 February 1917; PRO CAB 23/1/WC74, War Cabinet 19 February 1917.

48. PRO CAB 23/1/WC77, War Cabinet, 21 February 1917.

49. G. Hardach, *The First World War 1914-1918* (London: Allen Lane, 1977), 87; War Office, *Statistics of the Military Effort of the British Empire during the Great War 1914-1920* (London: Her Majesty's Stationary Office (HMSO), 1922), 484; PRO CAB 24/6/GT10, Worthington Evans, effect on munitions supply if ships are diverted from transport of materials to carriage of wheat, 8 February 1917. PRO CAB 23/2/WC87, War Cabinet, 5 March 1917.

50.PRO CAB 23/40/IWC5, Imperial War Cabinet 29 March 1917; PRO CAB 24/11/GT541, Devonport, Note by food controller on wheat supplies for the United Kingdom, 20 April 1917.

51.Barnett, *British Food Policy*, 103-5.

52.Herwig, *"Luxury Fleet,"* 149.

53.Churchill to Jellicoe 12 November 1914 and Jellicoe to secretary of the Admiralty, 14 November 1914, both in Patterson, *The Jellicoe Papers*, vol. 1, 86-92; Marder, *From the Dreadnought to Scapa Flow*, vol. 2, 60-64.

54.PRO CAB 23/1/WC40. War Cabinet 22 January 1917; Marder, *From the Dreadnought to Scapa Flow*, vol. 2, 409-11, and vol. 5, 158-59; J. Gooch, "The bolt from the Blue," in J. Gooch, *The Prospect of War. Studies in British Defence Policy 1847-1942* (London: Frank Cass, 1981), 15-17.

55.K. Neilson, "Kitchener: A Reputation Refurbished?" *Canadian Journal of History* 15 (1980); 207-27.

56.The actual breakdown was army--1.7 milllion tons; navy--2 million tons; Allies--1.8 million tons; Dominions and India--800,000 tons; ships on United Kingdom and Dominion registers trading abroad--1.8 million tons. PRO CAB 24/8/GT284, Statement by the shipping controller on the mercantile marine and the shipping program, 20 March 1917; PRO ADM 116/1805, Ministry of Shipping, statement showing the numbers of vessels engaged in the various theaters of war, 5 October 1917.

57.Admiralty, the British naval effort, 4 August 1914 to 11 November 1918, 24 December 1918, House of Lords Record Office Lloyd George mss F/116.

58.P. Hayes, "Britain, Germany, and the Admiralty's Plans for attacking German Territory, 1906-1915," in L. Freedman, P. Hayes and R. O'Neill, eds., *War, Strategy and International Politics. Essays in Honour of Sir Michael Howard* (Oxford: Clarendon Press, 1992), 99-116.

59.Kennedy, "The Relevance of the Pre-War British and American Maritime Strategies to the First World War and Its Aftermath," 178; E. A. Cohen and J. Gooch, *Military Misfortunes. The Anatomy of Failure in War* (New York: Vintage Books, 1991), 133-63.

60.PRO CAB 42/7/10. CIGS, The supply of rifles and small arms ammunition to the Russian army, 20 January 1916; PRO CAB 42/7/11, Note by the CIGS, 25 January 1916; PRO CAB 42/7/13, War Committee, 26 January 1916.

61.H. B. Jackson and A. J. Murray, An appreciation of the existing situation in the Balkans and Dardanelles, with remarks as to the relative importance of this situation in regard to the general conduct of the War, 9 October 1915, LHCMA Robertson mss I/9/8.

62.PRO CAB 42/13/2, Jackson, Memorandum, 3 May 1916.

63.PRO FO 800/178/Rus/17/22, Buchanan to FO, circ. to War Cabinet, 19 October 1917.

64.Marder, *From the Dreadnought to Scapa Flow*, vol. 4, 241-46.

65.PRO CAB 24/66/GT5962. Wemyss, Command of Allied Naval forces in the Aegean, 12 October 1918; PRO CAB 23/14/WC481A, War Cabinet, 2 October 1918.

66.Patterson, *Jellicoe*, 61.

67.PRO CAB 42/2/24. Fisher, Memorandum by the first sea lord on the position of the British Fleet and its policy of steady pressure, 25 January 1915.

68.Beatty to wife, 30 January 1917 in Ranft, *The Beatty Papers*, vol 1, 393-94; Patterson, *The Jellicoe Papers*, vol. 2, 143-44.

69.J. McDermott, "Total War and the Merchant State: Aspects of British Economic Warfare Against Germany, 1914-1916," *Canadian Journal of History* 21 (1986): 61-76; see also B. J. C. McKercher and K. Neilson, "The Triumph of Unarmed Force: Sweden and the Allied Blockade of Germany, 1914-1917," *Journal of Strategic Studies* 7 (1984): 188-94.

70.A. Offer, *The First World War: An Agrarian Interpretation* (Oxford: Clarendon Press, 1989), 25-65.

71.A point made forcefully by K. Neilson, "The British Empire Floats on the British Navy: British Naval Policy, Belligerent Rights and Disarmament, 1902-1909," in B. J. C. Mckercher, ed., *Arms Limitations and Disarmament. Restraints on War, 1899-1939* (Westport, Conn.: Praeger, 1992), 35.

72.PRO CAB 24/66/GT5967, Minutes of a conference held at Danny, Sussex, on Sunday, 13 October, 1918.

73.PRO CAB 24/76/GT6018, Wemyss, An inquiry into the meaning and effect of the demand for freedom of the seas, 17 October 1918; M. G. Fry, "The Imperial War Cabinet, the United States, and the Freedom of the Seas," *Journal of the Royal United Services Institute* 110 (1965): 353-55.

7

The American Navy, 1922–1945

Nathan Miller

On the night of 30 November, *New York Times* war correspondent Foster Hailey was on the bridge of the American destroyer *Grayson* off Guadalcanal. In the distance, he later recalled, "we could see the flashes of the guns as a United States South Pacific Task Force of cruisers and destroyers engaged a group of Japanese destroyers" with unhappy results in the Battle of Tassaforanga. Commander Frederick Bell, the *Grayson*'s captain, turned to Hailey and noted, "Eighteen years ago this month, we towed the *Washington* out to the drill grounds off the Virginia Capes and sank her in conformity with the terms of the 1921-1922 Washington Disarmament Conference. How Admiral Wright could use her in there tonight!"[1]

In the years of the "long armistice" between the two world wars, it was an article of faith among American naval officers that the Washington Conference was an unmitigated disaster for the U.S. Navy and contrary to the national interest. They charged that to meet the 5:5:3 ratio for capital ships and aircraft carriers established at the conference, the United States had scrapped modern vessels and newly laid-down hulls while other nations did little more than junk worn-out ships or tear up blueprints.

As late as 1947, six years *after* Pearl Harbor, Commodore Dudley W. Knox, the naval historian and propagandist, was still lamenting the outcome of the Washington Conference. In his introduction to the first volume of Samuel Eliot Morison's *History of U.S. Naval Operations in World War II*, Knox wrote, "The ships earmarked for scrapping from the American building program were those of superior design--the ones which would have been of most value in World War II."[2]

Yet, the U.S. Navy managed in those years to lay the keel for the most powerful fleet the world is likely to see. As Philip T. Rosen has pointed out in his study of the Treaty Navy, it was no accident that the service was able to send its fast carriers slashing into the heart of the Japanese Empire, mount a monumental amphibious campaign and wage the most devastating submarine campaign in history. "These accomplishments stemmed directly from naval policies shaped in the interwar years."[3]

Professor Hagan has ably discussed the Washington Conference in his chapter but I would like to touch upon one point. Despite the charges by navalists that the limitations imposed at the conference threatened the U.S. Navy with the same atrophy that followed the Civil War, the service fared better at the conference table than the critics were willing to admit. For the first time in history, the British had conceded parity in capital ships to the Americans, and the threat of a politically unpopular, financially crippling naval race between the two nations was lifted. In the Pacific, Japan was supposedly locked into a permanent position of inferiority, a situation unlikely to have been achieved had the postwar building race continued. Moreover, the Anglo-Japanese treaty of alliance, which irritated Americans, was abrogated.

Even the much-criticized agreement forbidding the establishment of bases in the western Pacific was merely a recognition of reality--that a parsimonious Congress was unlikely to provide funds for these projects. It should also be noted that Admiral William S. Benson, the conservative chief of naval operations, urged President Woodrow Wilson to support a Japanese mandate under the League of Nations of the Carolines and Marshalls because the Japanese would then be unable to fortify them.

The navy rid itself of the burden of obsolescent ships, while the battleships it retained were more efficient than many of those that remained in the British and Japanese fleets. Two of the unfinished battleships of the 1916 building program, *West Virginia* and *Colorado*, were completed. A pair of battle cruisers scheduled for the scrapyard were converted into the 33,000-ton aircraft carriers *Lexington* and *Saratoga*, a role in which they were of more benefit to the U.S. Navy. As battle cruisers, they would have been obsolescent by the outbreak of World War II, while as carriers they were still effective units of the fleet.

Eight of the eighteen remaining American battleships had been completed after the Battle of Jutland and incorporated developments in firepower and protection that had resulted from wartime experience. Only five of the ten Japanese battleships met this standard, and three of their twenty-two capital ships flew the white ensign of the Royal Navy.

Thus, the navy had fared better at the bargaining table than could have been expected. Moreover, despite the protestations of navalists, it was adequate to support the nation's existing foreign commitments. If the treaty later appeared to pave the way to naval inferiority, notes Allen Millett, "the source of difficulty was not the...treaty itself, but subsequent naval budgets."[4]

To most Americans of the 1920s, the very idea of coveys of admirals hunched over their game boards and multicolored war plans at Main Navy and the Naval War College would have seemed ludicrous--if they thought of it at all. Undoubtedly it would have been regarded as one more example of the celebrated obtuseness of the military mind. Peace prevailed except for a few minor-league colonial conflicts. Enjoying a giddy prosperity, the American people were in no mood to heed the dire warnings of the admirals about the possibility of future wars or, even more important, to provide funds for them.

The U.S. Navy grappled with several problems in the years between the wars. It had to maintain itself as a viable fighting force within treaty limitations. It faced the problem of dealing with new technologies, such as the airplane and the submarine and their vociferous advocates. It needed an enemy to justify its existence--and budgetary demands. Germany had been removed from this role by the outcome of world war, while the Washington Treaty had made war with Britain highly unlikely despite the lingering Anglophobia of some officers and numerous alarms throughout the 1920s. Only Japan remained.

War Plan Orange, the navy's strategic plan for use in case of war with the Japanese, had originally been promulgated in 1911 and was repeatedly revised by the Joint Army-Navy Board in the 1920s. But the basic premise of the plan never changed. If war came with Japan, the U.S. Army would conduct a holding operation in the Philippines until the battle fleet could thrust its way 5,000 miles across to the Central Pacific to relieve the besieged garrison and then defeat the Japanese in a massive Jutland-style engagement. By one count, officers attending the Naval War College during the 1920s and 1930s practiced for war with Orange at least 127 times.[5] The strongest elements of the U.S. fleet had been shifted to the West Coast as early as 1919.

But as Louis Morton has pointed out in his study of the Orange Plan, it was questionable whether the Philippines were either worth defending or whether they could be defended at all considering the advantages of time and distance possessed by the Japanese.[6] Admiral James O. Richardson may have supplied the real rationale for Orange when he stated that it provided "maximum justification for the necessary enlargement of the Navy."[7]

Foreign policy blunders compounded by American racism aggravated the unrest among the Japanese military over the inferior status imposed by the Washington Treaty ratios. The Johnson Act of 1924, which excluded Japanese immigrants from the United States, aroused widespread public anger in Japan and strengthened the hand of the militarists. It was followed by the laying down of a dozen eight-inch gun cruisers that secretly exceeded the 10,000-ton treaty limitation. In contrast, the backbone of the U.S. cruiser force was the aging 7,500-ton *Omaha* class armed with six-inch guns.

Precluded by the Washington Treaty from building new battleships, the U.S. Navy modernized its capital ships. Congressional appropriations remained nearly double those of 1916 in the years immediately following the Washington Conference, and most of the money was earmarked for the modernization and maintenance of the battle fleet. Although no U.S. dreadnought had fired its big guns in anger during the previous war, the navy's obsession with the Mahanian cult of the battleship was unabated. Modernization had its critics, however. Admiral William F. Fullam, for example, characterized it as "attempting to ressucitate a dying gladiator by vainly adding to the thickness of his shield or to the length of his lance."[8]

The remaining coal burners were converted to oil, electrical systems were improved and firepower was increased by the addition of new elevating systems for the turrets, which created a row with the British over whether or not this was a violation of treaty limitations. In 1922, *Langley*, the navy's first aircraft carrier, which had been converted from a collier, joined the fleet. Nearly 300 World War I-era "four-piper" destroyers provided an abundance of this type, and the U.S. Navy was deficient, in comparison to the Imperial Japanese Navy, only in cruisers.

Congressional enthusiasm for the navy soon cooled, however, reflecting the nation's mood of isolationism, economy and pacifism. With the falloff in funding, naval construction techniques lagged because there were fewer opportunities for experimentation and the testing of new designs. From 1922 to 1930, Congress authorized only thirty-one warships, and only ten had been laid down by the end of the decade. Manpower leveled off at about 100,000 officers and men, and prospects for promotion were limited. The Naval Academy class of 1923 were told upon graduation that they would be lucky to reach the rank of lieutenant commander.[9]

With economy the watchword of three successive Republican administrations, the navy's fighting capability became secondary to "bending the pencil." Naval officers spent much of their effort working out ways to operate their vessels with as little cost as possible. In an effort to win a fleet award for fuel economy, Hyman G. Rickover, the *Nevada*'s assistant engineering officer, reduced the heat in its living spaces to such frigid levels that a visiting admiral's staff pointedly wore their bridge coats in the wardroom.[10] Another officer suggested that the running lights of his ship be turned off, risking collision to save an amount of fuel so small it could not even be measured.

Battle competitions were often unrealistic, and tactical efficiency suffered accordingly. One senior officer told Morison, "The pencil became sharper than the sword as everyone tried to beat the target practice rules."[11] Mark 14 torpedoes cost $10,000 each so they were not tested, which concealed defects that should have been corrected long before they were revealed in the ruthless test of war. Jutland and the controversies that surrounded it dominated naval thinking. Students at the Naval War College scrutinized the battle with such intensity that one officer joked that it was "a major defeat for the U.S. Navy."

The navy's emphasis on the battleship was not unexpected considering the dominance of the "Gun Club" of battleship admirals in naval affairs. The three senior rear admirals on the General Board in 1922-23 had graduated from the Naval Academy before 1890 and "dreamed of the hammering of guns that beat out mastery of the sea." The battleship *was* the navy as far as they were concerned, and strategy, career advancement and organization all revolved around these vessels.

Threatened by such new technologies as the airplane and the submarine, the navy did not reject them out of hand, however. Rather, it did what it had always done when faced with a dramatic change—accommodate it within the familiar framework of the fleet. The submariners and aviators were guaranteed a part in the navy's future—but on the General Board's terms. The airplane and the submarine would be auxiliaries to the battle fleet, useful for scouting and screening but not a substitute for it.

Following the transatlantic flight of the NC-4, the board announced that "to put the United States Navy in its proper place as a Naval power, fleet aviation must be developed to the fullest extent."[12] But how was this to be done? Sharp infighting developed between the battleship admirals and carrier advocates, who saw a wider role for the airplane in naval operations. This new breed of naval officer asked, according to Captain

Edward L. Beach, the question that the "Gun Club" did not that to hear: "What use was a battle line with weapons of twenty-mile range if aircraft carriers could send weapons with greater accuracy ten times as far?"[13]

The navy's aging enfant terrible, Admiral William S. Sims, from his vantage point as president of the Naval War College, saw the traditional role of the battleship passing to the aircraft carrier. Two decades before the debut of the Fast Carrier Task Force, Sims introduced carriers into the school's war games. In future conflicts, he prophesied in 1925, the fleet with the strongest carrier force "will sweep the enemy fleet clean of its airplanes and proceed to bomb the battleships, and torpedo them with torpedo planes."[14]

Carrier advocates had a temporary ally in General "Billy" Mitchell, whose charges that the bomber had made the battleship "as obsolete as knights in armour after gunpowder had been invented," raised the hackles of the "Gun Club." Much of what Mitchell had to say was hardly revolutionary--Admiral Sims and others were saying the same thing--but his attacks attracted public attention and unwelcome questions about the navy's reliance on the very costly battleship.

Yet, the immediate response to the sinking of the former German battleship *Ostfriesland* by Mitchell's bombers in a staged test off the Virginia Cape was not the creation of an independent air force sought by Mitchell, but advancement of the cause of naval aviation. "The lesson is that we must put planes on battleships and get aircraft carriers quickly," declared Rear Admiral William A. Moffett, an articulate spokesman for naval air power.[15] To forestall possible transferrals of funds from the navy to the army air service, the navy, in effect, created its own air arm, with Moffett as its head. Under his able direction, it at least equaled those of Britain and Japan.

The "Gun Club," however, had no intention of abandoning the orthodox view that the battleship was the final arbiter of naval warfare. The primary task of the carrier and its aircraft, as far as the "Gun Club" was concerned, was to provide an aerial umbrella for the battle line and was to be tethered to it. But the aviators had important allies in the surface navy who saw the carrier as an offensive rather than a defensive weapon, among them Admiral William V. Pratt and Rear Admiral Joseph M. Reeves. Pratt had assumed the mantle of the navy's resident iconoclast previously held by Sims but, being less acerbic, eventually rose to the navy's highest pinnacle, chief of naval operations.

The test came in 1929 during Fleet Problem IX off Panama. Reeves was given permission by Pratt, the fleet commander, to break off from the main attacking force with the carrier *Saratoga* and a cruiser. Sweeping toward the Panama Canal at 25 knots, Reeves launched his sixty-five planes at the target. Surprise was complete. Most of the defending aircraft were caught on the ground, and the canal's locks were "destroyed."[16] Quickly recovering from the shock, the battleship admirals later ruled that the carrier had been sunk by the dreadnoughts. Three years afterward, planes from the *Saratoga* and *Lexington*, under the command of Rear Admiral Harry E. Yarnell, swept in from the sea one misty Sunday morning and launched a surprise attack on Battleship Row. The fast carrier task force had been born.

Yet, the problem of independent carrier operations was complicated by the fact that the Navy's pre-1922 battleships could make only twenty-two knots while the carriers were capable of thirty-three knots. If they were allowed to operate away from the battle line, they would be vulnerable to attack by enemy battleships. Yet, there were no U.S. battleships capable of keeping up with them, so the carrier task force could not attain full operation until the navy had fast battleships.

If the admirals disliked the airplane, they positively detested the submarine--possibly because it was too vivid a reminder of the vulnerability of their beloved dreadnoughts. They disdained the strategy of commerce raiding, or *guerre de course*, despite the near-fatal success of the Germans during the previous war. Like the British and Japanese admirals, they viewed the submarine as the weapon of the weak, not the strong. Besides, it was believed that an aroused world opinion would never permit a return to the brutalities of unrestricted submarine warfare as practiced by the U-boats. If it did not, the conventional wisdom held that introduction of convoys and, later, Asdic, or sonar, a system for detecting objects below the surface of the sea, had eliminated the submarine menace.

No effort was made to prepare for a war against commerce or to protect the nation's own commerce against underseas attack. Submarines were deployed as scouts and to protect the battle line in the annual war games. "Enemy" submarine captains who charged toward the dreadnoughts to make close-in attacks were branded as "reckless" violators of doctrine, and their fitness reports were damningly marked to reflect the stigma.[17]

But if submarines were to accompany the fleet and run interference for it, they had to be faster both on the surface and submerged and have longer range, heavy torpedo armament and better habability than the existing boats. This meant that the fleet submarine would be a large boat, upward of 1,500 tons. British efforts to develop a similar craft resulted in the disastrous steam-powered K-boats, and the 2,000-ton American V-class boats were only a shade better--slow in diving, awkward and cantankerous. Only six were completed by 1930, the entire U.S. submarine production for the decade. While still tinkering with the fleet submarine concept, the United States sought to have the submarine abolished altogether at the Geneva Naval Conference of 1927 and in London three years later.[18]

The scrapping of old battleships and restricting those remaining to specific levels did not bring the arms race to an end. Instead, it led to a significant precedent for future arms control negotiations. A half-century later, when the first Strategic Arms Limitation Talks (SALT) treaty limited the number of U.S. and Soviet long-range rockets, both sides responded by increasing the number of warheads, or MIRVs, on each missile. During the 1920s, the arms race shifted to smaller ships, especially cruisers. Efforts at subsequent conferences to fix proportionate numbers for these vessels failed because of conflicting needs and strategies, as well as deepening distrust among the naval powers.

The Geneva Naval Conference of 1927, the brainchild of President Calvin Coolidge, was aimed at imposing limitations on cruisers, destroyers and submarines but foundered on the issue of limitations on large cruisers. The United States, which lacked overseas bases, demanded a high ceiling on 10,000-ton ships armed with eight-inch guns and the extended cruising ranges needed for operations in the Pacific. Britain wanted strict limits on these ships but wished to build a large number of light cruisers armed with six-inch guns that could operate from its ample refueling stations. The American delegation believed that if it accepted the British position, it would not only accept permanent inferiority to the Royal Navy but give further advantage to Japan, which was already ahead of the U.S. Navy in all types of cruisers.

Relations between the United States and Britain soured in the wake of the failure of the Geneva Conference. The Joint Army-Navy Board began reworking its Plan Red, outlining the strategy for a war with Britain, fleet exercises were held in the Atlantic and Caribbean as a none-too-subtle warning and Coolidge asked Congress to approve funds for fifteen cruisers and an aircraft carrier, the latter to replace the *Langley*.[19] Two weeks later, Herbert C. Hoover, a Quaker who abhorred war, entered the White House. "Peace can be promoted by limitations on arms," he declared in his inaugural address.

Hoover, who pursued disarmament for budgetary as well as

humanitarian reasons, thought a large navy to protect the nation's overseas interests a needless luxury. He hoped to disengage from the Far East through Philippine independence and gradual abandonment of the Open Door policy in China. In order to pave the way for a new naval limitations treaty, he ordered work suspended on three of the five heavy cruisers authorized by Coolidge's navy bill. The bait was sufficient to snare the British, and the London Conference opened in January 1930.

Admiral Pratt, soon to be named by Hoover as Chief of naval operations (CNO), was the chief naval adviser at the Conference. Unlike many of his colleagues, Pratt saw Britain and the United States as natural allies against Japan and reached a compromise on the troublesome cruiser issue with the British while pacifying the Japanese. Essentially, limits were placed on total cruiser tonnage, with each nation able to build the type it preferred; the 5:5:3 ratio was continued for battleships and carriers, and Japan was allowed a ratio of 10:10:7 in cruisers and destroyers along with parity in submarines. The battleship "holiday" was extended for another five years and would end in December 1936.[20]

American naval strategists were disappointed by the outcome at Geneva. They considered a 25 percent fleet superiority in the Pacific essential for an American victory in case of war with Japan and contended this margin could not be achieved because of the increased numerical limits granted at London to the potential enemy. Pratt wanted a systematic long-term building program to replace the large part of the fleet that was becoming obsolete to maintain the U.S. Navy's edge, but events tripped him up. Even as the London agreement was being ratified by Congress, it was being rendered moot.

The Great Depression did the work a decade of arms limitation treaties had been unable to accomplish. Hoover slashed government spending, and the navy was forced to trim manpower, layup ships, reduce operations, place shipyards in caretaker status and release men on "furlough" without pay. Only part of the Naval Academy of 1933 was commissioned. Funding for ship construction all but dried up. Some officers doubted that the fleet could remain operational for very long without replacements.[21]

The election of Franklin D. Roosevelt, who had served as assistant secretary of the navy under President Wilson and was a "big navy" man, as president in 1932, was greeted by naval officers with relief and expectation. These expectations were immediately gratified. As part of the almost revolutionary first "Hundred Days" of his administration, Roosevelt earmarked $238 million of the emergency relief funds provided by the National Industrial Recovery Act for warship construction. Shipyards that had been all but abandoned again resounded to the clatter of rivet guns as work began on thirty-two new ships, including two 20,000-ton carriers, *Yorktown* and *Enterprise*, four cruisers, four submarines, two gunboats and twenty destroyers--the first since the old "four pipers."

To this was added a long-range building program sponsored the following year by Congressman Carl Vinson of Georgia, chairman of the House Naval Appropriations Committee. The Vinson-Trammell Act was designed to allow the navy to build up to the levels permitted by the naval limitations treaties and authorized seventy new warships and 730 additional naval aircraft to be built between fiscal year 1935 and 1939.[22] The act itself provided no funds, but as Table 7.1 indicates, a deteriorating international situation stirred Congress to approve ever-larger amounts for ship construction. In fiscal 1936, the appropriation more than tripled from the previous year to $133 million dollars.

Table 7.1
Naval Operation by Fiscal Year[23]

FY*	Total	Shipbuilding
	Approp. (in millions $)	Approp.** (in millions $)
1930	377	49
1931	400	49
1932	358	7
1933	338	35
1934	323	44
1935	311	41
1936	492	133
1937	528	169
1938	529	130
1939	624	191
1940	943	282
1941	3583	1048
1942	18682	3585

*Fiscal Year, for example, began on 1 July 1929 and ended 30 June 1930.
**Shipbuilding appropriations do not include $238 million from the National Industrial Recovery Act.

Paradoxically, the buildup to treaty limitations began at the moment the entire system of naval arms limitation was coming apart as Japan took the first step on the path that led to World War II. Power had passed to a reactionary military autocracy centered in the army and supported by fanatic nationalist associations. Through a campaign of political terrorism, they gained control of the government and set about establishing a new order in eastern Asia under the political and economic domination of Japan. This campaign began in 1931, when Japan seized Manchuria from China. Secretary of State Henry L. Stimson, restrained by President Hoover's reluctance to take overt action, unsuccessfully tried to persuade Britain and France to join in applying diplomatic pressure against Japan.

Unbridled, the Japanese, who were demanding the inadmissible--naval parity with the Anglo-Saxons--gave the required two years' notice in 1934 of their intention to end adherence to the naval limitations agreements--as of 31 December 1936. The 5:5:3 ratio, said one Japanese official, sounded "to Japanese ears like Rolls-Royce: Rolls-Royce: Ford."[24] That same year, the Japanese began constructing airfields in the Carolines and Marshalls--part of an interlocking network of "unsinkable" carriers. With both Japan and fascist Italy refusing to participate, the shaky equilibrium established at Washington a dozen years before had been upset, and further attempts to limit naval armaments collapsed.

Shrouded in secrecy, the Japanese began a massive program of warship construction that gave new life to the battleship. In 1937, they laid down the largest dreadnoughts ever built, the 68,200-ton *Yamato* class--roughly twice the size of any existing battleship--which mounted nine 18.1-inch guns. Reports that the Japanese were building superbattleships appeared in the Italian press, and the Office of Naval Intelligence (ONI) asked Lieutenant Edwin T. Layton, the assistant naval attaché in Tokyo, to make inquiries. The Japanese reply was a masterpiece of doubletalk: the Navy Ministry said it would not comment on "speculation in the Italian press over matters of no concern to the Italians." Surprisingly, Layton was advised by ONI to discontinue his inquiries.[25]

Other nations were also building new battleships by 1937. Unaware of the Japanese superdreadnoughts, Britain laid down the five 35,000-ton *King George* Vs; the Germans had nearly completed the 32,000-ton battle cruisers *Scharnhorst* and *Gneisenau* and were working on the 42,0000-ton *Bismarck* and *Tirpitz*. Not to be left out, the U.S. Navy ordered four classes of battleships prior to World War II--the 35,000-ton *North*

Carolinas; 35,000+ ton *South Dakotas*; 45,000+ ton *Iowas* and the 58,000-ton *Montanas*.

The Japanese, ignoring international opinion, which had proven completely ineffective in halting either the Italian invasion of helpless Ethiopia or their own aggression in Manchuria, launched an all-out invasion of China in 1937. Tension was also mounting in Europe, where Adolf Hitler had come to power in Germany in 1933. With the intention of reversing his country's defeat in World War I, he was rebuilding the German war machine.

The demise of naval arms limitation and the increasing boldness of Germany and Japan led to a revival of the 1916 policy of a navy "second to none." The Naval Act of 1938, shepherded through Congress by Carl Vinson, expanded the fleet beyond treaty limits for the first time. This ten-year $1.1 billion program increased fighting tonnage by 20 percent and authorized construction of three battleships, two carriers, nine cruisers, twenty-three destroyers and nine submarines, as well as a naval air arm of 3,000 planes, almost doubling the existing strength.[26]

The U.S. Navy was also developing new operational techniques and weaponry. Further improvements were made in the theory and practice of carrier warfare, including the refueling of the ships while under way; the fleet submarine reached the practical stage, and the marines were evolving a doctrine for amphibious warfare. Following the disastrous failure of the British landing at the Dardanelles in 1915, military strategists regarded any attempt to land on a hostile shore as doomed to defeat. Captain B. H. Liddell Hart, the British military commentator, observed that "it has now become almost impossible."[27]

Nevertheless, Plan Orange, which was constantly undergoing revision, required the capture of island bases. As early as 1921, Major Earl H. Ellis had suggested that, in case of war with Japan, marine striking forces be used to seize advance bases. Landing exercises were held in the Caribbean and Hawaii in 1924 and 1925 to test this theory but were hampered by a lack of landing craft and specialized equipment. The "Good Neighbor" policy that Roosevelt announced upon his inauguration in 1933 relieved the marines from their involvement in the "banana wars" in the Caribbean and Central America, and a sizable body of troops was now available for use as amphibious forces.[28]

Over the next eight years the Marine Corps was transformed from the navy's policeman into a hard-hitting force whose primary task was the capture of beachheads on enemy territory. Naval gunfire and close air support techniques were worked out, and specialized landing craft were designed. From these experiments followed an astonishing variety of landing craft, many of which proved their worth in the Pacific campaign.

Technological and design breakthroughs had also finally made the fleet submarine possible. The service settled upon a 1,400-ton boat armed with six to ten torpedo tubes with a range of 12,000 miles and capable of remaining on patrol for seventy-five days. These boats proved ideally suited for commerce raiding, although navy doctrine still proclaimed that they were to be used to support the battle fleet.

Of all the problems presented by Orange, none were more troublesome than the lack of defensible advanced bases in the western Pacific. In fact, as late as 1940, Congress refused to provide funds for the construction of a base at Guam. The navy dealt with the problem with a uniquely American solution--the fleet train, which supplied food, fuel, ammunition and repair facilities at sea. Although the number of ships involved was inadequate, navy planners expected in case of war to press civilian shipping into service until new construction became available.

World War II finally came on 1 September 1939, when German troops plunged into Poland. Two days later, Britain and France, after years of appeasing Hitler with the territory of his neighbors, finally went to war against him. Everywhere, the Nazi legions were victorious-- Poland, Denmark, Norway, the Low Countries and France. By the summer of 1940, the national strategies of the belligerents and major neutrals had been established. Britain would fight on, no matter what the cost; Hitler had decided to seize "living space" in the East from his ally, the Soviet Union; the United States began a massive military and naval buildup to preserve its national security and Japan had decided that war with the Westerners was preferable to abandoning its plans to build an Asian empire.

The naval rearmament measures enacted by the United States since 1933 had resulted in 600,000 tons of new warships. But after deducting some 365,000 tons of decommissioned, obsolescent vessels, the net increase for the period was only 235,000 tons. America's relatively slow buildup had not given the U.S. Navy any real superiority over Japan. The quantitative problem is demonstrated by Table 7.2.

The collapse of France created a crisis for the United States. Britain now stood alone against the full fury of the Nazi onslaught. Sooner than many Americans, President Roosevelt sensed the danger that the United States would face should Britain fall. With the Royal Navy dominant in the Atlantic, the U.S. Navy had, since 1922, been free to deploy its strongest units in the Pacific in readiness to deal with any threat from the

Japanese. If Britain went under, the United States would have no allies in the Atlantic or Pacific. Convinced that the survival of Britain was absolutely necessary to American security, Roosevelt decided to provide it all assistance "short of war."

Table 7.2
Comparative Fleet Strengths 1940[29]

	U.S.	Japan
Battleships	15	10
Carriers	5	6
Cruisers	36	37
Submarines	56	62

Three days after the German army entered Paris, Admiral Harold R. Stark, the CNO, went to Capitol Hill with a request for $4 billion for a "two-ocean" navy that would permit the United States to simultaneously fight two wars without allies. The appropriation, which was quickly approved, provided for a 70 percent increase in the size of the fleet, or 257 additional ships, including new, fast battleships as well as twenty-seven Essex-class fleet carriers, which were destined to carry the U.S. Navy to victory in the Pacific. Few of these ships would soon be available--"dollars cannot buy yesterday" is the way Admiral Stark put it--and Britain was on the brink of defeat.[30]

German U-boats operating from new bases on the French coast ripped the heart out of convoys, and the Royal Navy was short of escorts. Prime Minister Winston Churchill urged Roosevelt to let him have fifty of the old four-pipers being reconditioned for patrol work. Using hemispheric defense as a cover, the president made the vessels available by executive order in September 1940 in exchange for a ninety-nine-year lease on a chain of air and sea bases extending from Canada to the Caribbean. But the destroyers-for-bases deal deprived the U.S. Navy of a significant part of its reserve of antisubmarine vessels.

The election of Roosevelt to a third term in November 1940 began the final phase of America's slide into war. The Lend-Lease Act, passed in March 1941, ended the cash-and-carry provisions of the Neutrality Act and allowed the lending of arms, munitions and supplies to those nations "whose defense the President deems vital to the defense of the United States." Hitler, who was preparing to unleash an attack on the Soviet Union, chose to ignore these unneutral acts. The mistake of the rulers of imperial Germany in antagonizing the United States and the decisive effect that American intervention had on the outcome of World War I were in the forefront of his mind.

By 1941, America's total defense expenditures were greater than those of Germany or Japan, even though the nation was not at war. Increasingly, American policy was becoming Atlantic-oriented. Three battleships and the carrier *Yorktown*--nearly a quarter of the Pacific fleet-- were transferred from the Pacific to the newly established Atlantic fleet which was commanded by Admiral Ernest J. King. "If we lose in the Atlantic we lose everywhere," said General George C. Marshall, the army's chief of staff.[31] Admiral Stark reached the same conclusion. Navy planners produced the Plan Dog memorandum which turned the navy away from its concentration on the Pacific and assumed a two-ocean war.

Out of it grew the ABC-I Plan, worked out by the ranking military officers of the United States and Britain in March 1941, which governed Allied operations throughout World War II. The defeat of Germany was to have the highest priority, for only Hitler's Germany had industrial might and military capability to ensure an Axis victory. Preparations for war with Japan continued, but everyone hoped it could be delayed. Plan Orange was dropped as global strategy in favor of Rainbow Five, which established the details of the "Europe First" strategy. But the thrust across the central Pacific by the battle fleet remained basic to the navy's planning for a war against Japan.

The most immediate strategic challenge was getting Lend Lease supplies to Britain through the U-boat infested Atlantic. Roosevelt's movement toward providing convoys for these ships was like the shedding of the seven veils, and each veil that was dropped brought the United States closer to war in the Atlantic. By September 1941, the navy was committed to an undeclared war on the U-boats. Yet, as it girded for a struggle in the Atlantic, war erupted instead across the Pacific at Pearl Harbor.

"If I am told to fight...I shall run wild for the first six months or a year," declared Admiral Isoroku Yamamoto, the commander in chief of the Imperial Japanese Navy's Combined Fleet, as war brewed between the United States and Japan. "But I have no confidence for the second or third year."[32]

To prevent the war with the Americans from lasting into this "second or third year," Yamamoto launched a preemptive strike by 400 carrier-borne planes against the Pacific Fleet as it lay at anchor on the morning of 7 December 1941. Having seen America's industrial might at firsthand while a naval attaché in Washington, he realized that Japan needed a quick victory or would eventually fall victim to America's productive capacity. Once the American fleet had been knocked out, he hoped to gain enough time for Japan to erect a secure defensive perimeter around its newly won ocean empire, which pivoted on the crucial oil fields of the Dutch East Indies.

Sweeping over the green hills behind the base on that quiet Sunday as Admiral Yarnell's pilots had done nine years before, the Japanese destroyed the battle line of the Pacific fleet. But the Japanese had failed to destroy the three American carriers in the Pacific because they were elsewhere. Despite the heavy loss of life, the attack was a blessing in disguise. Although Yamamoto had achieved his aim of preventing the U.S. Pacific Fleet from interfering with the Japanese southward drive to the Philippines, Malaya and the East Indies, he compelled the U.S. Navy to abandon its reliance on the battleship and to turn, instead, to the carrier. The remaining battleships, too slow to keep up with the carriers, retreated to California while the flattops held the line in the Pacific. In previous actions in the European waters, the carriers' planes served as an extension of the big guns of capital ships; now it became the capital ship itself.

With only four carriers available, they usually operated separately in single task formations for several reasons: (1) many separate missions had to be carried on at the same time, (2) the fear of having too many eggs in one basket pervaded the high command and (3) early losses quickly reduced the number of available vessels.[33] Most of these early operations were small-scale affairs, such as launching the Doolittle raid upon Tokyo from the carrier *Hornet*. These operations were made possible only by the breaking of the Japanese naval code and the resulting advantage of knowing what the enemy was going to do next.

Yamamoto now realized that Pearl Harbor had failed to neutralize the U.S. Navy, and he planned a Mahan-type fleet action. This search for a modern Trafalgar led to the Battle of the Coral Sea, where the Japanese were turned back for the first time, and to the Battle of Midway, fought on 4-6 June 1942. Yamamoto again hoped to achieve surprise, but this time Admiral Chester W. Nimitz, the American Pacific theater commander, was forewarned by intercepts of the enemy's radio communications and sent in his three available carriers to lie in wait.

Luck favored the Americans. While the Japanese were reloading their aircraft after the initial attack on Midway, American dive bombers caught the Japanese carriers with bombs and torpedoes strewn about their decks. Four of them were turned into flaming pyres and sunk. Japan was thrown on the defensive for the first time in the war and now faced the long war with the United States that Yamamoto had warned against. Unable to match the productive capacity of American factories and shipyards, it was a war Japan could not win.

In the Atlantic, a handful of German U-boats reaped a deadly harvest of some 2.6 million tons of Allied shipping off the American coast in the first eight months of 1942. It was a greater disaster than even Pearl Harbor because, unlike the Japanese raid on Hawaii, it was not a surprise attack. Large shipping losses had been expected when the United States entered the war. But the eyes of Admiral King, now CNO, were fixed on the situation in the Pacific.

King's basic problem was a shortage of escorts. Like the British and Japanese, the U.S. Navy had almost totally ignored antisubmarine warfare in the interwar years. In case of war, the navy expected to build new escorts on short notice and fall back upon the four-pipers left over from the previous war until they were ready, but this reserve had been depleted by the destroyer-for-bases deal with the British. King saw his first duty as supplying escorts for troopships, and when these requirements were met, the Eastern Sea Frontier got what was left.

While King agreed that the situation was indeed "desperate," he refused to start convoys with the inadequate escorts on hand. Two contemporaries have faulted him for this decision. "I still do not understand the long delay in making all ships sail under escort," complained President Roosevelt. Jurgen Rohwer, a German naval historian, has said the American delay in adopting coastal convoys "was without doubt one of the greatest mistakes in the conduct of the Battle of the Atlantic."[34]

Some observers contend King resisted convoys because he was interested only in the Pacific war; others say he was opposed to convoys in general, while there are those who claim his virulent Anglophobia ruled, and he did not establish convoys merely because the British recommended them. All paint a false picture. King understood the importance of convoys, noting that "escort is not just *one* way of handling the submarine menace, it is the *only* way that gives any promise of success." But he was opposed to weakly defended convoys. "Inadequately escorted convoys are worse than none," he declared. They would merely mass unprotected targets for the U-boats.[35]

King's mistake lay in not learning from the hard-earned experience of the British and Canadians that even weakly defended convoys are better than no convoys. They had learned through three years of struggle that, in dealing with the U-boats, the best attack is defense--and the only defense against the U-boat is the convoy. Numbers had nothing to do with calculating what constituted an effective escort. A trained escort group of four ships was better than a poorly trained one of eight.

Once convoys were organized, Admiral Karl Donitz withdrew his boats from American waters and the Caribbean and returned them to the North Atlantic. The Atlantic battle itself was primarily a British and Canadian operation. As late as mid-1943, when the struggle was at its height of intensity, the Royal Navy was furnishing 50 percent of the convoy escorts, the Royal Canadian Navy 46 percent and the U.S. Navy only 4 percent.[36] The American contribution lay mainly in the central Atlantic, where "hunter-killer" groups built around small escort carriers dealt with U-boats hoping to pick off ships carrying supplies for the invasions of Sicily and Italy. In one two-month period, four of these groups accounted for thirteen German submarines. By the time the war in Europe ended on 7 May 1945, the Germans had lost 781 submarines; 191 were sunk by American ships and planes.

Could the Germans have won the Battle of the Atlantic? In the final analysis, Donitz was battling the productive capacity of American shipyards, rather than the convoy escorts. The Allied victory was won as much on the building waves as on the stormy waters of the Atlantic--by the simple fact that after July 1942, American workers produced merchant ships faster than Donitz's U-boats could sink them. In reality, July 1942, rather than March 1943, which is usually cited, marked the turning point of the Battle of the Atlantic. Germany's only chance to bring Britain to its knees by severing its maritime lifelines was in the early years of the war, when antisubmarine warfare (ASW) techniques were primitive and before America's prodigious industrial prowess came into play--not later than mid-1941. After that, the demands of the war in Russia made it impossible to allocate enough resources to win the U-boat campaign.

Luckily, Hitler was a land-bound strategist with no understanding of what he called "the eerie and sinister sea." Rather than building a large

U-boat force before the war, he had planned a conventional surface fleet of battleships and cruisers worthy of any of Mahan's acolytes. Donitz had but fifty-seven submarines in 1939, of which only half were capable of Atlantic operations and Germany was producing only four a month. "A realistic policy would have given Germany a thousand U-boats at the beginning" of the war, Donitz later told his captors.[37]

Donitz was a fine tactician, but once the United States had entered the conflict, his vaunted "tonnage war" was largely irrelevant. One need consider only a single set of statistics to gauge the truth of this statement. Between 1942 and 1945, the Allies lost 12,590,000 tons of shipping. But during the same period, the size of the Allied merchant fleet rose from 32 million tons to 54 million tons.[38] The effort required to make way against such a margin was beyond the capabilities of the U-boat command.

This is not to deny that the Atlantic battle was a bitter, hard fought struggle. Hindsight makes it clear that the Allied victory was inevitable, but those doing the fighting--and dying-- were unaware of this, and there were grim periods when the submarine offensive appeared to be coming close to achieving its objective of isolating Britain.

In 1943, General Douglas MacArthur had forecast that it would take many years to defeat the Japanese. A year later the U.S. Joint Chiefs of Staff argued at the Quebec Conference that it would take a year after the defeat of Nazism to bring about a Japanese surrender. The British Chiefs of Staff believed it would require two years, so the combined chiefs compromised on a prediction of eighteen months. Yet, the fighting in the Pacific ended in August 1945--only three months after the German surrender. How did this happen?

The Allied armies, the strategic bomber, the miracle of mass production performed by American workers--all contributed to the triumph. The Japanese made their own contribution by poor planning and strategy. Having expected to win the war in its opening months, they failed to plan for a defensive war. Once driven from their early conquests by a combination of American production, organization and training, they were unable to mount an adequate defense and were whipsawed between MacArthur's troops advancing up from the southwest Pacific and Nimitz's assault across the Central Pacific--War Plan Orange redux, but with a significant difference.

Rather than being led by the battleship, as originally envisioned by naval strategists, the decisive blows were administered by the submarine and carrier aircraft. Interdiction of the supplies of oil, coal, raw materials and food that had prompted the Japanese to gamble on war in the first place by carrier raids and undersea attack had ensured Japan's defeat long before the atomic bombs dropped on Hiroshima and Nagasaki induced Japan's leaders to surrender. Once regarded as mere auxiliaries of the capital ship, these weapons systems developed during the interwar years had become the new measure of sea power.

It had ended as Admiral Stark had predicted to Admiral Kichisburo Nomura on the eve of Pearl Harbor:

> If you attack us we will break your empire before we are through with you. While you may have initial successes due to timing and surprise, the time will come when you too will have your losses, but there will be this great difference. You will not only be unable to make up your losses but will grow weaker as time goes on; while on the other hand we will not only make up our losses but will grow stronger as time goes on. It is inevitable that we shall crush you before we are through with you.[39]

NOTES

1. Foster Hailey and Milton Lancelt, *Clear for Action* (New York: Duell, Sloan and Pearce, 1964), 129.

2. Dudley Knox, Introduction to Samuel Eliot Morison, *The Battle of the Atlantic 1939-1943* (Boston: Atlantic, Little, Brown, 1947), xxxv.

3. Philip T. Rosen, "The Treaty Navy," in Kenneth J. Hagan, ed., *In Peace and War* (Westport, Conn.: Greenwood, 1984), 402.

4. Allen R. Millett and Peter Maslowski, *For the Common Good* (New York: Free Press, 1984), 365.

5. Kenneth J. Hagan, *This People's Navy* (New York: Free Press, 1991), 309.

6. Louis Morton, "War Plan ORANGE: Evolution of a Strategy," *World History* (January 1959).

7. Edward S. Miller, *War Plan Orange* (Annapolis,: Naval Institute Press, 1991), 220.

8. Robert L. O'Connell, *Sacred Vessels: The Cult of the Battleship and the Rise of the U.S. Navy* (New York: Oxford, 1991), 289.

9. David A. Rosenberg, "Officer Development in the Interwar Navy," *Pacific Historical Review* (November, 1975).

10.Clay Blair, Jr., *The Atomic Submarine and Admiral Rickover* (New York: Henry Holt, 1954).

11.Samuel Eliot Morison, *The Two-Ocean War* (Boston: Little, Brown, 1963), 11-12.

12.Archibald D. Turnbull and Clifford L. Lord, *History of United States Naval Aviation* (New York: Arno Press, 1972), 161.

13.Quoted in Hagan, *This People's Navy*, 272.

14.Clark A. Reynolds, *The Fast Carriers* (New York: McGraw-Hill, 1968), 1.

15.O'Connell, *Sacred Vessels*, 285-286.

16.Hagan, *This People's Navy*, 273-274.

17.Ibid.

18.For the development of the fleet submarine, see Norman Polmar, *The American Submarine* (Baltimore: Nautical & Aviation, 1981).

19.William R. Braisted, "On the American Red and Red Orange Plans, 1919-1939, in Gerald Jordan, ed., *Naval Warfare in the Twentieth Century* (London: Croom Helm, 1977).

20.George T. Davis, *A Navy Second to None* (Westport, Conn.: Greenwood Press, 1940), Chapter 13.

21.Gerald E. Wheeler, *William Veazie Pratt* (Washington, D.C.: Naval History, 1974), 365-67.

22.Davis, *A Navy Second to None*, 360-61.

23.Dean C. Allard, "Naval Rearmament, 1930-1941: An American Perspective," *Revue Internationale d'Histoire Militaire*, No. 73, 1991.

24.Quoted in Thomas F. Bailey, *A Diplomatic History of the American People* (New York: Appleton-Century, 1946), 742.

25.Edwin T. Layton, *Oral History* (Nimitz Library: U.S. Naval Academy).

26.Allard, "Naval Rearmament."

27. B. H. Liddell Hart, *A History of the World War, 1914-1918* (London: Faber and Faber, 1934).

28.Jeter T. Isely and Philip A. Crowl, *The U.S. Marines and Amphibious War* (Princeton,: Princeton University Press, 1951), Chapters 2 and 3.

29.Millett and Maslowski, *For the Common Good*, 387.

30.Morison, *Battle of the Atlantic*, 27-30.

31.Hagan, *This People's Navy*, 292.

32.Gordon W. Prange, *At Dawn We Slept* (New York: McGraw-Hill, 1981), 10.

33.Reynolds, *The Fast Carriers*, 22-23.

34.Jurgen Rohwer, "The Operational Use of ULTRA in the Battle of the Atlantic," in C. Andrews and J. Noakes, eds., *Intelligence and International Relations 1900-1945* (Exeter, U.K.: University of Exeter, 1987), 284-85.

35.Dan van der Vat, *The Atlantic Campaign* (New York: Harper & Row, 1988), 242.

36.Morison, *Atlantic Battle Won* (Boston: Little, Brown, 1956), 20, note 10.

37.Morison, *The Battle of the Atlantic*, 4.

38.John Ellis, *Brute Force* (New York: Viking, 1990), 161.

39.John Major, "The Navy Plans for War 1937-1941, " in Hagan, *In Peace and War*, 445-46.

8

The British Navy, 1918–1945

G.A.H. Gordon

The Second World War differed in fundamental ways from the hypothetical war for which their lordships had assiduously planned. This discrepancy, a magnet of hindsight wisdom from the "bloody fools" school of historians, was not the product of serious incompetence or unrealism in interwar policy making.

Whether the Grand Fleet had fulfilled its "destiny" in the Great War was a matter that, in 1919, could be left to retired admirals. The one clear, major military victory over which the Admiralty had presided (albeit belatedly) was the confounding of Germany's post-Jutland campaign to defeat Britain with submarines. But owing both to the decisive mastery of the U-boat and to postwar international naval dynamics, the future of Britain's surface fleet of major warships preoccupied naval policymakers in the war's immediate aftermath. The key to that future lay in the balance of naval power on the other side of the world from the mists of the North Sea.

The alliance between Britain and Japan had serviced Jacky Fisher's concentration of fleet units in home waters in the first decade of the century and had enabled the Royal Navy to give its undivided attention to the German High Seas Fleet. The alliance had brought Japan into war against Germany in August 1914. Japanese forces had searched for Von Spee's cruiser squadron, had escorted Australian troops across the Indian Ocean and had helped themselves to Germany's Pacific possessions. But Japan was reluctant to get involved in hostilities outside the western Pacific area, and the impression that it regarded the Far East as an unsupervised adventure-playground gained credence from the Twenty-one Demands with which she confronted China and that brought Washington and London together in protest.

Not least suspicious about Japan's agenda was the U.S., and "Japanese-American relations at the end of the First World War were strained."[1] Both embarked upon huge construction programs and appeared committed to "big-time" naval arms competition. American popular opinion, agitated by the usual inventory of anti-British lobby groups, set itself the goal of breaking up the Anglo-Japanese Alliance, which was due for review in 1921.

It became clear that war-exhausted Britain would have to stop the new naval race or somehow win it, for otherwise it would find itself shoved from first to third among nations and its empire a hostage to the unlikely indulgence of others. Its predicament was aggravated by the fact that the Royal Navy's (RN) stock of capital ships comprised a Jurassic Park of worn-out, obsolescent, mostly coal-burning dreadnoughts that were no match for the hardware taking shape on postwar drawingboards. When the Americans invited the Pacific powers to discuss their differences, the British readily agreed.

In Washington, Great Britain and Japan were confronted with the concept of parity in capital ships at a level economically convenient to the United States, rather than commensurate with Britain's global defense liabilities, and with the requirement that they terminate their alliance with Japan.

How serious the Americans really were about the massive program bandied about by their naval lobby is a moot point, but the British negotiators were almost certainly underaware of the competitive and uncoordinated nature of policy making in U.S. government of which skillful use might have been made. Within the officer corps of the Royal Navy, the U.S. Navy had supplanted the Imperial Japanese Navy as the closest foreign service by virtue of the fact that toward the end of the war an American battle squadron had joined Admiral Beatty's Grand Fleet, and American destroyers had played an important part in the defeat of the U-boat. Regrettably, it proved a brief episode in transatlantic relations.

There was undoubtedly an element of racism in the preference of British officers for those with whom they had cultural affinity, but it is fair to suggest that the Japanese refusal to lend a couple of *Kongos* to the battle cruiser fleet, when asked to do so earlier in the war, had left the "hearts and minds" field clear for the Americans later on. Now that Germany's *Riskflotte* had been disposed of, the benefits to Britain of the Japanese alliance were less immediately obvious. Nevertheless, the preponderant political view was that its continuation would act as a restraint on Japan's future behavior, it was held by the Admiralty that

Britain should tell the Americans

> to go ahead with building what they liked and good luck to them.
> No one in Britain contemplated a war with the United States, and if
> the latter felt inclined to possess the largest fleet in the world,
> Britain had no cause for apprehension. But for Britain to tie her
> hands in the all-important matter of sea power, not only in relation
> to America but other countries too, was a fundamental mistake.[2]

Had the world not then been "living in an era of dreams [in which it]
would take [huge] doses of morphia,"[3] the American remedy could
probably have been dismissed on cogently argued rational grounds. But
in the atmosphere of moral righteousness that prevailed in 1921, "to
challenge the American President's arbitrarily chosen ratios would
probably mean wrecking the Conference, and it was thought most
inadvisable for Britain, as the American public's hereditary whipping-
boy, to risk doing that."[4]

The details of the settlement agreed to in Washington in 1922
scarcely require repetition. The British government, beset by war debts
and League-of-Nationism, overrode the Admiralty's reasoned objections
to the American package and accepted parity in capital ships. Japan was
allowed a 60 percent ratio to the big two; France and Italy, 35 percent
Other major warship types were also subjected to limitations, for a period
of ten years. To make the Far East accessible to the British battle fleet--
in compensation for the loss of the alliance--a naval base was permitted
at Singapore.[5] The termination of the Anglo-Japanese Alliance "was
softened and to some extent disguised by its merging in a multilateral
treaty between the US, Britain, Japan and France." In Ned Willmott's
words, "The arrangement was manifestly fraudulent and left the Japanese
resentful and hurt."[6]

For the Americans, despite ritual protests from their navalists that
they had been robbed, the deal promoted them "at a stroke into co-
equality with the strongest naval power without having to go to the
expense of building their way up to that position."[7] For the British
Empire, the settlement papered over an insidious strategic flaw, for the
alliance with Japan had been worth at least a squadron of battleships, and
Washington made sense only as long as the naval shipyards of
Continental Europe remained idle. At Washington were sown the seeds
of future appeasement.

Admiralty policy in the event of war with Japan was now expressed by the *ju-ju* "main fleet to Singapore." The "main fleet" was to comprise ten capital ships, and slowly, with stops and starts, a base fit to house it grew out of the mangroves of Singapore island. But the predicament of a global military power arms-limited by regional mathematics began to disturb the more farsighted almost immediately. At the 1923 Imperial Conference,

> that shrewd Boer Jan Smuts, Prime Minister of South Africa, believed that Japan was unlikely to attack unless she had support in Europe. If this were so, Smuts asked, would it be feasible to divide the Royal Navy?
> Leo Amery, First Lord of the Admiralty, had admitted in reply: "Of course it is perfectly feasible that, if there were a European combination against us at the same moment as war was declared against us by Japan, we should be in a position of extraordinary difficulty."[8]

The Americans now began to agitate for reductions in the Royal Navy's cruiser strength for the irrelevant reason that it did not need so many. Beatty celebrated its failure at the Geneva Disarmament Conference in 1927:

> Every nation in the history of the world has only attained Sea Power as the result of great achievements and the price of many lives and much money. The DAMNED Yanks thought they could get it for nothing!! I wish their ridiculous attitude under the guise of economy and disarmament could be made plain to the World.[9]

As Beatty's acerbic words[10] hint, the British were (as usual) losing the public relations battle, and the Americans' campaign strengthened the hands of British economists and pacifists. They were rewarded, against renewed Admiralty protests, at the 1930 London Naval Conference, which curtailed cruiser construction and extended the Washington moratorium on capital ships for a further five years. Significantly, France refused to comply through fear of German new construction, and Italy refused through alleged fear of France. The dormant naval yards of Europe were beginning to stir. In September 1931, Japan invaded Manchuria. In January 1933, Hitler arrived.

Doubt grew over the assumption that the British "Main Fleet" would be available, whenever needed, to defend the Far East. The passing of the Japanese Alliance was bitterly lamented. Britain had lost the freedom to concentrate its fleet. From this perspective it is unsurprising that appeasement's most dogged advocates were to be found in the Admiralty.[11]

Relentlessly, from 1933, Admiral Sir Ernle Chatfield, now first sea lord and chief of Naval Staff--"the dominant personality in the formulation of British strategic policy" before World War Two[12]--warned that Japan would surely strike *south but only if* the British navy became detained elsewhere. As early as December 1933, he told the Defence Requirements Committee that it was "imperative to do everything possible to keep on good terms with Japan."[13] In February 1934 he told the commander in chief in China, Admiral Sir Frederick Dreyer, that Japan "is unlikely to provoke this country too far until she knows that we have a danger nearer home to worry us." That first, preconditional danger would come, he predicted accurately, from Nazi Germany in five years' time.[14]

The next month the Cabinet discussed the need to get back "at least to our old terms of cordiality and mutual respect with Japan." The discussion shows the essentially naval character of imperial security, the beginnings of appeasement and the central role of Neville Chamberlain (chancellor of the exchequer). The secretary of state for India:

> pointed out that, at present, no nation had any influence with Japan, who was isolated. It would be a great advantage if Britain could recover our influence there.
>
> The chancellor of the exchequer agreed. He recalled that the Japanese were a sensitive people and that the termination of the Anglo-Japanese Alliance had been a great blow to their *amour propre*. The very fact of our offering to have a fresh discussion and some kind of bilateral understanding would tend to restore their ruffled feelings.
>
> Turning to the forthcoming second London Naval Conference, he gathered that the Americans wanted us to line up with them in opposing any alteration in the Japanese proportion of fleet strength. He could think of nothing more likely to give offence to the Japanese than this, and he thought we should make clear to the Americans that we could not pull the chestnuts out of the fire for them...he put as a basis of discussion the opposite point of view: we should decline to align ourselves with Washington; indicate that we were not prepared to submit ourselves to the limitations of a treaty

and say that we did not mind what the Americans chose to build. At the same time we might go to Japan and say that we had not linked ourselves with America. If this were done, Japan would be free of the fear that we might be united with America against it.[15]

Privately, Chamberlain wrote, "I have no doubt we could easily make an agreement with [the Japanese] if the USA were out of the picture. It is the Americans who are the difficulty."[16] His chief of staff at the treasury, Sir Warren Fisher, held that "the worst of our deficiencies is our entanglement with the USA" and that Britain should be prepared to sacrifice American friendship to regain the more valuable friendship with Japan.[17] Chamberlain undoubtedly agreed.

At the Second London Naval Conference, in 1935, the Japanese demanded a common upper limit for the fleet strengths of Japan, Britain and America but let it be known that they were "quite willing that the UK should have a stronger Navy than Japan." This (in the words of the Cabinet minutes), of course, "gave rise to an almost insoluble problem in as much as the US insisted on naval parity with ourselves."[18]

Meanwhile, Adolf Hitler repudiated Versailles and made clear his intention of building a new fleet of capital ships. Those responsible for imperial defense saw at once that "the demands made on the Navy by a war against Germany might threaten the whole basis of the planned Far Eastern strategy."[19] With the Anglo-German Naval Agreement of June 1935, the Admiralty was clearly leading Whitehall in appeasement. Its objective was to forestall the development in European waters of a threat so serious as to preclude the fleet's deployment to the Far East, and indeed Germany's senior naval officers considered their 1935 limit to rule out Germany and Britain as future adversaries.[20]

Then Italy attacked Abyssinia. It fell to Britain alone to provide the forces of so-called collective security, and it nearly found itself at war in the Mediterranean. Obviously, fences must be mended with Italy to leave the armed forces free "to deal with the Far Eastern menace."[21] Chatfield privately took the view that if Italy had a stake in Abyssinia its communications would then be hostage to British sea power, a state of affairs that should favor peace.[22]

In January 1937, the first sea lord, by now directionally impartial in his quest for appeasement, petitioned the professional head of the Foreign Office:

[a]s we cannot fight simultaneously in the East and the West, can we

make an agreement in one area or the other, not necessarily a permanent agreement, but one which will give us greater security than we have now during our slow period of rearmament? It appears impossible that we should make an agreement with Japan that would be of the same value as the old alliance. We might placate her by recognising Manchuku.[23]

A few weeks later the chiefs of staff hammered away that

the difficulties and dangers of conducting a war against Japan in the Far East, particularly if we were simultaneously engaged in Europe, are so great that it is manifest that no effort must be spared to establish such good relations with our former allies, the Japanese, as will obviate, as far as possible, the chances of their being aligned against us.[24]

First-generation history is mostly the celebration of victorious causes, and, until recently, historians have fallen over one another to associate with Churchill's supposed sagacity. Above all, they have obliged him by placing the appeasement issue solely in the European context. Even Martin Gilbert, in his otherwise excellent book on the *Roots of Appeasement*,[25] written before his Churchillian days, seems unaware of the empire's existence. In a purely European setting, appeasement fails to make complete sense and thus appears to warrant the tarnishing of its advocates with (in Margaret George's words) "sympathy for the goals of Hitler's Germany."[26]

To ascribe such motives to Chatfield and his naval staff would be fatuous. No doubt, at the time of the Spanish Civil War, British admirals privately tended to favor Franco; as men from a class collectively threatened by the rise of socialism, it would be surprising if they did not. But they were highly professional naval officers whose prime concern was global defense mathematics, and it may be mentioned that in 1939, after appeasement was seen to have failed, Chatfield, as minister for the coordination of defense, was to advocate alliance with Communist Russia as a means of containing Germany.

The British were not Europeans in the 1920s and 1930s; they were the center of a worldwide maritime empire, the core custodian of which was the navy. Only if one considers the defense of empire to have been either a lost cause or an unworthy one, can one echo Williamson Murray's opinion that the Chamberlain Government's "record...is unpardonably dismal. The Prime Minister and his advisers made the wrong choice on almost every strategic and diplomatic question that they faced."[27] To the Admiralty, which feared that peace, once broken somewhere, would prove to be hemispherically indivisible, appeasement was as obvious as any damage-limitation precaution before a possible collision at sea. It was simple strategic seamanship.

The Admiralty's insistent lobbying for appeasement probably deserves a book in its own right. The problem is not the shortage of documentary evidence, so much as its repetitive nature and the early exhaustion of the superlatives of doom. The sailors, of course, had friends.

Their greatest departmental ally was the treasury. The Foreign Office had understood the Achilles' heel of Britain's Far Eastern policy as long ago as 1925[28] but obtusely continued to imagine that Britain could respond to the dictators through weight of armaments alone--if the Government so wished. The almost emotional attachment of some historians to the Churchillian myth that the scale of rearmament was constrained by treasury meanness and that appeasement was therefore avoidable persists to this day. In fact, naval programs had taken up all specialized industrial capacity only a few months into rearmament in 1936.[29] By the time Chamberlain succeeded Earl Baldwin as prime minister, appeasement offered the only short-term solution to Britain's strategical nightmare. In his words, "a political adjustment with one or more of our potential enemies was absolutely vital."[30]

In July 1937, the secretary of the Committee of Imperial Defence, Sir Maurice Hankey, wrote to the new prime minister:

> In the interests of Imperial Defence it is very important that better relations should be established with Italy, permanently if possible, but in any event during the completion of our Defence Programme. We have not succeeded in making much progress in getting on better terms with Germany or Japan. With Italy our relations are unsatisfactory. We have therefore almost reached the position, against which the Chiefs of Staff have uttered so many warnings, where we have potential enemies in the West, the Far East, and athwart the main line of Imperial communications between the two. If war broke out in the Mediterranean, we should have to expect severe blows at the outset, affecting our prestige especially in the Near East. In the long run victory would be certain, provided we and Italy were left alone in the ring. But since we could only win by

uncovering our vital interests elsewhere, a world war would almost certainly be precipitated and for that we are totally unprepared. Neither we nor Italy could run the risk of a world war. Almost any sacrifice would be better for either nation.[31]

A week after receiving the above, Chamberlain had a warm and friendly talk with the Italian ambassador,[32] who went so far as to say that "England and Italy had been divorced for two years and might now be remarried."[33] However, problems remained in the way, such as recognition of Abyssinia and Italy's support for Franco, and the reunion was not to be.

In November 1937, Hankey joined the first sea lord in yet another strident call for "something [to be done] in the field of foreign policy to reduce our defensive commitments. With the greatest sense of responsibility, I must add my considered endorsement to the repeated warnings of the Chiefs of Staff that action ought to be taken to effect a permanent improvement in our relations with Italy." Chatfield doggedly "pointed out that an improvement in our relations with Germany or Japan is urgent."[34] He was desperately worried about the likelihood (as he perceived it) "that shortly after the commencement of a war [in Europe] we might have to send a fleet to the Far East, where we now have an enemy instead of an ally."[35]

That same month, the Admiralty's director of plans, Captain Tom Phillips, painted the stark strategical urgency of rapprochement. "If we could reach a satisfactory agreement with Germany, our other defence commitments would largely solve themselves, as Italy would never dare attack alone and even if Japan did not moderate her policies we should at least be in a position to deal with her." Chatfield considered Phillips's summary of the situation "very able" and sent it up to his Minister with the following covering remarks:

[t]he main proposal of this paper is that we should make an agreement with Germany because, in view of our Imperial responsibilities, we cannot afford to prolong our enmity....If we have to fight her it will probably also mean war with Japan and possibly Italy--a world war which may last for years with enormous loss of lives and money, and general misery in the world.[36]

After March 1938, only Europe appeared to offer scope for detente, for in that month Japanese intransigence obliged Britain and the United

States to cut themselves free from the remnants of the "Washington" restrictions. Only now, six months before Munich, did Britain accept that friendly relations with Japan were irrecoverable.

The import of this parting of the ways was plain enough to Captain Phillips and the planning chiefs of the other services. Appeasement was still vital, but now the only scope for it lay in Europe. In a paper on "The Military Implications of German Aggression against Czechoslovakia," they connected the Japanese threat directly with Britain's options vis-à-vis Hitler:

> [b]y no pressure that we can bring to bear, either by sea, on land or in the air, is it possible for us forcibly to prevent Germany from invading and overrunning Bohemia, and from inflicting a decisive defeat on the Czechoslovakian Army. We should then be faced with the necessity of undertaking a war with Germany, for the purpose of restoring Czechoslovakia's lost integrity, and this object would only be achieved by the defeat of Germany and as the outcome of a prolonged struggle...[meanwhile] the advent of Japan on the side of Germany and Italy would produce a situation which neither the present nor the projected strength of our defence forces is designed to meet. The British Empire would be threatened simultaneously in Western Europe, in the Mediterranean and in the Far East, by an immense aggregate of armed strength and would be faced with the gravest danger...
> We are therefore of the opinion that Great Britain should not risk the possibility of war except in the defence of interests that are vital to her [which obviously did not include Czechoslovakia].[37]

On March 1939, Hitler occupied Prague and tossed away both the Munich peace promises and the Anglo-German naval agreement. Appeasement had run its course. The Australian government immediately pressed for reaffirmation of Britain's post-1922 commitment to send the main fleet to Singapore in the event of Japanese aggression. It was Chamberlain's miserable task to frame an evasive reply, which, as A. J. Marder has written, came as a "bombshell" to the Australians, "referring, as it did to 'a combination never envisaged in our earlier plans,' namely, the possibility of Britain having to fight Germany, Italy and Japan at the same time."[38]

A few days later the Cabinet met to consider whether Britain should offer a guarantee of military aid to Poland. The admiral, who had spent six years burdened with imperial safety, said wearily that "if Poland were attacked, it [would be] politically impossible for us to stand aside."[39] For Britain's Far Eastern empire, those resigned words marked the beginning of what an Australian historian has called--with some bitterness--"the great betrayal."[40]

The same month as that Cabinet meeting saw the completion of the navy's supply arrangements for the first year of another world war. In this field, Britain's and the Admiralty's approach was based heavily on the experiences of the "total mobilisation" of the Great War, whose lessons were studied very carefully and taken to heart. The principles, organization and practicalities of the Admiralty's procurement preparations against a new total war were the subjects of my, study *British Seapower and Procurement between the Wars*. Some points that need to be kept in mind include:

•In the 1920s, helped by the Board of Trade, the three services organized themselves into a comprehensive, cooperative, procurement system, known as the Supply Board.

•The task of the Supply Board was (initially) to identify industrial capacity for war stores and earmark capacity for the use of the three services in wartime.

•Under the Supply Board, nine supply committees oversaw specific fields of industry and were each chaired by the service department with the greatest knowledge of that field. The Admiralty ran shipbuilding and general stores, for example; the War Office, armaments and Food; the Air Ministry, scientific stores and internal combustion products; the Board of Trade, machine tools, and so on. Contrary to popular cliche, uncoordination was virtually impossible.

•The task of earmarking capacity (and noting shortfalls)--in accordance with approved war hypotheses--was more or less complete by 1934-5.

•Then, rearmament provided the unplanned opportunity to educate firms in the work they would find themselves doing in wartime. At the same time, controversially, the treasury stumped up quite considerable sums of money to supply private firms with plant extensions to enlarge their potential for war stores and thus reduce the identified shortfalls.

•The challenges facing the three service departments in this process were different. Far more of the Admiralty's hypothesized needs were armaments, rather than munitions, than was the case with the other services (an armament being a munition that cannot be mass-produced), and thus most extensions on Admiralty account went to major arms firms already specializing in their planned war work.

•Almost from the start of rearmament, naval construction was constrained by the limits of industrial capacity (more precisely, skilled labor) and not by money. In three years, a sum equal to the cost of four fleet aircraft carriers was spent enlarging the capacity of the Admiralty's suppliers.

•By April 1939, the Admiralty had "allocated to them[selves] all the capacity that they will require at the outset of war."[41]

Of Vice Admiral Sir Reginald Henderson, controller of the navy during rearmament, the Director of Naval Contracts (DNC) was later to say "the people of this country will never know how much they owe to [his] wisdom and energy." He might well have extended the plaudits to Sir Warren Fisher, the permanent secretary of the treasury.

Prewar supply planning was weighted toward the construction of big-ship fleet units to a degree apparently unwarranted by actual needs in the Second World War. To some extent, it had to be, if the option was to be retained of expanding the fleet in wartime, for large warships are the "armaments" of naval construction, requiring highly specialized capacities--in contrast to escort vessels, minesweepers and so on, which are more like "munitions" and can be produced by semiskilled methods.

But obviously, it was also a product of the governing war hypothesis, the baseline of which was the active participation of France in a future war with Germany. France possessed the largest army in Europe, and it was inconceivable, given the millions who had died defending it in the First World War, that its surrender should be contemplated, still less planned for. There is, furthermore, evidence that if the chiefs of staff had been asked to plan for Britain's fighting on alone, they would have replied simply that it could not be done.[42]

With France in the war, the prospective situation in European waters would have been similar to that of 1918, with a major ally in the Mediterranean and with U-boats distanced from the Southwestern approaches by the long haul round Scotland and by a barrage across the Dover Straits. If you criticize the Admiralty's supply preparations, as the history of the Second World War invites you to do, you are really taking issue with the forecasts that governed them; and if you insist that Britain should have planned for war after the fall of France, I would like to hear you rehearsing how you would have told the French.

Nevertheless, "Jutland-itis" remains one of the easy, "wise" criticisms of Admiralty thinking in the 1930s.[43] In as much as this disease existed, it took the form of a determination not to have a rerun of Jutland (and may be represented by the building of what were, ton for ton, the world's most heavily armored fleet units). But the Naval Staff's predicament deserves further consideration.

It is reflected in a memorandum of June 1939 by the first lord (and ex-grenadier guardsman), the Earl of Stanhope. Assuming that the fleets of France and Italy would continue to cancel each other out, he projected that, between them, Germany and Japan would be level pegging with Britain in commissioned capital ships by 1941 and by 1944 would be in the lead. By the end of 1946 he was looking at 34 1/2 capital ships for Germany and Japan (the *Deutschlands* each counting for 1/2), as against 29 for the Royal Navy.[44] With such mathematics in the offing, only fools would have consigned the era of big-gun fleet actions entirely to the dustbin of history.[45] No wonder Stanhope wanted to enlarge battleship capacity from two to three per year and to throw a quick ship together using spare fifteen-inch mountings.

Yet, the Admiralty had been pursuing a strategically schizophrenic building policy for several months. Shortly after Munich, the constructors were told to draft a design for a fast escort vessel, which was to be robust and simple of construction. The hull, to quote the staff requirements, "should be capable of withstanding minor damage when handled by inexperienced personnel"--plain reference to civilians in uniform--and it was admitted that the ships were intended "to meet requirements that arise only in war."[46] The first ten Hunt-Class destroyers were ordered well ahead of parliamentary sanction; ten more followed soon after. Then, after Prague, a civilian contractor converted a whale-catcher into a rudimentary escort, and fifty-six Flower-class corvettes were ordered before war actually broke out.

It is a remarkable testament to the Admiralty's realism that it embarked in peacetime upon the construction of seventy-six utility warships that had no peacetime use. It has to be placed in the context of the Admiralty's oversanguine faith in "ASDIC" Submarine detection device and of the strategic expectations already mentioned. It is impossible to do justice to the cost of sea power paid by the British in the Second World War in a chapter of this length. A brief discussion of some broad strategic themes will help to illustrate the point, however.

Britain's naval situation and prospects differed in 1940 from those of 1914 in two gigantic and fundamental ways. First, there was no alliance in the Far East to secure the empire. Second, France was overrun by the Germans. The fall of France was not Britain's first strategic embarrassment. But it was the worst, and from it others followed, sequentially and causally.

With the defeat and occupation of France, Britain's strategic assumptions collapsed like a house of cards. Even if the United Kingdom were somehow to survive, there was no prospect of defeating Hitler in anything other than the longest term. The world had been turned upside down.

My father was in one of the ships that bombarded the French fleet at Oran. Nobody had an entirely convincing explanation for why they were attacking the French; it seemed (as indeed it was) merely a progression of the crazy events of the last few weeks, and there was no guessing what might or might not happen next. The only constant, familiar factor among all the turmoil was the navy--the ship, the routine, and Jack's incapacity for systematic worry. A few days earlier, when France had surrendered, Admiral Cunningham had asked his second in command why he was so cheerful. "We're bound to win now," John Tovey explained; "we have no allies left." But for those responsible for global strategy (if you can be "responsible" for something that is out of your control), the prospects were a nightmare.

The task of countering the Italian navy in the Mediterranean (hitherto accounted against France's five modernish capital ships) would now have to be shouldered by the Mediterranean fleet, which the Admiralty had mostly earmarked--in event of need--for Singapore. To leave the Mediterranean would be to lose it. The pressure of other priorities had caused work to be stopped on the four battleships of the *Lion* class. The flame of renewed battleship programs flickered on in the hearts of the naval staff for some time, but in a subtle, symbolic sense this was the beginning of the letting go of the Far East.

The orphaning of French colonies in Indochina, combined with Britain's life-or-death struggle in Europe, "offered all sorts of glittering opportunities to Japan,"[47] and the chiefs of staff met at the end of July to reassess the situation in the Far East. The papers placed before them and the comments added by the War Cabinet on 8 August,[48] depict exactly the strategical overstretch that the Admiralty had dreaded because:

> [u]ntil we have defeated Germany and Italy or have drastically reduced their naval strength, we are faced with the problem of attempting to defend our Far East interests in the absence of an

adequate fleet.

...the collapse of France, the development of a direct threat to the UK and the necessity for retaining in European waters a fleet of sufficient strength to match both the German and Italian fleets have made it temporarily impossible for us to despatch a fleet to the Far East should the occasion arise.

...Committed as we are in Europe...we must avoid an open clash with Japan. A general settlement, including economic concessions to Japan, should be concluded as soon as possible. Failing this settlement, our general policy must be to play for time, cede nothing until we must, and build up our defences as soon as we can.

For the information of the Commander in Chief Far East, this dismal material was packed off by surface mail in a steamer, which was captured in the Indian Ocean by a German merchant raider. Before long, the War Cabinet papers found their way, via the German Embassy in Tokyo, onto the desk of Vice Admiral Kondo; and the late James Rusbridger, in his otherwise scurrilous book, *Betrayal at Pearl Harbor*[49], makes out an impressive, if largely circumstantial, case for this intelligence windfall's being the catalyst that enabled Japan's naval "strike south" faction to gain ascendancy in the strategic debate over its army's "strike north" lobby.

Meanwhile, Churchill's priorities remained consistent with his antiappeasement stance, in his nonresponsible position outside government, in the late 1930s. Then the vulnerability of the empire--the "catch-1922" of British strategy--had been inconvenient to his aggressive stance toward Germany, and so he had belittled the threat from Japan and even disavowed the importance of the colonies. He had carried this expedient, tendentious and even wishful perspective into Downing Street in May 1940. To have the use of Australian troops for the Middle East, he had consistently to downplay the Japanese threat to Australia. Throughout 1940 and 1941 he considered Naval Intelligence "very much inclined to exaggerate Japanese strength and efficiency,"[50] but promised that if Australia were threatened with invasion, Britain would "then cut our losses in the Mediterranean and sacrifice every interest" to defend the Dominion.[51] He gambled on the debt's not being called in.[52]

At last, in the autumn of 1941, Churchill grudgingly agreed to send capital ships to Singapore, although only the minimum that he believed necessary to impress the Malayans and Australians and deter the Japanese. The tragic saga of *Prince of Wales* and *Repulse* is well known.

Some historians have suggested that when it became clear that the deterrence had failed to deter, it should have been withdrawn out of harm's way at once. But "it was inconceivable that the force sent to secure Malaya from attack should not give battle when that attack materialised,"[53] and when reports came through of landings in north eastern Malaya, its "duty seemed clear."[54]

Where Admiral Phillips had planned to take his ships, had they survived the foray into the South China Sea, is unknown. The War Cabinet, on the ninth, had more or less settled for Pearl Harbor, as a sort of consolation prize to the Americans; but decided to sleep on it. When it awoke in London on December 10, it was too late. All that remained of Britain's Far Eastern deterrent strategy were several hundred sailors swimming for their lives and a few acres of floating wreckage.

The Royal Navy had failed in what it had considered its primary strategic task: the defense of empire. It failed because of a danger that the Admiralty had seen coming ever since Washington had set the scene for a delayed "game of poker in which the stakes were the Empire itself and the bluff could be called by Japan declaring war concurrently with Germany."[55] Neither of the other two major Pacific powers, the U.S. or Japan, had been compromised in this fashion.

The widespread expulsion of British forces from Allied and colonial territories, in the earlier stages of the war, was the key to why the Royal Navy's war tasks differed markedly both in nature and in scale from those forecast in the war hypothesis upon which the Admiralty had based its contingency plans. There were two main themes to this difference: the drastically worsened task of protecting merchant shipping from submarine fleets based in France and the commitment of the navy, in Northwestern Europe and the Mediterranean, to warfare in coastal waters, usually under land-based air attack. Both themes militated toward smaller ships.

The degree of the difference can be illustrated by a comparison of warship construction in the two world wars. In the fifty-one months of the First World War, 1,661 naval ships, averaging 960 tons, were built for the Admiralty. In the first fifty-one months of the Second World War (up to the end of 1943), the figure was 4,490 ships, averaging just 400 tons.[56]

Another measurement can be found in the expenditure on armor plate (as a rule, only used in fleet units) as against spending on guns and ammunition. The 1939 figure for armor plate halved in 1940 and halved again in 1941 while the figure for guns and ammunition roughly doubled in 1940 and doubled again in 1941.

Undoubtedly, the most important sea power role that the White Ensign played in the Second World War was its unrelenting six year labor to husband, control and defend merchant shipping. The arteries of shipping circulated life support round the enormous sprawling animal of the Allied war effort. Had the net hemorrhage been too great, or the pump stopped, the consequences would have been terminal to every limb of that animal. The availability of cargo hulls, therefore, not only permitted Britain to survive but both enabled and defined the limits of, Allied campaigns to an extent not always fully appreciated by American commanders whose indisciplined use of shipping caused considerable British anger.[57] While it is certainly not my intention to diminish the contribution of other services, other navies or other nations, it is entirely justifiable to say that while the U.S. Navy strode massively past the British in the currency by which sea power was measured--major fleet units--the enormous part played by the British and Canadian navies in the preservation of merchant shipping stocks--tedious, costly and unglamorous though it may have been--was as crucial as the American dollar or the Russian soldier to the ultimate victory of the Allies over the Axis.

Earlier I said two major strategic factors differentiated Britain's position in 1940 from that of 1914--the absence of an alliance in the Far East and the fall of France. In fact, of course, there was a third. Liddel Hart, in his *History of the First World War*, doubts that Britain could have continued fighting Germany if the Schlieffen Plan had been executed properly, and France defeated, in 1914, on the grounds that the public then was simply not conditioned to perceive war in terms of total national commitment as opposed to the vocational pursuit of small professional elites. The matter is open to debate (in the light of the Napoleonic War); but unquestionably, in 1940, the British people, through the experience of the First World War and through government measures in the intervening years, understood and expected war to mean the total commitment of national productive and labor resources. Notwithstanding the discrepancy between war hypotheses and the real thing, in my view it is clear from the evidence that the British were far ahead of any other nation in planning for total mobilization and certainly many years ahead of the Germans. Britain did not just have a planning advantage (in which the Admiralty had played an absolutely central role). Britain had an attitude advantage. In the worst-case scenario, which came about, it was just as well.

NOTES

1.Russell Grenfell, *Main Fleet to Singapore* (London: Faber and Faber, 1951), 32

2.Ibid., 37.

3.Chatfield, *It Might Happen Again* (London: W. Heinemann, 1946), 5.

4.Ibid., 41.

5.See S. W. Roskill, *Naval Policy between the Wars*, vol. 1 (London: Collins, 1968); M. D. Kennedy, *The Estrangement of Great Britain and Japan 1917-35* (Manchester: Manchester University Press, 1969); J. R. Ferris, *Men, Money and Diplomacy: The Evolution of British Strategic Policy 1919-26* (Ithaca: Cornell University Press, 1989).

6.Willmott, *Empire in the Balance*, 36, 38.

7.Grenfell, *Main Fleet to Singapore*, 40.

8.Barnett, 379.

9.Beatty Papers, vol. 2.

10.Ironically, Beatty had not only commanded American forces in the Grand Fleet but also had an American wife. But it is fair to say that it is virtually impossible, in the Beatty Papers, to find an example of his speaking favorably of Anybody, apart from his unfortunate flag lieutenant. He certainly had no brief for the Japanese; indeed, he seems to have rejected the mechanisms of diplomacy as having any legitimate role at all in national security.

11.Part of what follows, on the link between the Admiralty's strategic concerns and Britain's prewar policy of appeasement, derives from Chapter 17 of my book, *British Seapower and Procurement between the Wars* (Basingstoke, Hants: Macmillan, 1988).

12.A. J. Marder, *Old Friends, New Enemies: The Royal Navy and the Imperial Japanese Navy* (Oxford: Clarenda Press, 1981), 30.

13.3rd DRC, 14 December 1933, CAB[inet] 16/109.

14.2 February 1934, Chatfield Papers, (CHT) 4/4/30. See also, 7 August 1934, Chatfield Papers, CHT 4/4/38; 3rd Defence Requirements Sub-Committee (DRC), CAB 16\109.

15.9(34), 14 March 1934, CAB 23/78.

16.N. H. Gibbs, Grand Strategy, vol. 1, Rearmament Policy (London: HMSO, 1976), 394-95.

17.Ibid., 94. See also C. A. MacDonald, *The United States, Britain and Appeasement 1936-1939*, (1981).

18.37(34), 29 October 1934, CAB 23/80.

19.Gibbs, Grand Strategy, 420. See also Joint Planning Committee (JP) Paper 105, "Defence Plans for War against Germany," 31 October 1935, CAB 55/7.

20.C. Bekker, *Hitler's Naval War* (London: Macdonald, 1974), 27.

21.Roskill, *Naval Policy between the Wars*, vol. 2 (1976), 354.

22.Chatfield to Dreyer, 16 September 1935, Chatfield Papers, CHT 4/4/72.

23.Chatfield Papers, CHT 3/2/192-200.

24.Gibbs, *Grand Strategy*, 398.

25.Martin Gilbert, *The Roots of Appeasement* (London: Weiderfeld and Nicolson, 1966).

26.Margaret George, *The Warped Vision: British Foreign Policy, 1933-1939* (Pittsburg, N. J.: Princeton University Press, 1965), 115-116.

27.Murray Williamson, *The Change in the European Balance of Power, 1938-1939* (Princeton, N. J.: Princeton University Press, 1984), 54.

28.193rd CID, 5 June 1925, CAB 2/4.

29.See Gordon, *British Seapower and Procurement between the Wars* (1988); G. C. Peden, *British Rearmament and the Treasury* (Edinburgh: Scottish Academic Press, 1979). The government's policy of noninterference with normal trade has been cited as evidence of its lack of commitment to rearmament. This is an error. By "normal trade" were meant exporting and the earning of foreign currency (in which Britain's engineering industries played the major part). There are three ways to defeat an island dependent trade: 1) invade it; 2) disrupt its sea communications; and 3) frighten it into diverting its exporting industries to domestic production and then wait while its gold and currency reserves are spent until it has to give up or starve. None of the meticulous plans to convert industry to war production would have been of any use if Britain had started the war without enough reserves to bear the loss of exports for a considerable period. The deliverance of Lend-Lease bears witness to how nearly Britain was defeated by method (3).

30.Gibbs, *Grand Strategy*, 401.

31.19/7/37, PREM[ier's Office], 1/276.

32.Ibid., 27/7/37.

33.Ibid., 28/7/37.

34."Defence Expenditure 1937-9," CAB 21/534.

35.Chatfield to Admiral Drax, 5 November 1937, Chatfield Papers, CHT 3/1/224.

36.10 November 1937, ADM[iralty] 116/3631.

37.JP 279, 16 April 1938, CAB 55/12 36. Marder, *Old Friends, New Enemies*, 40.

38.Marder, *Old Friends, New Enemies*, 40.

39.16(39), 30 March 1939, CAB 23/98.

40.See David Day's (1988) book by that name.

41.Advisory Panel of Industrialists, 26/4/39, SUPP3/40.

42.See Lord Ismay, *Memoirs* (London: Heineman, 1960), 153; also, N. H. Gibbs, *Grand Strategy*, vol. 1, 400.

43.Jon Sumida's recent paper on "The Development of British Fleet Tactics" makes an important contribution to this debate.

44.Board Memoranda, ADM167/104.

45.The 1939 Fighting Instructions, as a matter of interest, owe much more to Beatty's BCFOs than to Jellicoe's GFBOs.

46.Escort Vessels of 1939 Programme, Sketch Design 6 Legend, ADM1/9940.

47.Willmott, *Empires in the Balance*, 58.

48.COS(40)592, CAB 79/6; CAB 65/8.

49.James Rusbridger, *Betrayal at Pearl Harbor: How Churchill Lured Roosevelt into World War II* (New York: Summit Books, 1991).

50.Winston Churchill, *Their Finest Hour* (Boston: Houghton Griffin, 1950), 526.

51.Ibid., 351.

52.Churchill, *The Grand Alliance* (Boston: Houghton Griffin, 1951), 461.

53.Willmott, *Empires in the Balance*, 166.

54.Bennett, 43.

55.David Day, The Great Betrayal: Britain, Australia and the Onset of the Pacific War 1939-42 (North Ryde, Aust: Angus and Robertson, 1988), 10.

56.Hornby, *Factories & Plant* (London: H. M. Stationary Office, 1958).

57.See President's directive of 9th December 1944 to his senior theatre commanders, in C.B. Behren's *Merchant Shipping and the Demands of War* (London: Longman's, Green, 1955), 429.

9

Sea Power For Containment: The U.S. Navy In The Cold War

Colin S. Gray

The intellectual parents of this chapter are the somewhat odd couple of Julian Corbett and John Lehman. There are any number of ways to approach the subject of the U.S. Navy in the Cold War. I have elected, first, to pursue the thought expressed in the title of Chapter 1 of *England in the Seven Years' War*, "The Function of the Fleet in War"[1]; and, second, to explore the question implicit in the title of a slide in "The Maritime Strategy" briefing of 1985, "Objective: Making a Strategic Difference."[2] To conflate the parental influences, the purpose of this inquiry is to explore the function of the U.S. Navy in the Cold War and, above all, to speculate on the "strategic difference" that the navy made to the course and outcome of that conflict.

The Cold War, which now can be viewed as a bounded historical episode with a beginning, a middle, several peak "peril points"[3] and a definitive end, was a great balance-of-power struggle, as were World Wars I and II. Nonetheless, it seems unlikely that official or even semiofficial histories of the Cold War will be commissioned. The several belligerents' series of official histories of round two of the Great War, superior though many of them are, demonstrate all too clearly just how difficult it is to tell an environmentally specific military story in proper joint and combined-arms contexts. This chapter is drafted, therefore, naked of narrative support from a Samuel Eliot Morison of Cold War naval history.[4] However, even if a latter-day Morison had written at express speed a history of the U.S. Navy in the Cold War, such a narrative could provide only limited assistance for the task assumed here. It is important to know what the U.S. Navy actually did, and it is at least interesting to know what the navy planned contingently to do in times of crisis and war. But it is far more important to try to understand the function of the U.S. Navy in national and coalition strategy and the strategic difference that performance of that function did make or might have made.

The question that lies at the heart of this chapter--how important was the U.S. Navy to the course and outcome of the Cold War?--is unusually difficult to address and answer because of the expanding complexity of modern strategy. The question is familiar in kind and in character of difficulty to those who have sought to explain just what it was that Allied sea power contributed to the victories of 1918 and 1945. The British Royal Navy or the U.S. Navy did not win those wars against continentalist Germany--Japan is another matter entirely--but they enabled those wars to be won.[5] Unfortunately for the peace of mind of those who like very tidy analysis and clear judgments, victory in both wars was "enabled" by several contributing factors, the objective rank ordering among which is all but impossible to achieve. When a great chain of strategic-effect logic connects British geostrategic endurance, the U.S. economy, resilience and advantage on the eastern front, success in the Battle of the Atlantic, the defeat of the Luftwaffe over Germany, and the protracted multivectored coup de grace on the ground in 1944-45, just how does one proceed to estimate the relative value of U.S. or Allied sea power to the victory overall? Parallel exercises in strategic analysis can be performed for the Great War of 1914-18 and for the Great War against France. All that distinguishes the Cold War from those other cases are, first, that most of the action remained hypothetical and, second, that the number of claimants for relative strategic glory was larger than ever before. Both at the time and in historical retrospect, the evolving nuclear fact casts a giant shadow over all arguments concerning the "strategic difference" that the U.S. Navy did make, or might have made, in the age of containment.

COLD WAR AND THE CONTAINMENT OF A CONTINENTAL ADVERSARY

It is commonplace to claim that 1945 marked the end of an oceanic phase in the strategic history of U.S. naval power. After 1945, to follow the lead taken by Samuel P. Huntington in his seminal 1954 article,[6] the U.S. Navy assumed a transoceanic character. If that strategic concept means anything, presumably its authority was overtaken by a renewed *oceanic* concern for sea control in the twenty years from the mid-1960s to the mid-1980s, when the Soviet navy plainly emerged as a worthy adversary, even a worthy blue-water adversary. With the demise of the USSR, the relevant concept again is that of transoceanic naval power that will yield strategic effectiveness by exerting influence *from the sea.*[7]

When sea control is the United States' by default, because there is no plausible and competent naval adversary to contest the movement of U.S. ships, there is strictly no need for naval strategy. Indeed, slightly confused naval historians have been known to write articles claiming that "naval strategy is dead."[8] Of course, naval strategy is not dead; it is merely resting in preparation for its next strategic trial. The absence of a first-class, or even a formidable second-class, naval opponent in the late 1940s or the mid-1990s carries no strategic implications for the future.

Some naval theorists and commentators may find the U.S. Navy's post-Cold War blueprint *From the Sea* startlingly, even shockingly, novel. But theorists and commentators whose domain of concern is wider than naval operations should find the new concept less than revolutionary. "It is," as Jan Breemer argues, "unprecedented in that it codifies the decisions by a major naval power to relegate preparations to fight for command of the sea to a secondary concern."[9] Also, we are told, 1990s-style "[n]aval power from the sea signifies a 180-degree reversal of the classic relationship between sea control and power projection."[10] All of which may be true enough, at least for a while. But that argument threatens to obscure what ought to be the ever-dominant strategic point that naval power always, ultimately, has to have meaning for the course of events on land, where people live.

Naval power narrowly, sea power more broadly, most typically plays an enabling role in a noticeably joint and combined ground and military-strategic team endeavor. Naval power, latent and active, contributes to the total strategic effectiveness that our side generates for deterrence or in actual war. Even in the historically exceptional cases wherein the enemy is very significantly maritime in geostrategic character--for example, imperial Japan, notwithstanding that country's continental ambitions--naval success still needs translation into strategic effect for the course of the war as a whole. Given humankind's land-bound states' organization, war at sea can never be synonymous with war.

I have risked making heavy weather of the obvious here, because I suspect that navies as organizations necessarily focused upon maritime activity, and naval theorists and commentators who are understandably fascinated by ships, fleets and their immediate uses are apt to forget why countries finance prowess at sea. The conduct of operations from the sea and active campaign expression of the maritime strategy in a global and protracted all-but-conventional war fundamentally are strategically identical. The enemy lives on land, whether it has a large navy, a small navy or no navy, and whether sea control is a gift or a prize to be fought for. Everybody knows this but tends to forget it. Major, later Major General, Charles E. Callwell, was very much on target when he wrote in 1897: "The effect of sea-power upon land campaigns is in the main strategical. Its influence over the progress of military operations, however decisive this may be, is often only very indirect." [11]

It would be difficult to exaggerate the cumulatively revolutionary impact of the nuclear factor upon strategic possibilities after 1945, but it is not at all difficult to exaggerate the novelty of the strategic challenge posed the United States by the Soviet Union. It is true to claim that the U.S. Navy truly had come of age--won its Trafalgar--in the maritime theater of the Pacific from 1941 to 1945. It is also true to claim that the U.S. Navy was a variably and arguably more or less significant element in the conduct of three great balance-of-power contests against continental foes in Eurasia. Regarded geopolitically and geostrategically and, of course, with a caveat concerning the nuclear "wild card," just what was it about the Cold War that was so novel? The enemy in both world wars, certainly the principal enemy in World War II, fairly effectively comprised landlocked, or landlockable, continental coalitions. The United States contributed vitally via a maritime alliance in both great hot wars to the continental confinement of most of the enemy's power. The two world wars focused on Europe and concluded on land, but there was a most obvious sense in which they both were "decided" at sea--moreover, they could have been decided either way.

If the Cold War entailed, inter alia, the continental containment by a mixed maritime-continental coalition of a presumptively expansionist would-be continental hegemon, does that not sound remarkably familiar? On 4 April 1947, the vice chief of naval operations, Forrest Sherman, advised the secretary of the navy that the Mediterranean should be viewed as "a highway" for the projection of military power "deep into the heart of the landmass of Eurasia and Africa."[12] Sherman's thought reflected a commonsense appreciation of some particular strategic geography that was not radically dissimilar from British perspectives nearly a century before in their "grand raid" on the Crimea,[13] or indeed from some British preferences in the two world wars. Sherman's reference to "deep into the heart of...Eurasia" was a distinctly American strategic-cultural touch, as well as a recognition of the increasing reach of weapons from the sea.

It may well be a weakness of a strategic theorist such as this author to seek and, naturally, discover strategic parallels across time, adversary and technology. Be that as it may, and with such apology as is due to those who are more impressed by the rich particularity of unique historical episodes, almost (which is to say, nuclear matters aside) the most strategically remarkable feature of the Cold War is its lack of remarkability. Yet another great continental foe appeared to be threatening to run amok with unmatchable, or very hard-to-match, land power in peninsular Europe. If continental primacy were permitted to grow into hegemony and then into effective, preclusive empire, the insular power of the West assuredly could face the strategic problem that British geographer Halford J. Mackinder specified in 1919:

> The surrender of the German fleet in the Firth of Forth is a dazzling event, but in all soberness, if we would take the long view, must we not still reckon with the possibility that a large part of the Great Continent might some day be united under single sway, and then an invincible sea-power might be based upon it.[14]

To demonstrate conceptual continuity throughout the century, consider that National Security Council (NSC) 20/4 of 23 November 1948 judged that "Soviet domination of the potential power of Eurasia, whether achieved by armed aggression or by political and subversive means, would be strategically and politically unacceptable to the United States."[15] Forty-one years later President Ronald Reagan stated:

> [t]he first historical dimension of our strategy...is the conviction that the United States' most basic national security interests would be endangered if a hostile state or group of states were to dominate the Eurasian landmass, that area of the globe often referred to as the world's heartland. We fought two world wars to prevent this from occurring.[16]

N. A. M. Rodger has argued contentiously with reference to French naval power in the eighteenth century that the fungibility of defense potential as between different environments tends to be less than some historians--and alarmed commentator-theorists, perhaps--have assumed.[17] In other words, could a continentally undistracted France, or USSR, really generate world-class naval power, as opposed merely to a large number of ships?

Geostrategically viewed and as always thus far in this chapter nuclear issues aside, the Soviet foe in the Cold War was a substantially familiar beast. The assets of North Atlantic Treaty Organization (NATO)-Europe in particular--though not exclusively--as well as contributing the leading "prize" in the game, served as an American beachhead, possibly a springboard for more forward operations. In addition, Allied geography served as a "rimland" barrier helping to landlock the foe. The rimland Allies of the United States in Europe and Asia, therefore, both assisted in keeping the continental menace continentally distracted with unfinished imperial tasks on land and denied that menace ready and reliable maritime access to the wider world.[18]

The geostrategic structure of the Soviet challenge to U.S. statecraft, strategy and defense planning thus has always been plain enough in its essentials. The *possible* contributions of the U.S. Navy to the containment or military defeat of a putatively hostile Soviet Union have never been difficult to identify. The challenge, rather, then and now, is first to try to understand the strategic effect of the latent menace posed by the U.S. Navy upon deterrence, that is, upon the willingness of the intended deterree actually to be deterred. Second, it is necessary to consider what the U.S. Navy should or might have been able to do given the inconvenience both that conflict usually allows some choices to the enemy and that, in the hypothetical war in question, the naval dimension would constitute only a part of the total story. It is possible, but it is neither wise nor useful, to detach discussion of the strategic utility of the U.S. Navy in the Cold War from the whole framework of dynamic national and alliance policy and strategy vis-a-vis a geostrategically, and hence militarily, asymmetrical adversary.

THE NAVY AND THE NUCLEAR NUISANCE

In retrospect, the U.S. Navy from 1945 to 1989 seemed determined to prove that time is a cycle rather than an arrow.[19] To be specific, the navy's strategic preferences, possibly even its dominant operational expectations in the event of major war, had turned almost full circle. The passage of forty-three years, the total (i.e. combined) accumulation of possibly 70,000 nuclear weapons of all kinds and the conduct of a military competition across the board of the armed forces had produced in the mid- to late 1980s a very fair facsimile of the U.S. Navy's strategic concept of operations in global war of 1946-47 vintage.[20] This point is not registered as criticism but rather in some slight awe at the strategic unity of the Cold War era.

Nuclear weapons have been a great nuisance for postwar naval planners and theorists of sea power. At every level of analysis they have appeared to subvert, or at least diminish, the importance of naval power. The new nuclear fact threatened the strategic, operational, tactical and logistic integrity of the world that the navy knew. The advent of the atomic bomb more or less foreclosed preemptively upon what could have been a very vigorous professional and public debate over the relative utility of "strategic" bombing (taking its cues from the voluminous reports of the U.S. Strategic Bombing Survey team). But, in sharp contrast, "the bomb" cast a giant shadow over the strategic relevance of the U.S. Navy, at least of the navy that had just secured one of history's more memorable maritime triumphs. What could be the strategic role of the U.S. Navy in the containment of the USSR in an atomic, then nuclear, age? How could naval power, even sea power, contribute very usefully to the deterrence or conduct of a World War III?

As already noted, for some different reasons, though perhaps with a range of tolerably common instincts, naval theorists and planners in the mid 1940s and the mid 1980s shared a theory of victory in global war. In the 1940s, the U.S. Navy envisaged the conduct of a protracted and barely nuclear global war against the USSR, based on the assumptions of U.S. atomic scarcity and Soviet atomic incompetence. In the 1980s, maritime strategy envisaged a strategic environment rendered permissive for global, protracted, non-nuclear (or barely nuclear) war by the functioning of intrawar deterrence. In other words, the U.S. Navy assumed in the 1940s that not much nuclear war could be waged. In the 1980s, it was hoped--rather than assumed--both that the Soviet enemy would choose not to employ nuclear weapons on a large scale and that NATO's condition defending on the ground in Europe would not be so desperate as to oblige Supreme Allied Commander Europe (SACEUR) to demand prompt escalation. Obviously, the barely nuclear story of the 1940s was more robust than was that of the 1980s. It may be well to recall that the U.S. atomic stockpile comprised only nine (disassembled) weapons in 1946, thirteen in 1947 and fifty in 1948.[21] There was some excuse for defense planners in those years making preparations to refight

World War II, albeit with an atomic adjunct. In the 1940s, the atomic arsenal was too small to guarantee immediate victory in war, even though the enemy would have had no atomic bombs of its own. In the 1980s, the nuclear arsenals of both sides paradoxically were too large to guarantee victory in war; their very size, in fact, was key to their diminishing strategic utility.

From the time when the U.S. Joint Chiefs of Staff, with their Joint War Plans Committee, formally began the processing of developing contingency plans for war with the USSR, that is on 14 December 1945,[22] right through to the close of the Cold War, there was a nuclear shadow over the practicality of a U.S. maritime strategy for major war. That nuclear shadow was but faint in the 1940s, because of the small scale of the U.S. atomic arsenal and the absence of a Soviet atomic arsenal. In the 1950s, however, the relevance of maritime strategy for major war--in a sense that Julian Corbett would approve--was monumentally imperiled principally by the growth in U.S. and British, rather than Soviet, nuclear arsenals--not to mention the development of deliverable thermonuclear weapons. Happily, this is all speculation, but the conduct of a hypothetical World War III in the 1950s would have required little maritime prowess from a United States whose total nuclear arsenal climbed from 450 weapons in 1950 to 18,500 by 1960.[23] Whatever most directly would have shaped the course, and decided the outcome, of a World War III in the mid- to late 1950s and whatever that compound decision would have been (win-lose, lose-win or lose-lose), it would not have been sea power.

Tactically and operationally, the U.S. Navy has always worried about the vulnerability of its ships and task forces to nuclear assault. The vulnerability of the U.S. Navy that really mattered, however, was at the levels of high policy and of strategy. Nuclear weapons could function, so it was argued, as a great equalizer tactically, operationally, strategically and politically. Every such possibility was a menace to the U.S. Navy. Not only did nuclear weapons pose a most severe physical, tactical and operational threat to the integrity of the navy, but also they were allowed to shape the policy and strategy of NATO in such a way that naval power appeared to many people to be unlikely to "work" in wartime in its traditional manner as a great enabling agent. I must emphasize that these are not facts; the war in question was never waged.

I do not wish to reopen tired old debates about NATO strategy, but the West's Cold War coalition, in effect, was a client states' system of security fueled strategically by the military centrepiece of a nuclear guarantee and legitimatized politically by an informal, but fairly authoritative, doctrine of tolerable equality of risk. Virtually all aspects of the transatlantic security nexus of NATO, not even excepting the most obvious geographical one, were unfriendly to the strategic significance of the U.S. Navy. What is the geopolitical and geostrategic basis for this possibly controversial claim of mine?

First, although NATO looked like a maritime coalition and *might* function strategically even in war as a maritime coalition, the geostrategic terms of Soviet-American engagement rendered that possibility ever less probable as the 1950s marched on. To explain, pending the appearance of large numbers of mature and survivable Soviet nuclear forces in the 1960s, the great deterrent to Soviet aggression in Europe was the nuclear sword to be wielded very promptly, indeed principally, by the U.S. Strategic Air Command. The Soviet army held NATO-Europe hostage to U.S. good behavior. U.S. "air-atomic" striking power held the Soviet homeland hostage to Soviet good behavior. Rightly or wrongly, for good or ill, NATO-Europe believed that it could not field the ground and tactical air forces that just might stand a chance of defeating a Soviet invasion.

Second, the same maritime distance that could, in some strategic circumstances, render the outcome of a third Battle of the Atlantic the decisive struggle in war served politically all but to oblige the NATO countries to seek and find a nuclear short-cut to security. Not all Americans have understood that their European allies in the Cold War essentially saw NATO much more as a political guarantee against war than as a practical device for the organization of success in war. In NATO-European eyes, there was always a twofold residual problem of trust vis-a-vis the superpower guardian. Could the United States really be trusted to take the most serious of risks on behalf of societies an ocean away? In addition, could the United States be trusted to conduct military operations in a way that front-line allies would find compatible with their survival interests? Behind this second point lies the central difficulty for . Whereas the proximate "prize" in the Cold War lay on the doorstep of the Soviet army, *the* guardian power and the sources of its strength were thousands of miles distant. Nuclear threat could, or might, perform the military job for deterrence or for defense that geography rendered so difficult for NATO.

Third, nuclear dependence was not only economically and militarily expedient--and apparently just common sense, in the dominant view of the early to mid-1950s--but, also politically most desirable for the cohesion of the alliance. While NATO's ground forces in a forward defense mode should preclude successful aggression by coups de main, should be large enough to compel the aggressor to come in very large numbers and should defend exposed NATO territory briefly, U.S. nuclear forces would be "deciding" the war, by and large, east of the Curzon line. Nuclear dependence, in short, apart from being fashionable and modern, would oblige the guardian superpower to use the crown jewels in its arsenal promptly against the aggressor-superpower's homeland. This was transatlantic "linkage" on a magnificent scale.

Fourth, for reasons both genuine and expedient, NATO-European leaders believed that a nuclear-dependent "military" strategy offered the prospect of a superior quality of deterrence than would a strategy of defense or denial. As Soviet nuclear holdings burgeoned and matured in the late 1950s and the early to mid-1960s, so the United States came to insist upon some apparently radical modification of the military terms of its protection system. The concept of flexible response that was authoritative for NATO from 1967 until 1991 did not, however, quite have the character or the practical implications that its American, as opposed to its European, parents originally had intended.[24] Early McNamara-vintage flexible response envisaged NATO defenses so robust that it would be the USSR that would face the hopefully deterring burden of decision on nuclear escalation. American-style flexible response, the aspiration for the ability to effect an all-conventional defense in Europe, foundered partly on the economic and military demands of the Vietnam War after 1964/65, but even more on the rejection of its premises by NATO-Europe. European leaders neither believed that the nonnuclear defense of NATO-Europe was feasible nor wished it to be so. For the highest quality of an economical deterrence, NATO-Europe was always concerned to ensure that Soviet leaders would not believe that a war they initiated in Europe could be confined to Europe.

Finally, inherent in the structure of any conflict is an enemy with an independent will. User-friendly enemies litter the pages of ill-conceived prewar planning documents. Even if NATO could have imposed a conventional stalemate on Soviet arms, would Moscow have been so chastened as to seek a hasty armistice, or would it have been inclined to up the ante and escalate with nuclear weapons in search of a better verdict at a higher level of violence?

The purpose behind this lengthy discussion of the nuclear element, with its leading implication of a relatively short war, is to explain the political and strategic context for analysis of the role of the U.S. Navy in containment. My central claim is that at the European terminus of the putative transatlantic sea bridge, there was never a determination to provide very seriously for the actual local defense of NATO in Europe. On one hand, NATO's stopping power in Europe was dependent on that transatlantic sea bridges promptly and reliably delivering material support for the continental fight. On the other hand, no less critically, the strategic salience of that sea bridge and, ipso facto, the strategic utility of the naval effort to secure it were dependent on *both* the ability of SACEUR to hold on in peninsular Europe with a coherent "front" (that could make use of transatlantic supply) *and*--just possibly--the willingness of the Soviet Union to tolerate nonnuclear frustration.

Carl von Clausewitz advised:

> The first, the supreme, the most far-reaching act of judgment that the statesman and commander have to make is to establish by that test [of war as an instrument of policy] the kind of war on which they are embarking; neither mistaking it for, nor trying to turn it into, something that is alien to its nature. This is the first of all strategic questions and the most comprehensive.[25]

I am not suggesting that the U.S. Navy or NATO's naval power overall was unimportant to deterrence, or--with the exception of nuclear power projection from the sea--assuredly that it would have been strategically irrelevant in the event of major war. On the contrary, given the historic victory of NATO in the Cold War, the U.S. Navy played its role in implementation of a policy and evolving strategy that functioned more than adequately for deterrence. There are no very substantial grounds for criticism. My concern here with the larger context for naval activity in the Cold War has been triggered by reading histories that succeed in neglecting to tell their readers that, at least with reference to *grande guerre*, the U.S. Navy was committed to mission impossible. NATO's naval assets might secure the mobile zone of sea control necessary to permit the sea bridge to function well enough. But, as suggested previously, that sea bridge would have been constructed in aid of a continental defense that was designed to fail sooner rather than later. Indeed, the very prospect of relatively early failure on the ground provided the critical fuel for Soviet anxiety over NATO's propensity to exercise its nuclear escalatory options. It is no exaggeration to claim that there was intended to be deterrent success in a Soviet estimation of NATO's failure in conventional defense.

It may be objected that a chapter dedicated to consideration of the role and strategic utility of the U.S. Navy in the Cold War should not be pursuing fine points of nuclear theory and deterrence practice. My defense lies in the axiomatic truth well stated by Vice Admiral William Ledyard Rodgers: "In its nature maritime war is secondary to that on land."[26] Whatever the U.S. Navy attempted in aid of containment in the Cold War, the environment of ultimate reference was the land. With respect to the principal prize in the contest and the principal battlefield, that is, peninsular NATO-Europe, the U.S. Navy was operating in support of a military effort on land that was nuclear-dependent--and hence short-war likely--by geostrategical circumstance, by political design and by menace of Soviet decision.

It is tempting to retreat into empiricism and tell the story of U.S. Navy planning endeavors and of U.S. Navy activities, passing in silence over the political-military contextual questions that yield strategic meaning to that planning and activity. The U.S. Navy's activities in the Cold War, no matter how challenging and interesting in themselves, have strategic meaning for the success of containment only in relation to national and alliance performance overall.

THE U.S. NAVY AND THE COMPLEXITY OF DETERRENCE AND WAR

It may not be politic, but it is certainly accurate, to claim that in the Cold War the U.S. Navy was committed to support a coalition's continental defense effort that most members intended to fail militarily relatively early in trial by battle. Also, the U.S. Navy was committed to an important and arguably redundant mission of long-range nuclear bombardment as an integral component, or "leg," to what became known after 1960 as the strategic forces' "triad" (of long-range manned bombers, Inter-Continental Ballistic Misslies (ICBMs) and Sea-Launch Ballistic Missiles (SLBMs) on Ballistic Missile Firing Submarines (SSBNs). To cite these apparent limitations, however, of a land campaign intended to "fail," and of a strategic "deterrent" redundantly contributed for synergistic reasons (inter alia), is not, not even by implication, to pass negative judgment on the quality and quantity of the U.S. Navy's contribution to the policy of containment.

If it were merely politically correct to cite the growing complexity of modern strategy, it would be an elementary matter to cut through the nonsense and identify the essentials. Unfortunately, this is one case, at least, wherein the cliche holds true. The dimensions of war and deterrence keep expanding; indeed, they keep expanding into the zone where one cannot help but inquire whether the subject of this chapter really has historical integrity. This is a "joint" and "combined" world. At the levels of political and strategic logic and activity, the world persists without significant change, but the military referents for that political and strategic energy have exploded into an ever-increasing complexity.

In 1900, the strategic world had but two dimensions, the land and the surface of the sea. Since 1900, three previously militarily unexploited environments have staked their dynamic claims in the joint arena--the air environment, the space environment and the electromagnetic spectrum. Virtually as a "wild card" quite distinct from these environmentally focused forms of military power, the nuclear factor erupted as an element that had potentially radical implications for activity in each of the geographically defined dimensions of conflict.

It would be an understatement to note that there is no autonomous U.S. naval history of containment and successful deterrence in the Cold War. Quite aside from the obvious points that the Cold War provided only hypothetical armed conflict (against the USSR, at least)--meaning that there is an insoluble problem of negative evidence, and both a joint and a combined arms team for victory--high policy and overall military strategy constrained most severely what the U.S. Navy achieved and might have attempted.

Rarely have navies been unleashed to deter war or, if need be, to wage it in ways and for objectives selected by themselves with no practical need to consider other instruments of grand strategy. Rarely, if ever, though, has a navy been so politically constrained, militarily shepherded and menaced by what amounted to non-linear threats to strategic effectiveness, as was the U.S. Navy in the Cold War.

THE U.S. NAVY IN THE COLD WAR

It is necessary to begin this brief review of U.S. naval activity in the Cold War with the reminders both that the deterrence story is complex and ultimately indeterminate, and that the whole enterprise, taken as a whole, was a triumph for steadiness of purpose, persistence and prudent statecraft. This is a success story. There is no way in which the contribution of the U.S. Navy to NATO's success in the Cold War can be measured. We will each have our opinion on whether or not the USSR really needed to be deterred, or how much deterring it needed, and which threat or threats made the most strategic difference to Soviet minds. Suffice it to say that just as NATO's total blend of negative and positive sanctions self-evidently performed well enough to do the deterrence job that might most have needed performance, so also the U.S. Navy contributed well enough on the tasks it was assigned. The greatest of NATO's strategic triumphs lay in battles, campaigns and wars *not* waged. It is a little testing even of the methodology of social scientists to show how well the U.S. Navy really performed in wars that did not occur. Some war-game aficionados are wont to believe that they have cracked the code of future war, but I am skeptical.

When one considers the tricky questions of the roles and significance of the U.S. Navy (or Air Force or Army) in the Cold War, rapidly one discovers that there are two questions, not one, in need of answer. Moreover, as usual, the slightly concealed second question can prove the killer for otherwise tidy analysis. The questions are, first, what did the United States and NATO require of the U.S. Navy? What was it asked or told to do? So far so good; the question is straightforward, as should be the answer. We can discuss merrily how the U.S. Navy kept, or planned to keep, the sea-lanes open for friendly forces and shipping-- positive and negative sea control, in other words. Unfortunately, the second question is more stretching of the evidence, intellect and judgment: how important were, or might have been, the roles assigned the U.S. Navy? Brutally stated, even if the North Atlantic sea bridge could be constructed and kept open, did that prospect matter (1) for pre-war Alliance cohesion or (2) for pre- and intrawar deterrence?

This chapter is not so much an inquiry into what the U.S. Navy did, or tried to do and how well it did it. My purpose, rather, is to speculate in the murky waters of strategic significance. The distinction is between tactical proficiency and strategic utility. In this case, however, even the classical Clausewitzian dividing line between tactics and strategy does not work very well, because strategic utility was not, à la Clausewitz, the realm of "the use of an engagement for the purpose of the war,"[27] but instead the use of *hypothetical* engagement for the overriding purpose of deterrence in Cold War. Because the U.S. Navy, powerful institution of state though it is, does not exist to serve its own ends, the quality of external integrity, not internal integrity, of its contributions to success in the Cold War must contribute our center of gravity here.

Those of us who have plowed the barren fields of strategic nuclear weaponry, nuclear deterrence theory, doctrine for nuclear employment and nuclear war plans occasionally are reminded that great intellectual debates and exciting newspaper stories tend to imply more capability for agility than the real-world referents actually enjoy. The details of fashion in policy explanation, of our forces and Soviet forces and, of course, of targeting designs are all in near-constant flux at the margin. But the continuities tend to be massive and tolerably immune to shifting political, intellectual and doctrinal currents. There are good reasons this should be so. Moreover, I suggest that much the same should be said for maritime strategy and how a first-class navy contributes within the framework of maritime strategy.

Environmentally focused doctrine for the navy, as for the air force, and one day for a space force, for parallels, has to respect the opportunities and limitations specific to each environment. Clausewitz may have made only two references, en passant, to naval matters in *On War*,[28] but his stricture on the subject of the "grammar," as contrasted with the policy "logic," of war is entirely well taken.[29] The geography behind, as well as under and over, strategy, albeit modified in its significance by changing technology, still broadly shapes to enduring effect the missions that different kinds of armed forces can perform or perform well.

It follows that there is structural continuity, or nearly so, in navy missions throughout the Cold War, indeed, throughout history. In every decade of the Cold War, the U.S. Navy either had, or--in one case-- aspired to have, four missions. Those missions were *sea power* (positive and negative), *power projection*, *presence* and *strategic deterrence* (the threat of long-range--by and large, nuclear--bombardment of the shore). The difficulty of performance of these missions and the priorities among them did, of course, alter over time. The navy's mission area was, thus, stable in identity but fluctuating in its internal boundaries. Turning to the external significance of the U.S. Navy's missions, severally and all together they, too, altered over time as the NATO land and nuclear stories waxed and waned and waxed again and as the enemy's preferences and capabilities appeared noticeably cumulatively to shift. Therefore, two principal dimensions organize discussion of this subject: an evolving balance of effort among stable, broad mission areas and an evolving strategic meaning to the U.S. Navy's performance of those missions.

The 1940s

In the second half of the 1940s, the U.S. Navy played deterrent and prospective war-fighting roles essentially all but identical to those so recently performed in World War II. Strategic context is almost everything. The U.S. Navy, with noteworthy British assistance, again would connect a "victim Europe" with the war-making potential of the world beyond the seas. The "pincher" war plan of 1946 envisaged the pinching of an expanded Soviet continental domain on its very far-flung maritime flanks, especially to the south. Collectors of those historical parallels that are driven by geostrategic logic should compare the "pincher" vision with the metaphorical global-scale "callipers" that griped the USSR in the 1985 briefing on the U.S. Navy's maritime strategy.[30] As a World War II with a few, then some, atomic weapons added, World War III in the 1946-49 period would have seen the U.S. Navy engaged principally in the North Atlantic, but not the Arctic, and the east-central Mediterranean rather than the Pacific. The navy would have sought to attack the large Soviet submarine fleet "at home" and, by all prudent means, discourage it from perilous ventures on to the shipping lanes vital to the U.S.-United Kingdom sea bridge. The navy's duties vis-a-vis land battle in continental Europe would have been focused to assist and effect a successful replay of Operation Dynamo of May 1940. It seems improbable, however, that Anglo-American forces or residual other friendly forces in Europe, would have survived a Soviet assault in good-enough condition to be rescued from Dunkirk after the fashion of 1940.

In the 1940s, the U.S. Navy, in the eastern Mediterranean in particular, provided tangible, visible evidence that the United States cared about security in Europe. The navy could not defend Europe, in the short run could not even enable friendly land and land-based air forces to defend Europe, but its strategic paramountcy at sea all but guaranteed to a Soviet aggressor a long war and a global war against most of the world's economic assets in an increasingly atomic, and one-sidedly atomic, conflict. The navy itself could not deliver "the bomb" in most of this period. That fact carried some awesomely negative implications for the future political and strategic clout of the service, but the atomic arsenal was so modest and probably technically unreliable in these early postwar years that for a while, in reality, it scarcely mattered.

The 1950s

In this decade the Soviet threat to Western sea-lanes was large in numbers of submarines but both operationally unconvincing and overshadowed by the centrality of nuclear weapons in strategy. The U.S. Navy engaged in political "suasion" in its several forms throughout the decade[31] globally and from 1950 to 1953 reminded anyone in need of reminding that it is only within the framework of maritime strategy that the United States could engage in substantial hostilities abroad (except in Canada or Mexico). The navy enabled South Korea to be defended, just as it was to enable the postponement of North Vietnam's victory for a decade from 1965 to 1975.

Of geostrategic necessity, U.S. and British strategy in the mid- to late 1940s would have been of a maritime character. The continental story had to be subordinate and was distinctly tenuous. In the 1950s, however, especially after the spring of 1953, both U.S. and then NATO strategy embraced the law of the emerging instrument and made a virtue of the expedient availability of a newly abundant supply of nuclear weaponry. U.S. statecraft in the 1950s actually employed the framework of maritime strategy. The containing "rimland" of Eurasia was supported credibly by American sea power. Whether in action projecting power against the shore, as in Korea and after a fashion in Lebanon in 1958, or threatening to do so, as in Indochina in 1954 and off Quemoy and Matsu in 1955 and 1958, the U.S. Navy seemingly was ubiquitous as the agile military instrument of choice for the thwarting of continentalist Communist machinations.

With respect to the Great War that might occur, however, the record is a mixed one. The navy succeeded in jumping on board the atomic-offensive bandwagon. A. J. *Savage* auxiliary jet, heavy-attack aircraft, capable of carrying one atomic bomb, joined the fleet in September 1949, and the outbreak of the Korean War on 25 June 1950 triggered approval by the Truman administration of the first of the *Forrestal*-class supercarriers. In the 1950s, carrier aviation joined the air force in commitment to the nuclear offensive, submarine-launched, nuclear-armed *Regulus* cruise missiles became operational (in 1956) and *Polaris* A-1 SLBMs went on patrol after an amazingly truncated research, development and test program of only four and a half years' duration (1956-60).[32]

The navy in the 1950s believed that it had to be an integral part of the most glamorous and important national military mission, of nuclear deterrence. Also, the navy was determined to make sure that Soviet naval assets would be promptly serviced by U.S. nuclear striking power, and it even had some aspirations for seizing the nuclear retaliatory (for deterrence) mission all for itself with the impressively invulnerable SSBN program. Notwithstanding the growing number of seaborne platforms with nuclear strike, or strike-back, roles, the strategic story of the 1950s with reference to a World War III, was, overall, not of high significance for the navy or for a maritime cast to strategy. After 1953, U.S. and NATO strategy for the protection of the alliance in Europe was superficially continental but was pervasively nuclear in character. Neither maritime nor naval strategy would be likely to count for much when NATO's forward defenses were intended to register the unmistakable fact of a large attack and then hold on as best they could while medium- and long-range bombers transformed the USSR into "a smoking, radiating ruin at the end of two hours."[33] Moreover, even as the ever-more-nuclear context appeared to signal the demise of naval and maritime strategy for general war, so the navy's contribution to the nuclear deterrence and strike mission was dwarfed by the post-Korean expansion of the Strategic Air Command. In December 1960, for example, of 3,200 SIOP-assigned nuclear bombs and warheads, the Navy only had 32 (with SLBMs on board the first two SSBNs).[34]

The 1960s

In the 1960s, the U.S. Navy again demonstrated its indispensability for the conduct of regional or local warfare far overseas. Even all too close to home, in the Caribbean, the navy showed in October 1962 that its unparalleled ability to loiter with menace provided nearly desperate policymakers with policy choices worth their weight in plutonium.

Paradoxically, the 1960s witnessed both a growth in alliance strategic demand for the services of the U.S. Navy in the event of crisis or war in Europe and the intersection of trends that made it difficult for the navy to perform well. It is no great exaggeration to argue that the significance of the U.S. Navy in general war is related inversely to the promptness, scope and scale of nuclear-weapon employment. Soviet success in fielding an ultimately impressive mix of reasonably second-strike survivable nuclear armed forces by the early to mid-1960s, as well as the *absolute* quantity of damage that they threatened, drove American theorists and policymakers to insist upon a less immediately nuclear cast to Allied strategy.

It was a rule of NATO strategy in the Cold War that the United States, as *the* protecting power, could set the military terms of risk upon which protection was offered. It was also a rule of NATO strategy in the Cold War that the European Allies, having obligingly said "yes, in principle," to the latest American strategic fancy, were at liberty to resist the new American idea in policy preparation and practice. In the 1960s, the pure vein of American thought on a more flexible response was, as noted already, in favor of a NATO capability to wage a successfully all-conventional defense in peninsular Europe. Truly, this was "back to the future" with a vengeance. NATO-Europe was not inclined to offer itself as a conventional battlefield a outrance, always supposing that the USSR would agree to lose a nonnuclear war without rolling the nuclear dice.

The strategic concept of flexible response that NATO endorsed at long last in 1967 was a light-year removed from its American provenance, but still it did lay prospectively larger burdens upon alliance sea power. The new concept, enshrined in the document MC14/3, amounted to an attempt at more credible deterrence via escalation control in the form of linked plateaus of NATO ability to wage ever more violent conflict. NATO would seek to conduct a robust conventional defense on a scale, and long enough, hopefully to cause the Soviet aggressor to cease and desist, as the prospect of battlefield and then theater nuclear use became more likely. Similarly, NATO's concept intended that the measured use of battlefield and theater nuclear weapons would promote second thoughts in Moscow concerning the probability that the next and final stage of escalation was imminent. Publicly, NATO aspired to wage a fairly successful conventional defense for a few months; privately, it aspired to wage such a defense for a few weeks; and very privately it hoped to be able to effect a prenuclear defence for a few days. Formally, however, NATO navies now were obliged to prepare to wage quite protracted war at sea, given the ambitious goals set for conventional continental resistance in Europe.[35]

Trend one, then, was toward a renewed strategic significance for naval and maritime strategy imposed by NATO's adoption at U.S. insistence, of at least a variant of (less nuclear) flexible response. Unfortunately, trends two and three did not permit a reliable high-quality U.S. Navy performance on trend one. Trend two for the U.S. Navy was the distinctly mixed blessing of the cumulatively very impressive emergence of a genuinely first class, almost--though not quite--balanced Soviet fleet. The blessing was mixed in that, although Admiral Sergei G. Gorshkov's largely very new Soviet navy was the enemy from "central casting" of which naval planners dream, it was also sufficiently formidable as to cast into some question the ability of the U.S. Navy promptly to enforce a positive sea control, let alone be at liberty to indulge imaginatively in power projection. The third trend, no less disturbing, pertained to the size and quality of the U.S. Navy vis-a-vis its overly burdensome NATO tasks and the growing menace posed by the Soviet navy. The problem, simply, was that the 1960s were the last hurrah for the ships of the U.S. Navy constructed in such large numbers in the World War II construction programs and, in many cases, substantially refitted at intervals since that time. The problem of block aging of the fleet was compounded massively by year-after-year depredations upon procurement budgets effected by the current war expenditures in Vietnam.

The 1970s

The early 1970s witnessed a U.S. Navy profoundly unsure at its higher levels of its ability to prevail in its preferred style over a now unquestionably worthy Soviet naval adversary. For example, when writing to Secretary of Defense Melvin Laird in 1971 with regard to the fiscal year 1973 budget, Chief of Naval Operations Admiral Elmo R. Zumwalt, Jr., offered this pessimistic assessment:

> In my judgment...FY70 forces gave us a 55 percent probability of success if we became involved in a conflict at sea with the Soviet Union. . . . While I judge our naval forces today have only a 35 percent chance in an engagement with the Soviet Union, that level of confidence is reduced to 20 percent based on the potential consequences of the Tentative Fiscal Guidance. *It is perfectly clear that we are unable to support the fighting of a war overseas by the U.S. or allied forces should the Soviet Union challenge the U.S. for control of the seas.*[36]

Zumwalt's concerns reinforced the conclusions reached in a 1968-69 SACLANT study for NATO's Secretary-General Manlio Brosio of the NATO-Warsaw Pact naval balance. The Superior Allied Commander Atlantic (SACLANT)/Brosio study predicted NATO victory at sea, but only following an extensive and difficult campaign. Study after study in the first half of the 1970s expressed some measure of anxiety over the extant trend in combat prowess at sea.

The temper of the period with reference to possible land warfare in Europe continued to favor efforts to secure an all- conventional phase to operations, albeit in a context of growing uncertainty about the early wartime viability of the North Atlantic lifeline. The depth and breadth of Soviet nuclear modernization programs in all environments and for all ranges disinclined NATO governments to believe that any deterrent or war-fighting advantage could be secured by a return to the previous nuclear enthusiasm. U.S. and NATO nuclear modernization programs in the 1970s were viewed more as offsets to neutralize potential sources of Soviet leverage, than to regain the means for a lost measure of escalation dominance.

The 1970s began on a low note of professional anxiety for the U.S. Navy, as a less nuclear-dependent national and NATO strategy appeared to place more emphasis upon sea-lane security just when external and domestic threats to U.S. naval effectiveness were growing. However, the decade that began with a whimper went out with a bang. The successor Chiefs of naval operations (CNOs) to Zumwalt, Admirals James Holloway and Thomas B. Hayward, were not pessimistic over the future of the navy's relative combat prowess or potential strategic utility to nation and alliance. The defensiveness that suffused the Jimmy Carter administration's approach to the navy's tasks--and, indeed, that permeated U.S. Army doctrine in mid-decade--was rejected by the naval service. The somewhat overheralded maritime strategy of the 1980s had its immediate provenance in Pacific fleet and Navy Department studies in 1977-78.[37] The more distant provenance of much of the 1980s maritime strategy can, of course, be traced back intellectually first to the Forrest Sherman era of the late 1940s and very early 1950s. More distant still, the maritime strategy derived its inspiration from the plans and efforts of those leaders and theorists down the centuries--from Pericles, through Marlborough and Anson, to Corbett and Churchill--who sought to fashion maritime strategy for the effective conduct of war against great continental foes.

With reference to the strategic (nuclear) deterrence mission in the 1970s, modernization of the SLBM inventory with the Multiple Independent Reentry Vehicles (MIRV) *Poseidon* C-3 was important for target coverage and possibly as discouragement to Soviet breakout from the 1972 Anti-Ballistic Missile (ABM) Treaty, but really it provided insurance upon insurance. The strategic forces dyad of land-based ICBMs and long-range manned bombers already posed impossible problems in attack timing for the increasingly hard-target-counterforce capable Soviet strategic forces, even without the additional impossibility of neutralizing the U.S. SSBN force promptly and comprehensively. It was prudent to maintain a strategic forces' triad, a judgment vindicated by Soviet structural imitation. It is far from clear that the superpower peace needed to be kept in an active sense in the 1970s; but even if it did, there is no basis for claiming that the U.S. Navy's unique contribution to deterrence made the strategic difference in favor of peace. That is not a criticism of the SSBN/SLBM force in the 1970s.

The 1980s

We are much too close to the event to be able to offer confident judgment on why the Soviet imperium collapsed late in 1989, to be followed by the collapse of the USSR and even some of the Russian Empire over the next two years. It is important to recognize, however, that the U.S. Navy contributed arguably significantly, albeit not measurably, first, to the Soviet recognition of systemic crisis and second, to the ill-conceived and uncontrollable Gorbachevian halfhearted reforms that wrecked what they were intended to preserve.

The U.S. Navy's maritime strategy that appeared glossily in January 1986 in a "Supplement" to the U.S. Naval Institute *Proceedings*[38] had lurked in embryo in option 3 of "Seaplan 2000" of March 1978.[39] The strategy was rooted both in profound naval distaste for, and distrust in, the defensive approach to sea control that the Carter Administration favored and in the conviction that the world's premier navy should be able to make a strategic contribution to the deterrence or conduct of major war beyond the safeguarding of transatlantic seaborne transportation. In short, the U.S. Navy was disinclined to confine its strategic ambitions to the role of a maritime railroad company.

To my mind, at least, the many authors of the maritime strategy who asked the right central question--how can U.S. and NATO naval power make a strategic difference in a Great War against a continental enemy that has a large and competent navy?--came up with quite unremarkable commonsense *notional* answers and perfectly matched the political needs of the decade.[40] Consider the context. The maritime strategy and its umbilically connected demand for a 600-ship, 15-carrier-centered navy were the naval thrust of a generally newly aggressive American stance on East-West relations. The U.S. Army, under the influence of reform-minded theorists of operational art for decisive maneuver, was advancing what came to be known as AirLand Battle doctrine, while the administration at the highest level was recommending the overturn of the stale old orthodoxy that condemned strategic defense as destabilizing.[41]

The maritime strategy caught the Soviet attention and was all the more credible and formidable for reason of its broad political-military context. It was entirely plausible as the maritime element to the general "America is back" theme that was so publicly bruited by the actor/president Ronald Reagan. The maritime strategy was almost as controversial as the Strategic Defense Initiative (SDI) or, indeed, as Reagan's defense buildup overall. Regarded as political theater for Cold War strategic effect, however, these controversial ideas and programs arguably proved terminal in their consequences for Soviet statecraft.

At the time, the central strategic premise of the maritime strategy, that the Soviet Union would accede to the conduct of a protracted, global and nonnuclear war, certainly seemed to be in line with the visible and audible trend in authoritative Soviet defense thinking. In retrospect, we should be exceedingly grateful that the fairly heroic assumptions underpinning the maritime strategy were never put to the test.

CONCLUSIONS

What can be said by way of conclusions about "sea power for containment: the U.S. Navy in the Cold War?" Alas, I can offer only five surprise-free Parthian shots.

First, the U.S. Navy, as by far the most potent element in Western sea power, bound together what amounted to a global maritime coalition. From its central home base in North America, the U.S. Navy truly connected the Pacific and the Atlantic, the Sea of Japan and the Mediterranean. The transportation of heavy or bulky goods from North America had to be effected by sea, and the sea was safe for such transportation only because it was protected by superior naval force. Much of the "sharp end" of truly global strategy, with its swing-force referents, was naval. Truly the sea lanes of the world were the interior lines of communication of the Western coalition.

Second, the U.S. Navy in the Cold War did what a great navy always has done; it was present, forward, as sometimes visible, but unobtrusive, evidence of U.S. strategic concern (not necessarily political commitment). The Soviet Union was contained by a policy and strategy that effected its landlocking in Europe and Asia. The U.S. Navy, as an instrument of support for diplomacy and as a tool of choice for crisis response, played the role required of it to keep Soviet power and influence generally continentally confined.

Third, the U.S. Navy played sea power's traditional strategic "enabling" role, even vis-a-vis the calculated and unintended uncertainties of NATO's strategic concept of flexible response. Since sea control was never actively at issue in the North Atlantic in the decades of interest to this chapter, there can be no conclusive judgment on the navy's hypothetical military performance. Nonetheless, whatever was needed for deterrence by way of Soviet anticipation of U.S. naval prowess in sea control plainly was provided in adequate measure.

Fourth, the scale of, and balance within, the U.S. Navy allowed U.S. administrations responsibly to think and plan globally for the active conduct of cold or hot war. Very prominent among the distinctions of U.S. superpower was, and remains, its unique global military reach. That global reach is maritime in character for any operation with dimensions beyond those of a raid.

Finally, I am obliged to acknowledge yet again that the strategic contribution made by the U.S. Navy toward the containment of the Soviet Union in the Cold War is indeterminable with any precision. The navy was a team player, albeit often more of a team player than it would have preferred to be. I find modest consolation in the fact that the relative strategic contribution of naval power to victory in both the two hot world wars of this century, as well as in the great war during the French Revolution and Empire, is at least as uncertain as is the case of the recent Cold War.

NOTES

1.Julian S. Corbett, *England in the Seven Years' War: A Study in Combined Strategy*, vol 1 (London: Longmans, Green, 1918; first pub. 1907), Chapter 1.

2.House of Representatives, Committee on Armed Services, Seapower and Strategic and Critical Materials Subcommittee, *The 600-Ship Navy and the Maritime Strategy, Hearings*, June and September 1985, 99th Cong., 1st sess. (Washington, D.C.: Government Printing Office, 1986), 67.

3.I am grateful to Grant T. Hammond, *Plowshares into Swords: Arms Races in International Politics, 1840-1991* (Columbia: University of South Carolina Press, 1993), 254-55.

4. The closest approximation to date must be Robert W. Love, Jr., *History of the U.S. Navy, Volume 2, 1942-1991* (Harrisburg, P.A.: Stackpole Books, 1992).

5. An argument I develop in *The Leverage of Sea Power: The Strategic Advantage of Navies in War* (New York: Free Press, 1992), Chapters 6-8.

6. Samuel P. Huntington, "National Policy and the Transoceanic Navy," U.S. Naval Institute *Proceedings* 80 (May 1954): 483-93.

7. *From the Sea: Preparing the Naval Service for the 21st Century* (Washington, D.C.: Department of the Navy, September 1992).

8. Jan S. Breemer, "Naval Strategy Is Dead," U.S. Naval Institute *Proceedings* 120 (February 1994): 49-53.

9. Ibid., 52.

10. Ibid.

11. C. E. Callwell, *The Effect of Maritime Command on Land Campaigns Since Waterloo* (Edinburgh: William Blackwood and Sons, 1897), 29.

12. Quoted in Melvyn P. Leffler, *A Preponderance of Power: National Security, the Truman Administration and the Cold War* (Stanford, Calif.: Stanford University Press, 1992), 144.

13. See Andrew D. Lambert, *The Crimean War: British Grand Strategy, 1853-56* (Manchester, U.K.: Manchester University Press, 1990).

14. Halford J. Mackinder, *Democratic Ideals and Reality* (New York: Norton, 1962; first pub. 1942), 70.

15. Thomas H. Etzold and John Lewis Gaddis, eds., *Containment: Documents on American Policy and Strategy. 1945-1950* (New York: Columbia University Press, 1978), 208.

16. Ronald Reagan, *National Security Strategy of the United States* (Washington, D.C.: Government Printing Office, 1988), 1.

17. N. A. M. Rodger, "The Continental Commitment in the Eighteenth Century," in Lawrence Freedman, Paul Hayes, and Robert O'Neill, eds., *War, Strategy, and International Politics: Essays in Honour of Sir Michael Howard* (Oxford: Clarendon Press, 1992), 39-55.

18. I pursued this thesis in my *Maritime Strategy, Geopolitics, and the Defense of the West* (New York: National Strategy Information Center, 1986).

19. Stephen Jay Gould, *Time's Arrow, Time's Cycle* (Cambridge: Harvard University Press, 1987).

20. See Michael A. Palmer, *Origins of the Maritime Strategy: American Naval Strategy in the First Postwar Decade, Contributions to Naval History*, No. 1 (Washington, D.C.: Naval Historical Center, Department of the Navy, 1988).

21. David Alan Rosenberg, "U.S. Nuclear War Planning, 1945-1960," in Desmond Ball and Jeffrey Richelson, eds., *Strategic Nuclear Targeting* (Ithaca, N.Y.: Cornell University Press, 1986), 38.

22. Palmer, *Origins*, 22.

23. Thomas B. Cochran, William M. Arkin and Milton M. Hoenig, *Nuclear Weapons Databook, Volume 1, U.S. Nuclear Forces and Capabilities* (Cambridge, Mass.: Ballinger, 1984), 15.

24. Superior discussion is provided in David N. Schwartz, *NATO's Nuclear Dilemmas* (Washington, D.C.: Brookings Institution, 1983); J. Michael Legge, *Theater Nuclear Weapons and the NATO Strategy of Flexible Response, R-2964-FF* (Santa Monica, Calif.: Rand Corporation, 1983).

25. Carl von Clausewitz, *On War*, eds. and trans. Michael Howard and Peter Paret (Princeton: Princeton University Press, 1976; first pub. 1832), 88-89.

26. William Ledyard Rodgers, *Greek and Roman Naval Warfare: A Study of Strategy, Tactics, and Ship Design from Salamis* (480 B.C.) to Actium (31 B.C.) (Annapolis,: Naval Institute Press, 1937), 5.

27. Clausewitz, *On War*, 177.

28. Ibid., 220, 634.

29. Ibid., 605.

30. Roger W. Barnett and Jeffrey G. Barlow, "The Maritime Strategy of the U.S. Navy: Reading Excerpts," in Colin S. Gray and Roger Barnett, eds., *Seapower and Strategy* (Annapolis: Naval Institute Press, 1989), 325-27; and Palmer, *Origins*, Chapter 3.

31. See Edward N. Luttwak, *The Political Uses of Sea Power, Studies in International Affairs, No. 23* (Baltimore: Washington Center of Foreign Policy Research, School of Advanced International Studies, Johns Hopkins University, 1974).

32. The development story of *Polaris* and its successors is well told in Graham Spinardi, *From Polaris to Trident: The Development of U.S. Fleet Ballistic Missile Technology* (Cambridge: Cambridge University Press, 1994).

33. David Alan Rosenberg, "A Smoking Radiating Ruin at the End of Two Hours: Documents of American Plans for Nuclear War with the Soviet Union, 1954-1955," *International Security* 6 (winter 1981-82): 3-38.

34. Desmond Ball, "The Development of the SIOP, 1960-1983", in Ball and Richelson, *Strategic Nuclear Targeting*, 57.

35. See Joel J. Sokolsky, "Anglo-American Maritime Strategy in the Era of Flexible Response, 1960-80," in John B. Hattendorf and Robert S. Jordan, eds., *Maritime Strategy and the Balance of Power: Britain and America in the Twentieth Century* (New York: St. Martin's Press, 1989), 304-29; Joel J. Sokolsky, *Sea-Power in the Nuclear Age: The United States Navy and NATO, 1949-80* (Annapolis: Naval Institute Press, 1991), 112-16.

36. Quoted in Barnett and Barlow, "Maritime Strategy," 336.

37. See John B. Hattendorf, "The Evolution of the Maritime Strategy: 1977-1987," *Naval War College Review*, 41 (summer 1988): 7-28; Frederick H. Hartmann, *Naval Renaissance: The U.S. Navy in the 1980's* (Annapolis: Naval Institute Press, 1990).

38.James D. Watkins et al., *The Maritime Strategy*, Supplement to U.S. Naval Institute *Proceedings* 112 (January 1986).

39.Barnett and Barlow, "Maritime Strategy," 341.

40.The best explanation of the maritime strategy is Norman Friedman, *The U.S. Maritime Strategy* (London: Jane's, 1988).

41.The outstanding interpretive treatment is Samuel P. Huntington, "U.S. Defense Strategy: The Strategic Innovations of the Reagan Years," in Joseph Kruzel, ed., *American Defense Annual, 1987-1988* (Lexington, Mass.: Lexington Books, 1987), 23-43.

10

The Future Of Sea Power

Holger H. Herwig

At first glance, the title of this volume, *Navies and Global Defense*, may seem strange, if not downright oxymoronic. Anyone who has studied what William L. Langer half a century ago dubbed "the age of navalism" inaugurated by Alfred Thayer Mahan and the host of disciples who sought to realize Mahan's notion of sea power and sea control will see navies not as *defensive*, but rather as *offensive*, instruments of statecraft. Indeed, Andrew Lambert's superb study of the Royal Navy between 1856 and 1914 squarely addresses concepts such as "naval dominance," "war fighting" and "offensive capacity" and forcefully reminds us that the Royal Navy was much more than the celebrated "shield of the empire," as Arthur J. Marder put it. Donald Schurman eloquently writes about "imperial sea power" and passionately reminds us of the "maritime element in imperial history." Kenneth Hagan, citing Secretary of the Navy Benjamin F. Tracy in the 1890s, points out that while the U.S. Navy was always "defensive in principle," concurrently it was "offensive in operations."

This should not be surprising. The more pithy citations pertaining to naval activity that have come down to us since antiquity stress the ability of navies to dominate and control or, conversely, to deny to others what Mahan called the "well-worn paths" of the world's maritime "wide common." Cicero, for example, citing Themistocles, assured his fellow Romans "that whoso can hold the sea has command of the situation." Louis XIV is frequently credited with Lemierre's dictum that the "trident of Neptune is the sceptre of the world." Britain's most celebrated first sea lord in modern times, Admiral Sir John "Jacky" Fisher, foreshadowing the U.S. Navy's 1980s concept of power projection "from the sea," bluntly assured Englishmen before the Great War that the army "should be regarded as a projectile to be fired by the Navy."[1] Who does not instantly recall Winston S. Churchill's dire reminder from the First World War that Admiral Sir John Jellicoe, commander of the Royal Navy's Grand Fleet, was "the only man on either side who could lose the war in an afternoon?"[2]

But there were also more subtle historians of sea power from antiquity to the present. Thucydides, in defining the objectives of Athens's ill-fated Sicilian expedition, has Alcibiades describe sea power in what several authors in this volume term the "British way in warfare": "Our navy will enable us safely to stay, if successful, or to withdraw, as we shall be superior at sea to all the Siceliots put together."[3] Sir Francis Bacon put forth a similar interpretation of English sea power during the reign of Queen Elizabeth I: "He that commands the Sea is at great liberty, and may take as much and as little of the Warre as he will."[4] There, in a nutshell, is the intellectual path that eventually led to Sir Julian Corbett's definition of the "British way in warfare," which centered on concepts such as the "war of limited object," the interdependence of land and sea warfare, the "limited interference in unlimited war" of an army "disposal force" launched and, if need be, extracted, by naval power and the need for "combined operations."[5] As Geoffrey Till reminds us in his carefully crafted chapter, Corbett was the consummate theorist of the "controlled and careful application of maritime power," a naval theorist sufficiently astute to appreciate both the advantages and the limitations of sea power. After a careful reading of Carl von Clausewitz's *On War*, Corbett developed a sophisticated notion of the application of sea power in "limited interventions for limited objectives in unlimited wars," one that naval planners today would do well to read.

While intellectually we may agree with John B. Hattendorf's latest title, *Mahan Is Not Enough*,[6] it is almost impossible even today, a century later, to launch into a discussion of sea power without reference to Alfred Thayer Mahan. For Captain Mahan in 1890 synthesized numerous disconnected ideas about sea power into a coherent *philosophy* of sea power--one that bedazzled Germans and Japanese, Dutch and Mexicans, Turks and Brazilians alike. Why not? In 1890, the geophysical world was two-dimensional--the sea and the land; and of these, the sea constituted 70 percent of the globe's surface. But Mahan also offered a prescriptive set of underlying principles that, if followed to the letter, would accord any power a genuine shot at wealth and maritime dominance. Like Henri de Jomini and Karl Marx, but unlike Clausewitz, Mahan reflected the nineteenth-century fascination with discovering universal "laws" that, as he put it, "belong to the unchangeable, or unchanging, order of things."[7]

Mahan's six principal conditions for sea power--geographical position, physical conformation, extent of territory, number of population, national character and character of government--are well known and constitute truisms almost beyond question. But they need to be kept before us because for Mahan (and his disciples) they were the timeless "old foundations of strategy," principles that remained eternal "as though laid upon a rock."[8] Lest his readers in 1890 proved skeptical about his recipe for success, Mahan detailed another set of truisms that few dared refute: (1) the sea was superior to the land as an "influence" in history; (2) travel and traffic by water have always been, and will remain, "easier and cheaper than by land"; (3) the use and control of the sea were the "central link" in the chain by which wealth accumulates; and (4) production, shipping and colonies were the true "key to much of history."[9] Mahan assumed that we would accept as a fifth truism his major conclusion from his study of 150 years of British sea power: that battleships, whether small or large, arranged in symmetrical battle fleets were the loci of naval power.

Mahan seductively suggested that once all of his principles were in place, any nation that had ready access to the sea could be in "possession of that overbearing power on the sea which drives the enemy's flag from it, or allows it to appear only as a fugitive; and which, by controlling the great common, closes the highways by which commerce moves to and from the enemy's shores. This overbearing power can only be exerted by great navies."[10] Sea power accorded such a nation security from invasion by sea; the ability to reach and thus damage the enemy's shore; the opportunity to hurl a "disposal force" against the enemy at the place and time of its own choosing and to extract it, if need be; and the luxury to travel and trade upon the seas with impunity. In short, sea power for itself; sea denial to others.

Mahan the writer and publicist of the 1890s was an instant hit. Never even remotely a policymaker, Mahan the historian, as Hattendorf and Lambert argue cogently, sought on the basis of "selected evidence from aspects of a particular period of British history" to educate his own countrymen on the virtues of sea power and to promote his own service within the United States. Would-be maritime powers, especially, took from his writings whatever served their purposes. In Germany, Kaiser

Wilhelm II eagerly "devoured" *The Influence of Sea Power*. In Great Britain, Prime Minister William Gladstone called it "the book of the age." Lord Wolseley, the virtual commander-in-chief of British forces in the 1890s, only lamented that "it has taken a Yankee to wake up this generation to the meaning and importance of sea power." British naval writers contemporary to Mahan were somewhat less charitable. John Laughton thought *The Influence of Sea Power* "premature," while Julian Corbett deemed it "unhistorical," yet gave it a backhanded compliment when he called the book a "political pamphlet in the highest sense."[11] The extent to which scholars ever fully understood Mahan or were able to trace his influence on specific nations remains an open question. This confusion was perhaps best reflected by Barbara Tuchman in her Pulitzer Prize-winning book, *The Guns of August*, wherein she referred to Mahan as "the maritime Clausewitz, the Schlieffen of the sea."[12]

These disparate assessments of sea power and its application have been focused and placed in historical perspective by both the three theoretical treatises and the six case studies offered in this volume. Together, they lead us toward a middle road in assessing sea power, one whereby we can carefully weigh and balance "the influence of sea power upon history." No reader will go away with that feeling Corbett experienced at Greenwich in 1905, where he was unpleasantly surprised by "how difficult it was to present theory in a digestive form to the unused organs of naval officers."[13]

Admittedly, as historians we are all comfortable with Lord Byron's admonition that "the best of prophets of the future is the past." We are all sensitive to the fact that the writing of naval strategy, if it is to escape the narrow realms of iconoclastic "buffs" and ex-servicemen and to reach out to the larger world of professional scholars, must relate to foreign policy, land strategy, fiscal and economic determinants and political directives. Many of us already appreciate this need. Numerous historians of sea power in the age of the French Revolution and Napoleon, for example, have stressed in their writings the obvious example of the limits of sea power in the wars of Napoleon I: that, whereas the combined fleets of France and Spain were annihilated off Cape Trafalgar in October 1805, Napoleon nevertheless crushed the armies of Austria and Russia two months later at Austerlitz--and the vaunted Prussian Army one year later at Jena and Auerstadt--thereby attaining virtual mastery over continental Europe.

But there are other instances as well where preponderant sea power did not automatically translate into instant victory or even uninterrupted domination. In the Franco-Prussian War of 1870-71, for example, France possessed a mighty fleet of 400 ships (including 34 armored) against only 34 ships (including 5 armored) for Germany and yet lost the war disastrously.[14] In 1939, Adolf Hitler's *Kriegsmarine* was devastatingly outnumbered by the Royal Navy in battleships and battle cruisers (fifteen to five), light and heavy cruisers (fifty-nine to eight), and aircraft carriers (six to none).[15] Yet, despite the Royal Navy's crushing superiority at sea, Germany overran Poland, Denmark, Norway, Luxembourg, the Netherlands, Belgium, France, Yugoslavia and Greece in the first two years of the war. In the final analysis, as Corbett reminded his countrymen nearly a century ago and as Geoffrey Till here reminds us, "men live upon the land and not upon the sea"; and the land is where they ultimately exercise power.

Is it too far-fetched for me to suggest that had Hitler not invaded the Soviet Union, the European Community would still be called "Fortress Europe" and German would be its official language? Andrew Lambert and G.A.H. Gordon both confirm Britain's inability to bring to bear any power on the continent to deter Hitler from overrunning Czechoslovakia, Poland or France. Moreover, Karl Haushofer and Halford Mackinder may well have a cogent point in arguing that railroads, metallurgy and contiguous landmass were critical to the strategic algebra of the Great Powers. But none of this is, *eo ipso*, to deny the great importance of the real "muscle" of sea power. Why, indeed, must we always confront a Hobson's choice between army or navy? Must there always be--in the British case, for example--an "open choice" (to use Donald Schurman's words) between what Michael Howard and, later, Paul Kennedy termed the "continental commitment" and Corbett's or Mahan's stress on the importance of sea communications and battle fleets? Is the time not propitious, instead, to develop what Geoffrey Till calls a "synergistic relationship between army and navy"? David French and G.A.H. Gordon may debate the Royal Navy's relative "victory" in the Battle of Jutland; neither dismisses the navy's crucial role of keeping the world's maritime commerce routes open for Britain's eventual victories in the two world wars of this century. As Colin Gray reminds us in *The Leverage of Sea Power*, our strategic world today is no longer two-dimensional, but rather five-dimensional, with the addition of air, space and the electromagnetic spectrum.[16]

As a historian of the German variant of "navalism"--which, although not formally considered in this volumne, is frequently alluded to--I would argue that the concept of sea power is both fragile and complex. Physical and political geography and cultural-strategic orientation have determined its development during the last hundred years. A great gray host of capital ships anchored either at Wilhelmshaven or Kiel, I have suggested on a number of occasions, did not by themselves constitute sea power.

With regard to physical geography, neither Admiral Alfred von Tirpitz nor Admiral Erich Raeder ever grappled with the basic strategic dilemma that Britain blocked Germany's access to the Atlantic sea-lanes simply by its physical location--much as Mahan had pointed out that Ireland potentially blocked Britain's way to the ocean in the same manner. It remained for Lieutenant Commander Wolfgang Wegener to lecture his fellow officers in 1915 and (as vice admiral) again in 1925 and yet again in 1928 that sea power consisted of two things: "the tactical fleet" and the "strategic-geographical position" from which it could operate.[17]

Political geography placed Germany in the very center of Europe, flanked on either side by major powers (France and Russia). Chancellor Otto von Bismarck had taken great pains in 1888 to drive that geography lesson home to German explorers and would-be imperialists of Africa when he lectured Eugen Wolff: "Your map of Africa is very nice, indeed. But my map of Africa lies here in Europe: here is Russia, and here lies France, and we are in the middle. That is my map of Africa."[18] Not surprisingly, the second empire's generals quickly discovered that not even Tirpitz's "dream fleet" (which had been designed as anything but a "deterrent fleet") of sixty capital ships could have prevented a French or Russian entry into Berlin in a continental war. General Alfred von Waldersee, chief of the General Staff, expressed this view perhaps most brutally: "The Navy more and more cultivates the notion that future wars will be decided at sea. But what will the Navy do if the Army should be defeated, be it in the East or in the West? Those good gentlemen do not like to think that far ahead."[19] During the Second World War, when the admirals of Hitler's *Kriegsmarine* happily divided the world with Japan at seventy degrees longitude, thereby claiming the Indian Ocean, the Mediterranean Sea and the Atlantic Ocean as their own, Chief of the General Staff Franz Halder laconically commented, "These people dream in continents."[20]

Cultural-strategic orientation pertains to such "soft" concepts as psychology and tradition. No matter how often German admirals stressed that their nautical roots reached back to the Vikings and to the Hanseatic League, they constantly lived in the shadow of the Royal Navy, whose officers, in the words of Andrew Lambert, exuded an overbearing "arrogance" born of a "legacy of victory." Already in Tirpitz's time, the great Prussian novelist Theodor Fontane brilliantly summed up the dour German naval *mentalite*: "We do not have a trace of this confidence....We are not mentioned in the Old Testament. The British act as though they *had* the promise." Admiral Reinhard Scheer, commander of the High Seas Fleet at Jutland in May-June 1916, agreed: "The English fleet had the advantage of looking back on a hundred years of proud tradition which must have given every man a sense of superiority based on the great deeds of the past."[21]

The U.S. Navy, basking in the glow of Mahan and victory in two world wars, certainly exuded (and still exudes) cultural and psychological confidence. Its attitude was perhaps best encapsulated by Secretary of War Henry L. Stimson's interwar exasperation over what he termed the "peculiar psychology of the Navy Department, which frequently seemed to retire from the realm of logic into a dim religious world in which Neptune was God, Mahan his prophet, and the United States Navy the only true Church."[22]

I would like to throw out a few "principles" of my own to stimulate future research and writing in naval history. I begin with the *limits* of sea power:

1. Naval battles, as virtually all authors in this volume suggest, are rarely, if ever, decisive on their own. History abounds with examples. Austria won the Battle of Lissa in 1866 but lost the war against Piedmont-Sardinia (and France) on land. Britain scored spectacular successes at Aboukir, Copenhagen and Trafalgar, but it took almost a decade more of land warfare to defeat Napoleon. Again, Britain won the Battle of Jutland strategically, but the Great War was not decided for another two years and not until the arrival of almost 2 million American "doughboys" on the western front. Although the United States crippled the Imperial Japanese Navy at Midway in 1942, once more it took three years of fighting and two nuclear devices to end the Second World War.

2. Fleets are costly, high-risk instruments of state policy, as they take a generation and enormous treasure to create. Few nations can afford to gamble fleets "in an afternoon"; most prefer to maintain them as classic "fleets-in-being" to be used for bargaining leverage at the postwar settlement. The simple but powerful truth is that ships sink. Shattered armies, as Leon Gambetta showed in France in 1870-71, can be reconstituted almost over night, quickly and

cheaply. Imperial Germany's concern over its High Sea Fleet in 1914-18 and the U.S. Navy's current worry about the survivability of its aircraft carriers attest to this observation.

3. The very notion of sea control is difficult for nonsailors to appreciate. The sea cannot be dominated and occupied in the same way as the land. Sea control often is indirect and nearly always imperceptible.

4. Sea control and/or sea denial generally are unspectacular and slow in coming--and they hardly attract CNN television coverage like F-18s and cruise missiles. Perhaps Admiral Arleigh Burke of the U.S. Navy hit the nail on the head in 1952 when he compared the nature of sea power with that of a "virtuous woman": neither "is spectacular," and neither "causes long editorials" in the media. In the final analysis, Burke argued, sea power depends on "long, dull hours of hard work." Eventual success is built "upon a series of small successes."[23]

5. Sea power is a concept that is constantly in flux. Radical change is often dictated by technology. Admiral "Jacky" Fisher, the Royal Navy's first sea lord from 1904 to 1915, was a case in point with his various leaps of faith over turbines, oil-fired burners and air power. So, too, was Admiral Rickover in the United States with his new "capital ship," the nuclear submarine, and Admiral James Watkins, the chief of naval operations of the U.S. Navy, when he committed what was tantamount to "sea heresy" in 1983 with his seditious suggestion that "space power is sea power."[24]

When we try to determine what sea power *can do* today, we turn almost by default to the U.S. Navy. A few years ago we could have had a stimulating conference centered on U.S. Secretary of the Navy John Lehman's "maritime strategy." I well remember discussing its broad strategic contours with Admiral Watkins at Newport and later trying to explain its global logistical implications ("arsenal of democracy") for both the Atlantic and Pacific theaters to a group of highly skeptical naval reservists at Treasure Island in San Francisco. But the advisability of landing "disposal forces" (U.S. Marines) on the Jutland and Kamchatka peninsulas, supported by high-risk carrier groups, is no longer valid. For all intents and purposes, we are down to one dominant navy in world affairs, and that institution, in the words of the naval historian David A. Rosenberg, has replaced product with process,[25] a frightening suggestion that haunts anyone currently involved in advanced education.

That leads me to my final point: sea lift and power projection "from the sea." As the former Canadian commander in Bosnia-Herzegovina, General Lewis MacKenzie, conceded, only the United States has the ability to transport and maintain significant mobile forces in the "new world order." American sailors, as Kenneth Hagan and Nathan Miller document in their studies, have always understood the pivotal role of sea lift. Anglo-American control of sea communications translated into the safe passage of nearly 3 million American soldiers to Europe and the construction of 1,000 bulk cargo carriers of 3 million tons in 1917-18.[26] At the height of the American war effort in the summer of 1918, one troop transport or cargo vessel left the United States for France every five hours; seven soldiers and their equipment were landed in France every minute of every day and night. During the Second World War, the United States built an incredible 5,777 freighters and tankers, sufficient to transport major armies to Europe and Asia--not to mention 427,000 trucks and jeeps, 18,700 aircraft and 10,000 tanks to the Soviet Union.[27]

Certain "truisms" remain valid even in the five-dimensional strategic culture of the 1990s. The seas still make up seven-tenths of the globe. Water transport remains cheaper than land transport. Ships, rather than railroads, are the prime movers of goods. While rapid air strikes and massive air transport may put out small international brushfires, they still can not accord even the United States more than fleeting control at such flash points--witness Somalia and Bosnia. Sea lift alone can provide influence (and eventually victory) in protracted conflicts. An obvious case in point is the Gulf War of 1990-91, in which the U.S. Navy shipped 325,000 soldiers and 2.5 million tons of equipment halfway round the globe.

In conclusion, let me suggest that navies will remain a very significant part of the strategic culture for at least the rest of our lives. Airpower may demolish the infrastructure of Baghdad. Space power may some day target land sites with lasers. Land power will certainly continue to occupy and hold land. But sea power alone can accord or deny a nation the ability to move massive amounts of men and materiel to major or minor theatres of war, be they in the Balkans, the Middle East or Africa.

In a protracted conflict, as Colin Gray has convincingly documented in his breathtaking overview of 2,500 years of warfare, sea power will remain critical. It alone allows a power the luxury of time, the ability to reorganize old or constitute new coalitions, to choose the time and place of future combat, to exploit the weak points, especially of an overextended land power, and, if need be, to recover from defeat.[28] There is no chance that the naval establishment, especially in the United States, will fade away. Nathan Miller has provided ample evidence for this assertion with regard to the American naval "Gun Club" in the interwar period. In the knowing words of one of the U.S. Navy's erstwhile and most prominent assistant secretaries, Franklin Delano Roosevelt, the "Na-a-vy" is like a "feather bed." "You punch it with your right and you punch it with your left until you are finally exhausted, and then you find the damn bed just as it was before you started punching."[29]

NOTES

1. Robert K. Massie, *Dreadnought: Britain, Germany and the Coming of the Great War* (New York: Random House, 1991), 454.

2. Winston S. Churchill, *The World Crisis, 1911-1918*, vol. 2 (London: Thorton Butterworth, 1938), 1015.

3. Thucydides, *The History of the Peloponnesian War* (London: Oxford University Press, 1960), 283.

4. Paul M. Kennedy, *The Rise and Fall of British Naval Mastery* (New York: Charles Scribner's Sons, 1976), 27.

5. See Julian S. Corbett, *Some Principles of Maritime Strategy* (Annapolis: Naval Institute Press, 1988).

6. John B. Hattendorf, *Mahan is Not Enough*.

7. Alfred Thayer Mahan, *The Influence of Sea Power Upon History 1660-1783* (New York: Hill and Wang, 1957), 76.

8. Ibid.

9. Ibid., 25.

10. Ibid., 121.

11. William E. Livezey, *Mahan on Sea Power* (Norman: University of Oklahoma Press, 1961), 63-66. A critical reinterpretation of Mahan's influence is John B. Hattendorf, ed., *The Influence of History on Mahan: The Proceedings of a Conference Marking the Centenary of Alfred Thayer Mahan's The "Influence of Sea Power Upon History, 1660-1783"* (Newport, R.I.: Naval War College Press, 1991).

12. Barbara W. Tuchman, *The Guns of August* (New York: Macmillan, 1962), 333.

13. Cited in Donald M. Schurman, *Julian S. Corbett 1854-1922: Historian of British Maritime Policy from Drake to Jellicoe* (London: Royal Historical Society, 1981), 44.

14. Theodor Ropp, *The Development of a Modern Navy: French Naval Policy 1871- 1904* (Annapolis,: Naval Institute Press, 1987), 22.

15. Edward P. Von de Porten, *The German Navy in World War II* (New York: Galahad Books, 1969), 31-32.

16. Colin S. Gray, *The Leverage of Sea Power: The Strategic Advantage of Navies in War* (New York: Free Press, 1992), 2.

17. See my Introduction to Wolfgang Wegener, *The Naval Strategy of the World War [Classics of Sea Power]* (Annapolis: Naval Institute Press, 1989).

18. Cited in Holger H. Herwig, *Hammer or Anvil? Modern Germany 1648-Present* (Lexington: D. C. Heath, 1994), 132.

19. Cited in Holger H. Herwig, *"Luxury" Fleet: The Imperial German Navy 1888-1918* (London: Ashfield Press, 1987), 92.

20. Franz Halder, *Kriegstagebuch* (Stuttgart, 1964), 111, 455. Entry for 12 June 1942.

21. Cited in Herwig, *"Luxury" Fleet*, 147. Those still in confusion about who "won" the Battle of Jutland would do well to read Scheer's after-action report of 4 July 1916.

22. Henry L. Stimson and McGeorge Bundy, *On Active Service in Peace and War* (New York: Harper and Brothers, 1948), 506. The "peculiar psychology" of Admiral Hyman Rickover and the nuclear "silent service" might some day make an interesting study.

23. David Alan Rosenberg, "Process: The Realities of Formulating Modern Naval Strategy," in James Goldrick and John B. Hattendorf, eds., *Mahan Is Not Enough: The Proceedings of a Conference on the Works of Sir Julian Corbett and Admiral Sir Herbert Richmond* (Newport, R.I.: Naval War College Press, 1993), 144.

24. Cited in Gray, *Leverage of Sea Power*, 25-26.

25. Rosenberg, "Process," 141-75.

26. David F. Trask, *Captains & Cabinets: Anglo-American Naval Relations, 1917-1918* (Columbia: University of Missouri Press, 1972), 292, 363; Allan R. Millett and Peter Maslowski, *For the Common Defense: A Military History of the United States of America* (New York: Free Press, 1984), 339.

27. See George Baer, "U.S. Naval Strategy, 1890-1945," *Naval War College Review*, 44 (winter 1991), 21; Gray, *Leverage of Sea Power*, 242-43.

28. See Gray, *Leverage of Sea Power*, 29.

29. Marriner S. Eccles, *Beckoning Frontiers: Public and Personal Recollections* (New York: Alfred A. Knopf, 1966), 336.

Selected Bibliography

Ball, Desmond and Jeffrey Richelson, eds. *Strategic Nuclear Targeting.* Ithaca, N.Y.: Cornell University Press, 1986.

Barnett, L. M. *British Food Policy during the First World War.* London: Allen and Unwin, 1985.

Bell, A. C. *A History of the Blockade of Germany 1914-18.* London: Historical Section, CID, 1937.

Bekker, C. *Hitler's Naval Wars.* London: Macdonald, 1974.

Benians, E. A., J.R.M. Butler and C.E. Carrington eds. *The Cambridge History of the British Empire*, vol. 2. Cambridge: Cambridge University Press, 1940..

Blair, Clay, Jr. *The Atomic Submarine and Admiral Rickover.* New York: Henry Holt, 1954.

Braisted, William R. *The United States Navy in the Pacific, 1909-1922.* Austin: University of Texas Press, 1971.

Brown, Neville. *Strategic Mobility.* London: Chatto and Windus, 1963.

Buxton, Ian. *Big Gun Monitors.* Annapolis: Naval Institute Press, 1978.

Cable, James. *Gunboat Diplomacy: Political Applications of Limited Naval Force*, 2nd ed. London: Chatto and Windus, 1981.

Callwell, C. E. *The Effect of Maritime Command on Land Campaigns Since Waterloo.* Edinburgh: William Blackwood and Sons, 1897.

Chandler, David G. *Great Battles of the British Army, as commemorated in the Sandhurst Companies.* London: Arms and Armour Press, 1991.

Cogar, W. B., and P. Sine, eds. *Naval History. The Seventh Annual Symposium of the U.S. Naval Academy.* Wilmington, Del.: Scholarly Resources Inc., 1988.

Cohen, E. A., and J. Gooch. *Military Misfortunes. The Anatomy of Failure in War*. New York: Vintage Books, 1991.

Compton-Hall, Richard. *Submarines and the War at Sea, 1914-1918*. London: Macmillan, 1991.

Corbett, J.S. *England in the Seven Years War*, vol 1. London: Longmans, Green, 1907.

_____. *Drake and the Tudor Navy*. London: Longman's, Green, 1917.

_____. *Naval Operations*. London: Longman's, Green, 1920.

Davis, George T. *A Navy Second to None*. Westport, Conn.: Greenwood Press, 1940.

d'Egville, Howard. *Imperial Defence and Closer Union*. London: P. S. King and Son, 1913.

Dorwar, Jeffery M. *The Office of Naval Intelligence: The Birth of America's First Intelligence Agency, 1865-1918*. Annapolis: Naval Institute Press, 1979.

Duffy, M., ed. *Parameters of British Naval Power 1650-1850*. Exeter: University Press, 1992.

Eccles, Henry E. *Military Concepts and Philosophy*. New Brunswick, N.J.: Rutgers University Press, 1965.

_____. *Military Power in A Free Society*. Newport: Naval War College Press, 1985.

Ehrman, John. *The Navy in the War of William III, 1689-1697*. Cambridge: Cambridge University Press, 1953.

Freedman, L., P. Hayes and R. O'Neill, eds. *War, Strategy and International Politics. Essays in Honour of Sir Michael Howard*. Oxford: Clarendon Press, 1992.

French, D. *British Economic and Strategic Planning, 1905-1915*. London: Allen and Unwin, 1982.

_____. *British Strategy and War Aims, 1914-1916*. London: Allen and Unwin, 1990.

_____. *The British Way in Warfare: 1688-2000*. London: Unwin Hyman, 1990.

Friedman, Norman. *The U.S. Maritime Strategy*. London: Jane's, 1988.

Fuller, William. *Strategy and Power in Russia: 1600-1914*. New York: Free Press, 1992.

Gallagher, John, Ronald Robinson and Alice Denny. *Africa and the Victorians*. London: Macmillan, 1961.

Gat, Azar. *The Development of Military Thought in the Nineteenth Century*. Oxford: Oxford University Press, 1992.

Gleaves, Albert. *Life and Letters of Rear Admiral Stephen B. Luce, U.S.*

Navy. New York: G. P. Putnam's Sons, 1925.

Goldrick, James. *The King's Ships Were at Sea*. Annapolis: Naval Institute Press, 1984.

_____, and John B. Hattendorf. *Mahan Is Not Enough: The Proceedings of a Conference on the Works of Sir Julian Corbett and Admiral Sir Herbert Richmond*. Newport, R.I.: Naval War College Press, 1993.

Gooch, J. *The Prospect of War. Studies in British Defence Policy 1847-1942*. London: Frank Cass, 1981.

Gordon, D. C. *The Dominion Partnership in Imperial Defence: 1870-1914*. Baltimore: John Hopkins University Press, 1965.

Gordon, G.A.H. *British Seapower and Procurement Between the Wars*. Basingstoke, Hants: Macmillan, 1988.

Gould, Stephen Jay. *Time's Arrow, Time's Cycle*. Cambridge: Harvard University Press, 1987.

Graham, Gerald S. *The Politics of Naval Supremacy: Studies in British Maritime Ascendancy*. Cambridge: Cambridge University Press, 1965.

Gray, Colin. *Maritime Strategy, Geopolitics, and the Defense of the West*. New York: National Strategy Information Center, 1986.

_____. *The Leverage of Sea Power: The Strategic Advantage of Navies in War*. New York: Free Press, 1992.

_____, and Roger W. Barnett, eds. *Seapower and Strategy*. Annapolis: Naval Institute Press, 1989.

Grenfell, Russell. *Main Fleet to Singapore*. London: Faber and Faber, 1951.

Hagan, Kenneth J. *This People's Navy*. New York: Free Press, 1991.

_____, ed. *In Peace and War: Interpretations of American Naval History, 1775-1984*, 2d ed. rev. Westport, Conn.: Greenwood Press, 1984.

Hailey, Foster, and Milton Lancelt. *Clear for Action*. New York: Duell, Sloan and Pearce, 1964.

Hammond, Grant T. *Plowshares into Swords: Arms Races in International Politics, 1840-1991*. Columbia: University of South Carolina Press, 1993.

Hartmann, Frederick H. *Naval Renaissance: The U.S. Navy in the 1980's*. Annapolis: Naval Institute Press, 1990.

Hattendorf, John B. "The Evolution of the Maritime Strategy: 1977-1987," *Naval War College Review* 41 (summer 1988): 7-28.

_____. *The Influence of History on Mahan: The Proceedings of a*

Conference Marking the Centenary of Alfred Thayer Mahan's "The Influence of Sea Power upon History, 1660-1783." Newport, R. I.: Naval War College Press, 1991.

_____, ed. *Ubi Sumus: The State of Naval and Maritime History*. Newport, R.I.: Naval War College Press, 1994.

_____, and Lynn C. Hattendorf, comp. *A Bibliography of the Works of Alfred Thayer Mahan*. Newport: Naval War College Press, 1986.

_____, and R. S. Jordan, eds. *Maritime Strategy and Balance of Power. Britain and America in the Twentieth Century*. London: Macmillan, 1989.

Hayes, and J. B. Hattendorf, eds. *The Writings of Stephen B. Luce*. Newport, R. I.: Naval War College Press, 1975.

Herrick, Walter R., Jr. *The American Naval Revolution*. Baton Rouge: Louisiana State University Press, 1966.

Herwig, Holger. *"Luxury Fleet": The Imperial German Navy 1888-1918*. London: Allen and Unwin, 1980.

_____. *Hammer or Anvil? Modern Germany 1648-Present*. Lexington: D. C. Heath, 1994.

Hough, Richard. *The Great War at Sea 1914-1918*. New York: Oxford University Press, 1983.

Howard, Michael. *The Franco-Prussian War: The German Invasion of France, 1870-1871*. London: Haert Davies, 1961.

_____. *The Continental Commitment*. London: Temple Smith, 1972.

Howarth, Stephen. *To Shining Sea: A History of the United States Navy, 1775-1991*. New York: Random House, 1991.

Huntington, Samuel P. "National Policy and the Transoceanic Navy", U.S. Naval Institute *Proceedings* 80 (May 1954): 483-93.

Isley, Jeter T., and Philip A. Crowl. *The U.S. Marines and Amphibious War*. Princeton: Princeton University Press, 1951.

Jane, F. T. *Heresies of Seapower*. London: Longmans, Green, 1906.

Johnson, F. A. *Defence by Committee*. Oxford: Oxford University Press, 1960.

Jordan, Gerald, ed. *Naval Warfare in the Twentieth Century*. London: Croom Helm, 1977.

Kennedy, Paul. *Samoan Tangle*. New York: Barnes and Noble, 1974.

_____. *The Rise and Fall of the British Naval Mastery*. Florida: Robert E. Krieger, 1976.

_____. *The Rise of the Anglo-German Naval Antagonism, 1860-1917*. London: Allen and Unwin, 1980.

_____. *Strategy and Diplomacy 1870-1945*. London: Fontana, 1983.

King, J. W. *The Warships and Navies of Europe in 1880.* London: Oxford University Press, 1982.

Klatchko, Mary, and David F. Trask. *Admiral William Shepherd Benson, First Chief of Naval Operations.* Annapolis: Naval Institute Press, 1987.

Knox, Dudley W. *The Eclipse of American Sea Power.* New York: American Army and Navy Journal, 1922.

Lambert, A. D. *Battleships in Transition: The Creation of the Steam Battlefleet.* London: Conway Maritime Press, 1984.

_____. *The Crimean War: British Grand Strategy against Russia, 1853-1856.* Manchester, U.K.: Manchester University Press, 1990.

_____. *The Last Sailing Battlefleet: Maintaining Naval Mastery 1815-1850.* London: Conway Maritime Press, 1991.

_____, ed. *Steam, Steel & Shellfire: The Steam Warship 1815-1905.* London: Conway Maritime Press, 1992.

Leffler, Melvyn P. *A Preponderance of Power: National Security, The Truman Administration and the Cold War.* Stanford, Calif.: Stanford University Press, 1992.

Legge, J. Michael. *Theater Nuclear Weapons and the NATO Strategy of Flexible Response.* Santa Monica, Calif.: Rand Corporation, 1983.

Love, Robert W., Jr. *History of the U.S. Navy, Volume 2, 1942-1991.* Harrisburg, P.A.: Stackpole Books, 1992.

Luttwak, Edward N. *The Political Uses of Sea Power.* Baltimore: Washington Center of Foreign Policy Research, School of Advanced International Studies, Johns Hopkins University, 1974.

Mackinder, Halford J. *Democratic Ideals and Reality.* New York: Norton, 1962; first pub. 1942.

Mahan, Alfred Thayer. *The Influence of Sea Power Upon History, 1660-1783.* Boston: Little, Brown, 1890.

_____. *The Influence of Sea Power Upon The French Revolution and Empire.* Boston: Little, Brown, 1892.

_____. *Nelson: The Embodiment of the Sea Power of Great Britain.* London: Marston Low, 1897

_____. *Sea Power in Its Relations to the War of 1812.* Boston: Little, Brown, 1905.

_____. *Naval Strategy Compared and Contrasted with the Principles and Practice of Military Operations on Land: Lectures Delivered at the U.S. Naval War College, Newport, R.I., between the Years 1887 and 1911.* Boston: Little, Brown, 1911.

_____, ed. *Some Neglected Aspects of War*. London: Simpson, Low and Marston, 1907.

Marder, Arthur J. *The Anatomy of British Seapower: A History of British Naval Policy in the Pre-Dreadnought Era, 1880-1905*. London: Alfred A. Knopf, 1940.

_____. *From the Dreadnought to Scapa Flow: The Royal Navy in the Fisher Era. 5 Vols*. London: Oxford University Press, 1961-70.

_____, ed. *Fear God and Dreadnought: The Correspondence of Admiral of the Fleet Lord Fisher of Kilverstone*, vol. 3. London: Oxford University Press, 1959.

Martel, Gordon. "The Meaning of Power: The Decline and Fall of Great Britain," *International History Review* 13:14 (November 1991): 662-94.

Massie, Robert K. *Dreadnought: Britain, Germany. and the Coming of the Great War*. New York: Random House, 1991.

Masterston, Daniel M. *Naval History: The Sixth Symposium*. Wilmington, Del.: Scholarly Resources, 1987.

Miller, Edward S. *War Plan Orange: The U.S. Strategy to Defeat Japan, 1897-1945*. Annapolis: Naval Institute Press, 1991.

Millett, Allan R., and Peter Maslowski. *For the Common Defense: A Military History of the United States of America*. New York: Free Press, 1984.

Milner, Marc, ed. *Military History and the Military Profession*. Ottawa: Carleton University Press, 1992.

Morison, Samuel Eliot. *The Battle of the Atlantic 1939-1943*. Boston: Atlantic, Little, Brown, 1947.

_____. *The Two-Ocean War*. Boston: Little, Brown, 1963.

Morris, A.J.A. *The Scaremongers: The Advocacy of War and Rearmament, 1896-1914*. London: Routledge and Keegan Paul, 1984.

Neilson, Keith. *Strategy and Supply: The Anglo-Russian Alliance, 1914-17*. London: Allen and Unwin, 1980.

_____. "'Greatly Exaggerated': The Myth of the Decline of Great Britain before 1914," *International History Review* 13:14 (November 1991): 697-725.

O'Connell, Robert L. *Sacred Vessels: The Cult of the Battleship and the Rise of the U.S. Navy*. New York: Oxford, 1991.

Offner, John L. *An Unwanted War*. Chapel Hill: University of North Carolina Press, 1992.

Palmer, Michael A. *Origins of the Maritime Strategy: American Naval*

Strategy in the First Postwar Decade. Washington, D.C.: Naval Historical Center, Department of the Navy, 1988.

Parker, Foxhall A. *Fleet Tactics under Steam.* New York: D. Van Nostrand, 1879.

Parker, W. H. *Mackinder: Geography as an Aid to Statecraft.* Oxford: Clarendon Press, 1982.

Parkes, O. *British Battleships.* London: Arms and Armour Press, 1956.

Partridge, Michael. *The Military Planning for the Defence of the United Kingdom 1814-1870.* New York: Greenwod Press, 1989.

Patterson, A. Temple, ed. *The Jellicoe Papers. Volume 1, 1893-1916.* London: Naval Record Society, 1966.

Polmar, Norman. *The American Submarine.* Baltimore: Nautical and Aviation, 1981.

Prange, Gordon W. *At Dawn We Slept.* New York: McGraw-Hill, 1981.

Pollen, Anthony. *The Great Gunnery Scandal: The Mystery of Jutland.* London: Collins, 1980.

Ranft, Bryan. *Technical Change and British Naval Policy: 1860-1939.* London: Hodden and Stoughten, 1977.

_____, ed. *The Beatty Papers. Selections from the Private and Official Correspondence of Admiral of the Fleet Earl Beatty.* London: Scholar Press and Naval Records Society, 1989.

Reynolds, Clark A. *The Fast Carriers.* New York: McGraw-Hill, 1968.

Richmond, Herbert. *The Navy and the War of 1739-48,* 3 vols. Cambridge: Cambridge University Press, 1923.

_____. *Imperial Defence and Capture at Sea in Wartime.* London: Hutchinson, 1932.

Rodger, N.A.M. *The Wooden World: An Anatomy of the Georgian Navy.* London: Collins, 1986.

Rodgers, William Ledyard. *Greek and Roman Naval Warfare: A Study of Strategy, Tactics, and Ship Design from Salamis (480 B.C.) to Actium (31 B.C.).* Annapolis: Naval Institute Press, 1937.

Ropp, Theodore. *The Development of a Modern Navy: French Naval Policy 1871- 1904.* Annapolis: Naval Institute Press, 1987.

_____. *The Creation of a Modern Navy.* Annapolis: Naval Institute Press, 1988.

Rosenberg, David Alan. "A Smoking Radiating Ruin at the End of Two Hours: Documents of American Plans for Nuclear War with the Soviet Union, 1954-1955," *International Security* 6 (winter 1981-82): 3-38.

Roskill, S. W. *Naval Policy Between the Wars.* vol. 1. London:

Collins, 1968.

———, ed. *Documents Relating to the Naval Air Service. Volume 1. 1908-1918*. London: Naval Records Society, 1969.

Schurman, Donald M. *The Education of a Navy: The Development of British Naval Strategic Thought, 1867-1914*. London: Cassell, 1965.

———. *Julian S. Corbett, 1854-1922: Historian of British Maritime Policy from Drake to Jellicoe*. London: Royal Historical Society, 1981.

Schwartz, David N. *NATO's Nuclear Dilemmas*. Washington, D.C.: Brookings Institution, 1983.

Seager, R. *Alfred Thayer Mahan*. Annapolis: Naval Institute Press, 1977.

———, and Doris D. Maguire, eds. *The Letters and Papers of Alfred Thayer Mahan*. (Annapolis: Naval Institute Press, 1975.

Sokolsky, Joel J. "Anglo-American Maritime Strategy in the Era of Flexible Response, 1960-80." In John B. Hattendorf and Robert S. Jordan, eds., *Maritime Strategy and the Balance of Power: Britain and America in the Twentieth Century*. New York: St. Martin's Press, 1989.

———. *Sea-power in the Nuclear Age: The United States Navy and NATO, 1949-80*. Annapolis: Naval Institute Press, 1991.

Spector, Ronald H. *Professors of War: The Naval War College and the Development of the Naval Profession*. Newport: Naval War College Press, 1977.

———. *Admiral of the New Empire: The Life and Career of George Dewey*. Columbia: University of South Carolina Press, 1988.

Spinardi, Graham. *From Polaris to Trident: The Development of U.S. Fleet Ballistic Missile Technology*. Cambridge: Cambridge University Press, 1994.

Steinberg, Jonathan. *Yesterday's Deterrent: Tirpitz and the Birth of the German Battle Fleet*. London: Macmillan, 1965.

Taylor, A. J. P. *The Struggle for Mastery in Europe 1848-1918*. Oxford: Clarendon Press, 1954.

Till, Geoffrey. *Air Power and the Royal Navy 1914-1945*. London: Macdonald and Janis, 1979.

Tracy, N. *Attack on Maritime Trade*. London: Macmillan, 1991.

Trask, David F. *Captains & Cabinets: Anglo-American Naval Relations, 1917-1918*. Columbia: University of Missouri Press, 1972.

———. *The War with Spain in 1898*. New York: Macmillan, 1981.

Tunstall, Brian. *The Realities of Naval History*. London: Allen and

Unwin, 1936.

_____. *The Cambridge History of the British Empire.* vol. 3. Cambridge: Cambridge University Press, 1959.

Turk, Richard W. *The Ambiguous Relationship: Theodore Roosevelt and Alfred Thayer Mahan.* New York: Greenwood Press, 1987.

Turnbull, Archibald D., and Clifford L. Lord. *History of United States Naval Aviation.* New York: Arno Press, 1972.

Turner, J. *British Politics and the Great War. Coalition and Conflict 1915-1918.* London: Yale University Press, 1992.

Vat, Dan van der. *The Atlantic Campaign.* New York: Harper and Row, 1988.

von Clausewitz, Carl. *On War.* Edited and translated by Michael Howard and Peter Paret. Princeton: Princeton University Press, 1976; first pub. 1832.

Von de Porten, Edward P. *The German Navy in World War II.* New York: Galahad Books, 1969.

Wegener, Wolfgang. *The Naval Strategy of the World War.* Annapolis: Naval Institute Press, 1989.

Wheeler, Gerald E. *Admiral William Veazie Pratt, U.S. Navy.* Washington: Government Printing Office, 1974.

Index

About The Editors And Contributors

ELIZABETH JANE ERRINGTON teaches history at the Royal Military College of Canada. She is a historian of colonial America.

DAVID FRENCH is a Reader in History at University College, London. His publications include *The British Way in Warfare, 1688-2000* (1990) and *British Strategy and War Aims: 1914-1916* (1986).

G. A. H. GORDON is a private scholar who lives in London. He is the author of *British Seapower and Procurement between the Wars: A Reappraisal of Rearmament* (1988).

COLIN S. GRAY belongs to the Department of Politics at the University of Hull, Hull, England. Among his publications are *Maritime Strategy, Geopolitics and the Defense of the West* (1986) and *Leverage of Sea Power: The Strategic Advantage of Navies in Major Wars* (1992).

KENNETH J. HAGAN is an Archivist and Professor of History at the U.S. Naval Academy Archives in Annapolis. He is the editor of *In Peace and War: Interpretations of American Naval History 1775-1984* (1984) and author of *American Gunboat Diplomacy and the Old Navy* (1973).

JOHN B. HATTENDORF is an Ernest J. King Professor and Coordinator of Research at the U.S. Naval War College, Newport, Rhode Island. He is the author of *Mahan on Naval Strategy: Selections from the Writings of Rear Admiral Alfred Thayer Mahan* (1991).

HOLGER H. HERWIG is a Professor of History at the University of Calgary, Calgary, Alberta. Among his publications are *Germany's Vision of Empire in Venezuela: 1871-1914* (1986) and *Politics of Frustration: The United States in German Naval Planning: 1889-1941* (1976).

ANDREW D. LAMBERT teaches at King's College, London. He is the author of *Battleships in Transition: The Creation of the Steam Battlefleet* (1984) and *Warrior: The World's First Ironclad Then and Now* (1987).

NATHAN MILLER is a private scholar in Washington, D.C. He is the author of *The U.S. Navy: A History* (1990) and *Theodore Roosevelt: A Life* (1992).

KEITH NEILSON teaches history at the Royal Military College of Canada. He writes on Anglo-Russian relations.

DONALD M. SCHURMAN is a Naval Historian and a Professor Emeritus at the Royal Military College of Canada. Among his many publications are *The Education of a Navy: The Development of British Naval Strategic Thought, 1867-1914* (1965) and *Julian S. Corbett, 1854-1922: Historian of British Maritime Policy from Drake to Jelicoe* (1981).

GEOFFREY TILL is the Dean of the Royal Naval College, Greenwich, United Kingdom, as well as a noted naval historian. He is the author of *Maritime Strategy and Nuclear Age* (1982) and the *Modern Sea Power: An Introduction* (1987).

ISBN 0-275-94898-6

EAN

HARDCOVER BAR CODE